T0243401

GUIDE TO CHICAGO'S TWENTY-FIRST-CENTURY ARCHITECTURE

Publication supported by a grant
from the Furthermore Foundation:
a program of the J. M. Kaplan Fund.

Manufactured in the United States of America
P 5 4 3 2 1
♾ This book is printed on acid-free paper.

Library of Congress Cataloging-in-Publication Data
Names: Hill, John, 1973– author. | Chicago Architecture Center, author.
Title: Guide to Chicago's twenty-first-century architecture / Chicago Architecture Center & John Hill.
Other titles: Guide to Chicago's 21st-century architecture
Description: Urbana: University of Illinois Press, [2021] | Includes index.
Identifiers: LCCN 2020051235 (print) | LCCN 2020051236 (ebook) | ISBN 9780252085710 (paperback) | ISBN 9780252052620 (ebook)
Subjects: LCSH: Architecture—Illinois—Chicago—History—21st century—Guidebooks. | Chicago (Ill.)—Buildings, structures, etc.—Guidebooks. | Chicago (Ill.)—Guidebooks.
Classification: LCC NA735.C4 H48 2021 (print) | LCC NA735.C4 (ebook) | DDC 720.9773/11—dc23
LC record available at https://lccn.loc.gov/2020051235
LC ebook record available at https://lccn.loc.gov/2020051236

GUIDE TO CHICAGO'S TWENTY-FIRST-CENTURY ARCHITECTURE

CHICAGO ARCHITECTURE CENTER

& John Hill

Harlem Ave 7200W
9 mi
Narragansett Ave 6400W
8 mi
Central Ave 5600W
7 mi
Cicero Ave 4800W
6 mi
Pulaski Ave 4000W
5 mi
Kedzie Ave 3200W
4 mi
Western Ave 2400W
3 mi
Ashland Ave 1600W
2 mi
Halsted St 800W
1 mi
State St 0W
State St 0E
Cottage Grove Ave 800E
1 mi
Stony Island Ave 1600E
2 mi
20
O'Hare
Airport
Devon Ave
Bryn Mawr Ave
Lawrence Ave
Irving Park Rd
Belmont Ave
Fullerton Ave
Lake
Michigan
North Ave
Chicago Ave
Madison
Madison
Roosevelt Rd
Cermak Rd
31st St
Pershing Rd
47th St
55th St
63rd St
71st St
79th St
11
10
9
12
13
8
6
7
2
14
4
3
1
21
15
5
16
17
19
18
Midway
Airport

Contents

Foreword

Chicago has long defined itself The City of Architecture—a place where designers gather to explore new methods for building awe-inspiring structures that shape urban life all around the globe.

This commitment to experimentation is deeply embedded in the city's civic and business ideal. The Great Fire of 1871 provided the opportunity for visionaries, including Daniel Burnham and Louis Sullivan, to rebuild a soaring, fireproof downtown. In the first half of the twentieth century, Frank Lloyd Wright and Ludwig Mies van der Rohe responded to the work of their predecessors with deeply personal designs for commercial, residential, and institutional buildings throughout the city. Beyond the postwar era, designers such as Bertrand Goldberg, Fazlur Kahn, Stanley Tigerman, and Margaret McCurry brought forth an even broader range of structural forms to the skyline—and so forth.

Both physically and psychologically, the projects these outsize figures built cast long shadows across the city, looming particularly large over the drafting tables of contemporary designers. Architects from around the world travel to Chicago to see our iconic buildings. And when they receive a Chicago commission, they take great care knowing that their designs may literally stand up next to buildings that they and their colleagues recognize as iconic. The past two decades have repeatedly demonstrated that many of our most innovative practitioners are still here in town creating tomorrow's iconic buildings, places where we will work, sleep, study, play, and gather together for years to come.

Broadly speaking, the best new building is one that complements the architecture and community surrounding it while also demonstrating something visionary, purposeful, and responsive to the modern world. This guide provides a broad survey of some of the projects that meet this high bar of design excellence. In addition to emphasizing innovations in form, materials, and amenities, the sites here highlight efficient land use in an increasingly dense city, creative infrastructure improvements, state-of-the-art high rises, dignified senior housing, neighborhood-focused social services, and energy-efficient construction in an era defined by climate change.

The Chicago Architecture Center (CAC), founded in 1966, is a model for architecture centers worldwide. Though we are proud of Chicago's design legacy, it is our mission to inspire people to discover why design matters *today*. We offer a range of activities, including tours, gallery exhibitions, lectures, special events, and youth and adult education programs, all of which promote a broad and inclusive understanding of the built environment both locally and nationally. CAC challenges audiences of children and adults to consider how design shapes our lives and ways each of us can participate in the design process to help make our world better.

In August 2018, the CAC opened our new home above the Chicago River at Michigan and East Wacker. This dazzling space includes exhibits on Chicago's architectural legacy and innovative skyscrapers from around the world. The star attraction of the Center is our Chicago City Model, featuring more than 4,000 buildings and interactive elements that tell amazing stories of Chicago's growth after the fire through today. The public embraced this new "first stop" for design-minded visitors as a launching pad to explore the city. The *Guide to Chicago's Twenty-First Century Architecture* will help readers discover breathtaking new building designs that consider the triumphs and challenges of the past while pointing the way to a sustainable and resilient future.

Lynn J. Osmond, Hon. AIA
President & CEO
Chicago Architecture Center

Acknowledgments

After writing my first book, a guide to contemporary architecture in New York City published in 2011, I knew I would need help to make another similar book feasible—guidebooks are a lot of work! Having grown up in the suburbs of Chicago and worked in the city as an architect for close to ten years after architecture school, Chicago was a natural choice for another guidebook. And the Chicago Architecture Center (CAC) was a natural choice for collaboration.

So, thanks go first of all to CAC President and CEO Lynn Osmond for having faith in the project; it took a while from our first meeting until the book became a reality, but the time devoted to making a quality document of the city's architecture in the first two decades of this century is worth it. Thanks to Matthew Kuhl and Ray Clark for their part in setting up that first meeting all those years ago.

Thanks to the team at CAC—both past and present—especially Jen Masengarb whose knowledge of the city's architecture, keen insights, sharp editing, and unending patience made this book so much better than it would have been with me alone. Jen assembled a crack team of CAC docents and volunteers who shared their collective expertise and fact-checking talents. A special thank you to Roberto Valazquez who compiled all the relevant transit stops covering over 234 square miles of Chicago and its neighboring suburbs. Thanks also to Eric Huck, Billy Shelton, Adam Rubin, and Dan O'Connell for their work with the University of Illinois Press and their behind-the-scenes work in moving the project forward every step of the way.

Thanks to the CAC staff who created and assembled the many photographs and renderings that make this guidebook as beautiful as it is useful—Anne Evans, Anna Munzesheimer, and Eric Allix Rogers, in addition to a long list of additional and equally talented photographers whose images appear in these pages. Thanks in particular to a few friends who provided photos for buildings I couldn't capture myself: Lynn Becker, Don Guss, Frank Hashimoto, Margo Hill, Jeff Parfitt, and John Zacherle. Thanks to Walton Chan for making the maps. Thanks to my sister Margo for giving me a place to stay on my numerous visits to Chicago that were needed to research and write this book. Thanks to Lynn Inman for her indispensable advice early in the project. And thanks to Karen and Clare for putting up with yet another book project that devoured our free time together—I'll make up for it when we return to Chicago with guidebook in hand.

GUIDE TO CHICAGO'S TWENTY-FIRST-CENTURY ARCHITECTURE

Introduction

An architecture symposium at the Art Institute of Chicago in 2000 asked the assembled architecture critics and prominent local architects, "Where in the World Is Chicago?" A few years later, in a January 2003 edition of the *Chicago Reader*, critic Lynn Becker demanded that architects and their clients "Stop the Blandness!"[1] a sentiment echoed by then Mayor Richard M. Daley, who spoke out in February of the same year against the "bland concrete hulks that are blighting the cityscape."[2] Yet by the time Becker's and Daley's words hit the streets, there were signs of a turnaround that would eventually tip the scales and see the good elevated over the bad.

If we look to the years leading up to the millennium, when developers and institutions were building like crazy after the heavy recession of the early 1990s, years when people were actually moving (back) into the city following decades of population decline, this weight appears to have stifled creativity, as very few notable pieces of architecture were realized. The mediocre became the norm, even for buildings that warranted excellence. To wit, *Chicago Tribune* architecture critic Blair Kamin labeled the evolution of North Michigan Avenue, the city's richest and most trafficked thoroughfare, "The Mediocre Mile."[3]

But it wasn't always like this. Chicago's architectural history abounds with larger-than-life personalities whose impacts were felt far beyond the city's borders: Louis Sullivan, Frank Lloyd Wright, and Ludwig Mies van der Rohe, three of the greatest architects of the modern era. Sayings attributed to them—"Form follows function," "Less is more," and "God is in the details," in particular—still serve as mantras for architects, as does Daniel H. Burnham's famous dictum, "Make no little plans; they have no magic to stir men's blood." Less than two decades after Burnham oversaw the "White City" of the 1893 World's Fair, he and Edward H. Bennett created the 1909 *Plan of Chicago*, one of the most influential planning documents of all time. Add to these well-known personalities that the city rebuilt itself after the Great Chicago Fire of 1871, that Chicago is often considered the birthplace of the skyscraper (William Le Baron Jenney's Home Insurance Building was erected in 1885 as one of the first tall buildings with a structural steel frame), and that the city was home to the tallest building in the world from 1974 until 1998 (Skidmore, Owings & Merrill's Sears Tower, now Willis Tower)—it's no wonder that architects in Chicago have a heavy weight on their broad shoulders.

Evidence of an apparent 180-degree shift in Chicago's architectural climate—from bland to beautiful—can be found in the pages of this guide to two decades of contemporary architecture in the city and suburbs. But how did this happen? How did local architects move from bland to brilliant in less than a decade? Answers can be found in a man, a plan, and what the two represent.

RICHARD M. DALEY

Richard M. Daley—first son of Richard J. Daley, who served as Chicago mayor from 1955 to 1976—surpassed his father's tenure when he stepped down in 2011 after leading Chicago for 22 years and six terms. From when he took office in 1989, Richard M. Daley made the physical aspects of the city a priority. He cleaned up the Loop and activated it to become a place to live and play, not just work. He encouraged the transformation of warehouses and other industrial buildings near the Loop into living spaces geared at young professionals. He focused on tourism, particularly through the conversion of Navy Pier into an entertainment venue that became the most-visited tourist spot in Chicago. He rerouted Lake Shore Drive—its north- and south-bound lanes previously split around the Field Museum and Soldier Field "island"—to create the Museum Campus, another well-trafficked part of the city for visitors. And, beyond developments in the downtown area, he promoted green building initiatives and street plantings, which earned him the nickname "Mayor Daisy." But the greatest stamp he left on Chicago is undoubtedly Millennium Park.

MILLENNIUM PARK

The plan for the 24.5-acre park started as a simple one when it was first proposed by the Daley administration in 1997—a green platform over the railroad tracks that long separated Michigan Avenue from Grant Park and Lake Michigan beyond. By the time Millennium Park opened in 2004, it had ballooned into a half-billion-dollar collection of gardens, pavilions, cultural venues, artworks, and big-name architecture. The first chapter of this book goes into plenty of detail on Millennium Park, but suffice it to say here that it is a place that lives up to its hype. Sure, the assemblage of art, architecture, and landscape is an odd mix of styles and surfaces, but the 21st-century public space skillfully combines leisure, entertainment, and beauty to stimulate the senses and offer something for tourists and residents alike. With contributions by a Pritzker Prize–winning architect from Los Angeles via Canada, an artist from Spain and one born in India, a landscape architect from the Pacific Northwest, and a Chicago-based master planner with eleven offices in five countries, Millennium Park is also a symbol of Chicago's global situation.

THE GLOBALIZATION OF CHICAGO ARCHITECTURE

It could be said that obviously we are all global, since we can buy fruits from another hemisphere at our local grocery store and video chat with friends or colleagues anywhere at any time. But very few cities can boast of being global and Chicago is one of them. Its global-city status was cemented in the minds of many in 2001, when Boeing decided to move its international headquarters to Chicago; but that is only one sign of the way the city manages and controls global flows of money, goods, services, and information. Yes, cities like New York, London, and Tokyo are the dominant global cities, but Saskia Sassen, an expert on the phenomenon, wrote in 2004: "Others, like Chicago, are relatively young, products of the Industrial Revolution, manufacturing giants that grew from raw labor pools to places of power and sophistication in little more than a century. These cities are reinventing themselves now for the first time."[4]

Chicago's "reinvention" was already evident when the critics and architects assembled at the Art Institute in 2000 to respond to the question "Where in the World is Chicago?" The most notable projects "on the boards" at the time were Los Angeles architect Frank Gehry's billowing bandshell in Millennium Park, Italian architect Renzo Piano's modernist expansion of the Art Institute, and Dutch architect Rem Koolhaas's "L"-wrapping student center for the Illinois Institute of Technology. Architects from outside Chicago designed these buildings—a sure sign of globalization, but one that perturbed local architects who would have preferred that those commissions went to them instead. Not content to whine, a number of local architects have partaken in the global flows that the city is an integral part of by exporting their services to other cities and countries: numerous Chicago firms have opened offices in other cities and countries this century, some of them to realize the world's tallest buildings—what now takes place in parts of Asia rather than the US. More relevant here, many Chicago architects responded to this expansion of the architectural battlefield by elevating the quality of their architecture at home.

Rahm Emanuel took over as mayor in 2011, when the city was struggling to build after the Great Recession. By the time he left office eight years later, Chicago was in the midst of yet another boom that would reshape the city's iconic skyline and see many postindustrial areas slated for development. Daley had Millennium Park and Emanuel had the Riverwalk. But Emanuel also had the Chicago Architecture Biennial, which debuted at the Chicago Cultural Center in 2015, alternates with the more famous Venice Architecture Biennale but further embeds the city in global architectural culture.

At the end of the second decade of the 21st century—a decade and a half after Millennium Park opened and in the early days of Mayor Lori E. Lightfoot's administration following three decades of Daley and Emanuel—architecture in Chicago is a vibrant, verdant scene that deserves a guide of its own. This book serves as that guide, to aid in traversing the best buildings and landscapes produced in Chicago since the turn of the millennium.

SELECTION CRITERIA

This guide to contemporary architecture shares a number of traits with my first book, *Guide to Contemporary New York City Architecture* (W. W. Norton, 2011), including the criteria for what to include. The more than 200 buildings and spaces found in this guide are hardly an objective list of the best architecture in Chicago since 2000. If such a list were possible, it would have to include buildings and interiors not visible by or accessible to the public, as well as the shops, bars, restaurants, and other creative designs that are often short-lived—intentionally or otherwise. The main two criteria for selecting the entries are that projects are visible or accessible in one form or another, and that the buildings and spaces are long-term additions to the cityscape.

Limiting the projects in terms of design quality is a subjective exercise based on my experience as an architect—first in Chicago and then in New York—and then as a writer and editor on architecture. I did not let awards, publications, or other semi-objective rankings dictate what is considered good or what should be in this book, even though many of the projects have justifiably won their fair share of awards. In matters of taste there are always disagreements, so readers as well as architects may quibble about projects left out of the book.

There has also been a concerted effort to go beyond the Loop and nearby neighborhoods, the usual purview of most guides to Chicago. Rightly called a city of neighborhoods, Chicago's excellence in architecture this century has thankfully reached out into the places where people live, learn, and play. It is recommended that those new to the city venture beyond the downtown area to see what the city's neighborhoods—and the suburbs—have to offer.

HOW TO NAVIGATE THE CITY

Following the Land Ordinance of 1785, Chicago is laid out on a rational grid that divides the city into square-mile sections and locates major commercial streets on the miles and half-miles, starting from "0,0" at the intersection of State Street and Madison Street in the Loop. Easy enough, but streets and addresses happen at the rate of 800—or eight blocks—per mile, which can make navigating the city a little tricky at first for visitors. A couple of hypothetical examples to illustrate: a building at 2400 West Madison Street is exactly three miles west of State and Madison, and a building at 1200 North State Street is one and a half miles north of the intersection. It wasn't always this rational; not until Edward P. Brennan cleaned up Chicago's messy street numbering and naming system in 1909 to give us the orderly 800s we have to this day. A few exceptions to the 800-rule exist on the Near South Side, where Roosevelt Road (1200 South) is found only one mile south of Madison and 800-to-a-mile addresses don't resume until 31st Street.

A major trick in navigating the city is learning which named street, avenue, or boulevard is which number. Not all readers of this book are expected to know that the hypothetical building at 2400 West Madison Street sits at the intersection of Western Avenue, or that the one at 1200 North State Street is at the corner of Division Street, so addresses and directions in the guide are made as clear as possible, aided by the maps that indicate the major thoroughfares and their numbers. Beyond thinking in eights instead of tens, it's important to note that even-numbered addresses are on the north and west sides of the street, and odd-numbered ones are on the south and east sides of the streets. With this in mind, anybody can find an address in Chicago without having to look at a smartphone.

HOW TO USE THIS GUIDE

Three sections comprise this guide:

- Two hundred projects, or main entries, make up the bulk of the book. Clearly numbered 1–200 and keyed to maps, they are organized into neighborhood chapters.
- About one hundred more projects, some of them in-progress or under construction, are inserted into the appropriate chapters as sidebars.
- Supplemental material: glossary, selected bibliography, and indexes by architect, building name, and building type.

The main projects include the following information.

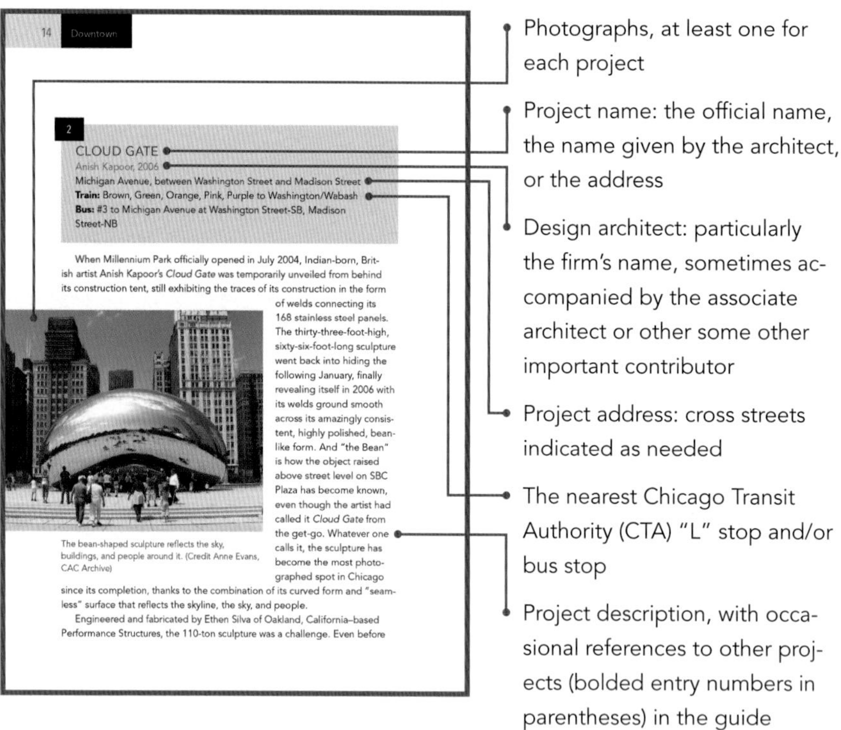

14 Downtown

2

CLOUD GATE
Anish Kapoor, 2006
Michigan Avenue, between Washington Street and Madison Street
Train: Brown, Green, Orange, Pink, Purple to Washington/Wabash
Bus: #3 to Michigan Avenue at Washington Street-SB, Madison Street-NB

When Millennium Park officially opened in July 2004, Indian-born, British artist Anish Kapoor's *Cloud Gate* was temporarily unveiled from behind its construction tent, still exhibiting the traces of its construction in the form of welds connecting its 168 stainless steel panels. The thirty-three-foot-high, sixty-six-foot-long sculpture went back into hiding the following January, finally revealing itself in 2006 with its welds ground smooth across its amazingly consistent, highly polished, bean-like form. And "the Bean" is how the object raised above street level on SBC Plaza has become known, even though the artist had called it *Cloud Gate* from the get-go. Whatever one calls it, the sculpture has become the most photographed spot in Chicago since its completion, thanks to the combination of its curved form and "seamless" surface that reflects the skyline, the sky, and people.

Engineered and fabricated by Ethen Silva of Oakland, California–based Performance Structures, the 110-ton sculpture was a challenge. Even before

The bean-shaped sculpture reflects the sky, buildings, and people around it. (Credit Anne Evans, CAC Archive)

- Photographs, at least one for each project
- Project name: the official name, the name given by the architect, or the address
- Design architect: particularly the firm's name, sometimes accompanied by the associate architect or other some other important contributor
- Project address: cross streets indicated as needed
- The nearest Chicago Transit Authority (CTA) "L" stop and/or bus stop
- Project description, with occasional references to other projects (bolded entry numbers in parentheses) in the guide

The two hundred projects are broken down into twenty-one chapters focusing on one or more neighborhoods. The chapters are grouped into five regions, starting at the Loop and then moving to the North Side, the West Side, the South Side, and into the suburbs.

While separated into digestible chunks, this book is not meant to be a strict turn-left-here-and-look-at-this-building walking guide. The ordering of the numbered projects, aided by the accompanying maps, offers an implied route, but veering from a connect-the-numbers path is encouraged. This is aided through the maps' highlighting of nearby buildings and spaces: well-known landmarks and open spaces, other projects mentioned in the book, and sidebar projects. In addition to the names of streets and parks, the maps show the "L" lines and stops.

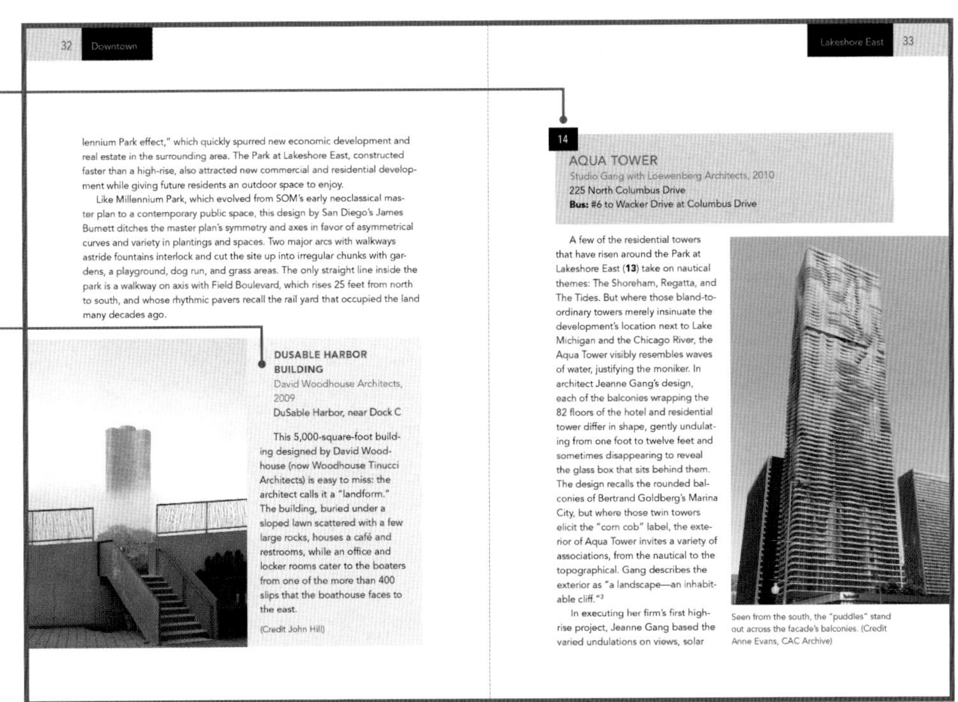

32 Downtown

lennium Park effect," which quickly spurred new economic development and real estate in the surrounding area. The Park at Lakeshore East, constructed faster than a high-rise, also attracted new commercial and residential development while giving future residents an outdoor space to enjoy.

Like Millennium Park, which evolved from SOM's early neoclassical master plan to a contemporary public space, this design by San Diego's James Burnett ditches the master plan's symmetry and axes in favor of asymmetrical curves and variety in plantings and spaces. Two major arcs with walkways astride fountains interlock and cut the site up into irregular chunks with gardens, a playground, dog run, and grass areas. The only straight line inside the park is a walkway on axis with Field Boulevard, which rises 25 feet from north to south, and whose rhythmic pavers recall the rail yard that occupied the land many decades ago.

DUSABLE HARBOR BUILDING
David Woodhouse Architects, 2009
DuSable Harbor, near Dock C

This 5,000-square-foot building designed by David Woodhouse (now Woodhouse Tinucci Architects) is easy to miss: the architect calls it a "landform." The building, buried under a sloped lawn scattered with a few large rocks, houses a café and restrooms, while an office and locker rooms cater to the boaters from one of the more than 400 slips that the boathouse faces to the east.

(Credit John Hill)

Lakeshore East 33

14
AQUA TOWER
Studio Gang with Loewenberg Architects, 2010
225 North Columbus Drive
Bus: #6 to Wacker Drive at Columbus Drive

A few of the residential towers that have risen around the Park at Lakeshore East (**13**) take on nautical themes: The Shoreham, Regatta, and The Tides. But where those bland-to-ordinary towers merely insinuate the development's location next to Lake Michigan and the Chicago River, the Aqua Tower visibly resembles waves of water, justifying the moniker. In architect Jeanne Gang's design, each of the balconies wrapping the 82 floors of the hotel and residential tower differ in shape, gently undulating from one foot to twelve feet and sometimes disappearing to reveal the glass box that sits behind them. The design recalls the rounded balconies of Bertrand Goldberg's Marina City, but where those twin towers elicit the "corn cob" label, the exterior of Aqua Tower invites a variety of associations, from the nautical to the topographical. Gang describes the exterior as "a landscape—an inhabitable cliff."[3]

In executing her firm's first high-rise project, Jeanne Gang based the varied undulations on views, solar

Seen from the south, the "puddles" stand out across the facade's balconies. (Credit Anne Evans, CAC Archive)

Downtown

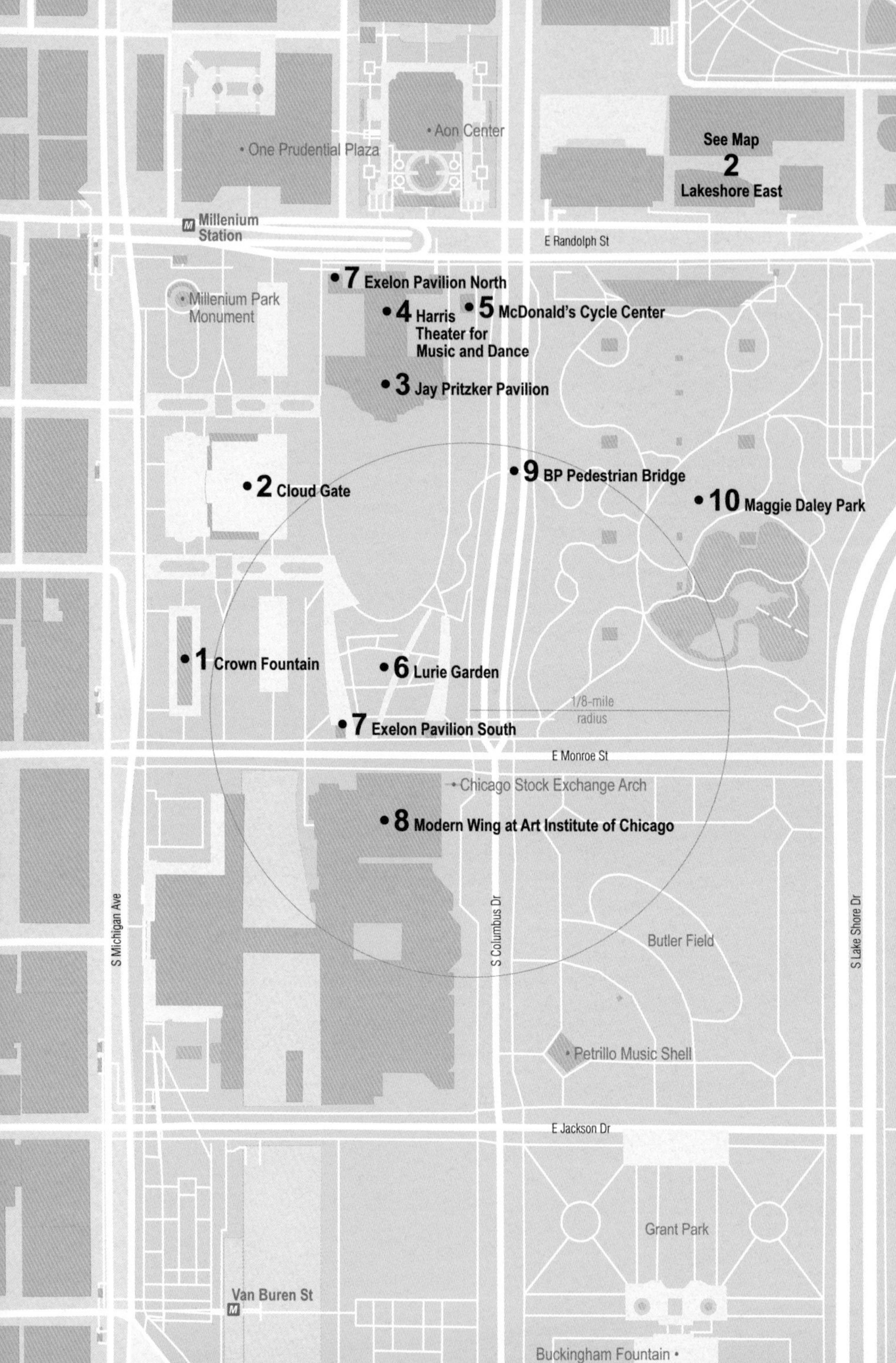
One Prudential Plaza
Aon Center
See Map
2
Lakeshore East
Millenium Station
E Randolph St
7 Exelon Pavilion North
Millenium Park Monument
4 Harris Theater for Music and Dance
5 McDonald's Cycle Center
3 Jay Pritzker Pavilion
9 BP Pedestrian Bridge
2 Cloud Gate
10 Maggie Daley Park
1 Crown Fountain
6 Lurie Garden
1/8-mile radius
7 Exelon Pavilion South
E Monroe St
Chicago Stock Exchange Arch
8 Modern Wing at Art Institute of Chicago
S Michigan Ave
S Columbus Dr
Butler Field
S Lake Shore Dr
Petrillo Music Shell
E Jackson Dr
Grant Park
Van Buren St
Buckingham Fountain

1 Millennium Park

More than a sign of Chicago's global-city ambitions and cultural transformations, Millennium Park illustrates the physical evolution of the city and represents how political and economic decisions can have long-ranging impacts.

If we look back in time far enough—as recently as about 16,000 years ago—the land that Chicago is built upon was underwater. By the time glacial Lake Chicago drained and receded, only the area east of present-day Michigan Avenue remained submerged. In 1852, the city made a deal with the Illinois Central Railroad, where the latter built a breakwater just east of Michigan Avenue in exchange for a right-of-way along a swath of the lakefront from the city's southern limits to Randolph Street. Trains ran east of downtown on a trestle between the breakwater and a recreation lagoon, ending in a depot and yards on the land now occupied by the Prudential Center, Illinois Center, and Lakeshore East development.

Jump ahead to 1989, when Richard M. Daley started his first of six terms as mayor, and the situation was much different: the depot was long gone, the lagoon east of Michigan Avenue was long ago filled in, and the yards were underused, a victim of the decline of railroads and rise of trucking in the middle of the 20th century. The future site of Millennium Park was a 24.5-acre hole in the northwest corner of Grant Park. The tracks, used only for passenger service by this time, were located below street level, thanks to electrification of the line in the 1920s, but much of the site was empty, used as a quasi-parking lot. Only a narrow strip along Michigan Avenue, with parkland atop a parking garage, was of any use to the public.

In 1998, after the Daley administration found a means of taking back the land from the railroad, Skidmore, Owings & Merrill (SOM) devised a master plan that would have placed a Beaux Arts–style park on decking over the tracks and on a sizable parking garage covering the eastern half of the site—total price tag: $150 million. Under the direction of former Chicago Park District architect Edward Uhlir, the plan quickly departed from its neo-traditional design and became more ambitious, thanks also to the fund-raising skills of

Sara Lee CEO John Bryan. The latter was necessary since Daley vowed to pay for the park solely with private funds and the parking garage revenue, which certainly couldn't cover the costs of the project topping out at $475 million. Soon Chicago businesspeople and corporations were giving millions for the park elements bearing their names, from an ice rink and tree-lined promenade, to the ambitious artworks and architecture that are described in this chapter. Since opening on July 16, 2004, Millennium Park has received more than 4 million visitors annually, making it the city's most popular destination after Navy Pier. But more than a tourist attraction, Millennium Park is a dense cultural assemblage that has injected life into downtown, spurred (primarily residential) development in the area, and paved the way for cities around the world to use landscapes and public space to do the same—"The Millennium Park Effect."

1

CROWN FOUNTAIN

Jaume Plensa with Krueck Sexton Partners, 2004
Michigan Avenue, between Madison Street and Monroe Street
Train: Brown, Green, Orange, Pink, Purple to Washington/Wabash
Bus: #3 to Michigan Avenue at Monroe Street

From the early days of SOM's master plan for Millennium Park, the southwest corner of the park was the intended site of a fountain. It was drawn as a small circular fountain bracketed by curved plantings on the south edge, in effect mirroring the reconstructed peristyle at the northwest corner of the park and recalling the grander Buckingham Fountain in the center of Grant Park. Yet *Crown Fountain* is as far removed from those neoclassical precedents as could be imagined—it is a water feature for the 21st century, merging computer technologies, innovative materials, and interactive spectacle to create something that hardly recalls any fountain built before. Illuminated faces on fifty-foot-high glass blocks look at each other across a shallow granite pool, spouting water every five minutes, to the delight of children who would be told to stay out of the more formal Buckingham Fountain.

The fountain is named for the family of businessman Lester Crown, who, with the Goodman family, donated $10 million toward its realization. The

Over a thousand people from all parts of Chicago adorn the fountains. (Credit Anne Evans, CAC Archive)

Crowns were instrumental also in finding Spanish artist Jaume Plensa, who was their choice after holding an informal competition among a few artists. Inspired by old Roman fountains, his concept of gargoyle-like faces on large cascading glass blocks astride a shallow pool is remarkably consistent with what was built, something that required the help of architects Ron Krueck and Mark Sexton. They worked with engineers and manufacturers to develop an internal stainless steel frame to laterally brace the "towers" and support the over 20,000 white glass blocks that were handmade in Pittsburgh. The LED lights that display the faces on the fronts and colors on the sides sit directly behind the glass, while, in the middle, is a system of piping for recirculating water from an underground reservoir.

Crown Fountain is a staggeringly complex construction, which was criticized by some in its early stages as too large, too Disney, and potentially upstaging Anish Kapoor's *Cloud Gate* (**2**). Rather, Plensa's work manages to move the attention from the fountain and its displays to the joy taking place between them, even in the winter when the water stops flowing.

2

CLOUD GATE

Anish Kapoor, 2006

Michigan Avenue, between Washington Street and Madison Street

Train: Brown, Green, Orange, Pink, Purple to Washington/Wabash

Bus: #3 to Michigan Avenue at Washington Street-SB, Madison Street-NB

When Millennium Park officially opened in July 2004, Indian-born, British artist Anish Kapoor's *Cloud Gate* was temporarily unveiled from behind its construction tent, still exhibiting the traces of its construction in the form of welds connecting its 168 stainless steel panels. The thirty-three-foot-high, sixty-six-foot-long sculpture went back into hiding the following January, finally revealing itself in 2006 with its welds ground smooth across its amazingly consistent, highly polished, bean-like form. And "the Bean" is how the object raised above street level on SBC Plaza has become known, even though the artist had called it *Cloud Gate* from the get-go. Whatever one calls it, the sculpture has become the most photographed spot in Chicago since its completion, thanks to the combination of its curved form and "seamless" surface that reflects the skyline, the sky, and people.

The bean-shaped sculpture reflects the sky, buildings, and people around it. (Credit Anne Evans, CAC Archive)

Engineered and fabricated by Ethen Silva of Oakland, California–based Performance Structures, the 110-ton sculpture was a challenge. Even before its erection on site, the parking garage below the plaza had to be reengineered to accommodate its weight. Much of the tonnage is thanks to an internal steel structure that the 168 panels are loosely attached to, allowing the skin to expand and contract with Chicago's wide temperature swings. Most amazing is that the surface appears continuous, something unheard of when Kapoor proposed the idea. The curved form gives funhouse reflections of the streetwall along Michigan Avenue and the people looking at themselves in the surface, the latter culminating in the disorienting, navel-like "omphalos" (as it's called) tucked deep inside the structure.

3

JAY PRITZKER PAVILION

Gehry Partners, 2004
201 East Randolph Street
Train: Brown, Green, Orange, Pink, Purple to Washington/Wabash
Bus: #3 to Michigan Avenue at Randolph Street

When the Pritzker family, owner of Hyatt Hotels and patron of the Pritzker Architecture Prize (considered the profession's Nobel Prize), ponied up the money for Millennium Park's music venue, they insisted a recipient of their eponymous award design it. They wanted Frank Gehry—more than that, they wanted *a Gehry*. But one of the Los Angeles–based, Canadian-born architect's first schemes was more Mies than Gehry, a gentle arc rising up and across the raised artificial landscape. Yet as the billowing sheets of stainless steel attest, the architect was persuaded to

The large trellis arching over the lawn supports the speakers and creates a sense of enclosure. (Credit Anne Evans, CAC Archive)

The billowing "headdress" as seen from the west along Washington Street. (Credit John Hill)

design something unmistakably Gehry, with echoes of the Guggenheim in Bilbao, Spain, and just about each of his commissions since that museum was completed in 1997.

The Jay Pritzker Pavilion, which serves the Grant Park Music Festival and other concerts, is made up of three architectural elements: a fairly plain box containing the stage and the back-of-house functions, the billowing metal-clad "headdress," and a steel-pipe trellis that arches over the lawn. The stage area is lined with a ceiling and walls of Douglas fir—a warm counterpoint to the stainless steel flowing around it—and outfitted with large sliding glass walls to close the stage off from the elements and for private events. Other parts of the stage and back-of-house are concealed from view by the headdress and by building down as much as possible, just like the Harris Theater (**4**), which the pavilion backs up against and shares facilities with.

The second element, the curling panels of stainless steel, understandably grabs the most attention, since the panels appear to be frozen in an explosion radiating from the proscenium. Projecting forward, outward, and upward to conceal catwalks and lighting, the billowing pieces shelter some of the 4,000 fixed seats and are clad with brushed stainless steel to cut down on the inevitable glare. Described by Gehry as "a bouquet of flowers in the park,"[1] they are a joy to behold whatever metaphor is applied to them. They also greatly exceed the height limitations on buildings in Grant Park, a situation remedied easily when Gehry called his creation a sculpture. Be sure to take a peek around the side and rear to see the "truth"; the substantial structure required to give the "flowers" their shape and support.

The third and last element is the interlocking trellis that sits on round concrete columns in the perimeter walkway and span across a lawn larger than two football fields, enough room for 7,000 more spectators. Wanting to get away from speakers mounted to pylons that block views of the stage, Gehry worked with acoustical consultant Talaske Group to create the overhead armature for speakers with technological enhancements that ensure all 11,000 concertgoers hear the performances equally well, while blocking out traffic and other noises of the city. Gehry might not have been able to get his way with the simplified bandshell design he first proposed, but the trellis comes close to it both in form and in "enclosing" a space with the most minimal of means.

4

HARRIS THEATER FOR MUSIC AND DANCE

Hammond Beeby Rupert Ainge Architects, 2003
205 East Randolph Street
Train: Brown, Green, Orange, Pink, Purple to Washington/Wabash
Bus: #3 to Michigan Avenue at Randolph Street

The Joan W. and Irving B. Harris Theater for Music and Dance opened the doors to its 1,500-seat performance space in November 2003, eight months before the official opening of Millennium Park. This fact is telling, since the theater is the one park element that comes across as slightly removed from it rather than an integral part of it. The theater is oriented to Randolph Street rather than the park, it is primarily hidden below grade, and it is a subdued

Outwardly, the theater is a simple glass box facing Randolph Street. (Credit Anna Munzesheimer, CAC Archive)

design relative to the other park elements. (It is also much more subdued than Thomas Beeby's 1991 Harold Washington Library Center in the Loop.) It serves as an integral part of Millennium Park, since it brings a much-needed midsized performance venue to the city, and it shares back-of-house facilities with the Jay Pritzker Pavilion (**3**).

Practical constraints and functional requirements drove much of what happens in the building, from restrictions on building heights in Grant Park and its location next to double-decker Randolph Street to the location of loading docks and the need to accommodate a wide range of performance types (ballet, chamber music, dance, jazz, and opera). Beeby's restrained design, which buries most of the theater's volume below the street and the level of Lake Michigan, pops up the entry with a boxy enclosure oriented toward Randolph Street, where glass walls carefully frame Louise Nevelson's stage curtain for *Orpheus and Eurydice* and hint at what happens underground.

5

McDONALD'S CYCLE CENTER

Muller+Muller, 2004

239 East Randolph Street

Train: Brown, Green, Orange, Pink, Purple to Randolph/Wabash

Bus: #3 to Michigan Avenue at Randolph Street

The roof of the glass building is angled slightly for the PV panels. (Credit Anna Munzesheimer, CAC Archive)

Regardless of its harsh winters, Chicago is an ideal place for biking, mainly thanks to its flat landscape and the slow but steady incorporation of bike lanes and other means of making riding safer and more enjoyable. As one way to encourage bicycling, the city incorporated a facility for storing, renting and repairing bikes into Millennium Park, tucking it into the northeast corner at Columbus and

Randolph. The cycle center, with parking for 300 bikes, is a three-story structure with two stories below grade (where showers and lockers are also found) and one story popping above as a glass atrium that is capped by photovoltaic panels angled to the south and flanked by blue awnings on the side.

6

LURIE GARDEN

Gustafson Guthrie Nichols, 2004
Monroe Street, at Columbus Drive
Train: Brown, Green, Orange, Pink, Purple to Adams/Wabash
Bus: #3 to Michigan Avenue at Monroe Street

The presence of the built past in any city exists on a gradient from preserved buildings and landscapes, re-created ones, and traces or hints at what came before. In Millennium Park, preserved buildings are nonexistent; a re-creation of a classical curved peristyle (designed in 1917 by Edward H. Bennett, coauthor of the *Plan of Chicago*) is found in the park's northwest corner; and a trace of the past lies in the opposite corner. Here is the competition-winning Lurie Garden designed by Seattle's Kathryn Gustafson with planting designer Piet Oudolf and theater set designer Robert Israel. In their design narrative, an arcing "seam" with a boardwalk, water feature, and stone wall follows the path of an old retaining wall that separated the Illinois Central tracks from Lake Michigan

Seen from the seam, the city's skyline rises beyond the garden's flowers and shoulder hedge. (Credit Anne Evans, CAC Archive)

for much of Chicago's history. This history became a trace, a mark across the raised artificial landscape that subtly makes the visitor aware of the city's expanding shoreline.

Metaphors continue with the large, steel-framed "shoulder hedge" that brackets the garden on the north and west and references the "City of the Big Shoulders" line in Carl Sandburg's famous "Chicago" poem. The 30,000 perennials of 240 varieties, shrubs, grasses, and trees in the garden—technically a green roof atop the 2,126-car parking garage—are separated into two halves via the seam. To the east is the "dark plate," raised and naturally darker through the presence of trees, and to the west is the "light plate," a four-season explosion of color thanks to groupings of the majority of the perennials and bulbs in a sunny opening. The whole garden expresses the City of Chicago's Latin motto "Urbs in horto," which translates to "City in a Garden." Stand on the seam and look at the skyline of tall buildings beyond the plants and above-shoulder hedge—from here that statement is the beautiful truth.

7

EXELON PAVILIONS

Hammond Beeby Rupert Ainge Architects, Renzo Piano Building Workshop, 2004

Randolph Street and Monroe Street, between Michigan Avenue and Columbus Drive

Train: Brown, Green, Orange, Pink, Purple to Adams/Wabash

Bus: #3 to Michigan Avenue at Madison Street

When walking about Millennium Park there are very few indications that its venues, sculptures, and gardens sit atop a huge 2,126-car parking garage. After all, the vehicle entrances are found on Columbus Drive, below the BP Pedestrian Bridge (**9**) and away from the crowds. Yet, access to the parking garage for pedestrians happens at four small pavilions—two on the north and two on the south—that do make the garage known, but in a very subtle manner. Designed respectively by the architects of the Harris Theater (**4**) and the Art Institute's Modern Wing (**8**), the pavilions make only subtle marks on the raised landscape while also incorporating other functions into them.

One of the south pavilions designed by Renzo Piano. (Credit Ruhrfisch CC-BY-SA)

Thomas Beeby's north pavilions are boxes that continue the language of his Harris Theater. But these smaller pieces are covered with glass on all sides, dark glass that selectively incorporates photovoltaic panels. The Welcome Center at Millennium Park is tucked inside the northwest pavilion. In a similar fashion, Renzo Piano's south pavilions are like scaled-down versions of his Modern Wing across Monroe Street: parallel stone walls on the east and west sides bracket glass walls that face the park and the street.

8

MODERN WING AT THE ART INSTITUTE OF CHICAGO

Renzo Piano Building Workshop with Interactive Design Inc., 2009
Monroe Street, between Michigan Avenue and Columbus Drive
Train: Brown, Green, Orange, Pink, Purple to Adams/Wabash
Bus: #3 to Michigan Avenue at Monroe Street

When Renzo Piano was hired by the Art Institute of Chicago in 1999 for what would become a 264,000-square-foot expansion adding 65,000 square feet of gallery space, the Italian architect was *the* go-to architect for museum commissions. Around that time, he also started working on designs for museums in Atlanta, Dallas, and Switzerland, and by the time the Modern Wing, as it came to be known, opened to the public across the street from Millennium Park, Piano had completed close to 15 other museums since the Centre Georges Pompidou in Paris in 1977 (with Richard Rogers). Needless to say, hopes were high that Piano would give Chicago, like Gehry across the street, a signature design that would help draw even more people.

The Art Institute dates back to 1893, occupying the only permanent building from that year's World's Fair that was not built in Jackson Park. The

The north facade of the Modern Wing as seen under its pedestrian bridge linked to Millennium Park. (Credit © Nic Lehoux)

museum sits on a highly visible site in Grant Park where Adams Street meets Michigan Avenue. It is one of the few exceptions to the restrictions that prohibited buildings being erected in Grant Park since the efforts of Aaron Montgomery Ward and Daniel Burnham in the late-19th and early-20th centuries. In the words of James Cuno, director of the museum from 2004–2011, "The Art Institute has been almost in perpetual construction and renovation since its first building opened,"[2] with additions flanking its original building and bridging the Illinois Central tracks toward Columbus Drive. The museum Piano encountered when he started designing was a classical edifice facing the city that tumbled into an odd assemblage of additions toward the park.

An initial idea of bridging the

Skylit Griffin Court is the main spine of the addition. (Credit © Nic Lehoux)

The galleries and third-floor sculpture terrace take advantage of singular views of Millennium Park. (Credit © Nic Lehoux)

tracks was shelved in favor of placing the addition over the site of the former Goodman Theatre near the intersection of Monroe and Columbus. This location positions the building on axis with Frank Gehry's Jay Pritzker Pavilion (**3**) and gives the museum an entrance from the north, from both street level and the slender pedestrian Nichols Bridgeway (also designed by Piano's firm) that touches down in the middle of Millennium Park. The addition is organized into three zones, defined by parallel, north-south limestone walls with expansive glass walls between them. The most extraordinary feature of Piano's design is the "flying carpet," a huge skylight roof propped on slender steel columns over the boxy eastern portion of the three-story addition. The louver-like skylight allows diffuse north light to enter the top-floor galleries, and its substantial cantilever shades the glass walls from direct sunlight in the warm months. The slender western portion of the addition, next to the tracks, houses more galleries, including those devoted to architecture. Between those is the generous Griffin Court, which is capped by its own skylight and connects to the rest of the museum. Not to be missed are the rooftop sculpture terrace with its views of Millennium Park and the Terzo Piano restaurant, designed by Dirk Denison Architects.

9

BP PEDESTRIAN BRIDGE

Gehry Partners, 2004

Columbus Drive, between Monroe Street and Randolph Street

Train: Brown, Green, Orange, Pink, Purple to Adams/Wabash

Bus: #3 to Michigan Avenue at Monroe Street

The second Frank Gehry–designed piece in the park is a curling, nearly 1,000-foot-long pedestrian bridge that spans six lanes of traffic on Columbus Drive to connect Millennium Park to Maggie Daley Park (**10**). Clad in stain-

The snaking, titanium-clad bridge is unmistakable Gehry. (Credit Anne Evans, CAC Archive)

less steel panels like the Jay Pritzker Pavilion (**3**), yet concealing the bridge's structure behind the metal skin, the curling walkway appears to be just "Gehry being Gehry," but the snaking form has a reason: accessibility by those with disabilities. The bridge needs to be long and at a low slope to get enough clearance over the roadway for trucks and to eliminate elevators, handrails, and intermediate landings. The back-and-forth of the curling line reorients the gaze of people to the surroundings as they move along the wood walkway from one park to the other.

10

MAGGIE DALEY PARK

Michael Van Valkenburgh Associates, 2015

337 East Randolph Street

Train: Brown, Green, Orange, Pink, Purple to Randolph/Wabash

Bus: #60 to Randolph Street at Columbus Drive

The closest precedent for park-atop-a-parking-lot Millennium Park once sat just across Columbus Drive. Opened in 1977, the Richard J. Daley Bicentennial Plaza, made up of a formal garden, tennis courts, and other recreational amenities, was built atop a 3,700-car parking garage. When Lake Shore Drive was reconfigured in the mid-1980s, the park expanded to 20 acres to include the Cancer Survivor's Garden and Peanut Park. Spurred by much-needed repairs

The skating ribbon and climbing walls anchor the northwest corner of the park. (Credit CAC Archive)

to the parking garage and the construction of Millennium Park, the whole site was renamed Maggie Daley Park in 2012 (in honor of Mayor Daley's late wife) and envisioned as a single continuous park rather than three distinct pieces. Like its neighbor to the west, the design by New York's Michael Van Valkenburgh departs from Grant Park's classical symmetry and axes, in this case favoring what he describes as "curvilinear, topographically dramatic, and relentlessly heterogeneous."[3]

The southwest corner of the park is given over to a three-acre play garden. (Credit CAC Archive)

Perhaps inspired by Frank Gehry's snaking pedestrian bridge (**9**), which delivers people into the middle of the park from Millennium Park, paths here curl across the site, wending around its two main components: the climbing park and skating ribbon in the northwest corner, and the play garden in the southeast corner near Lake Shore Drive. These areas are amped up for recreation and play while a stretch of grass running from the southwest to the northeast invites relaxation and repose. Tripodlike light poles stand out above all other park features, but in time the trees will grow higher and help make the park a popular destination for play and rest.

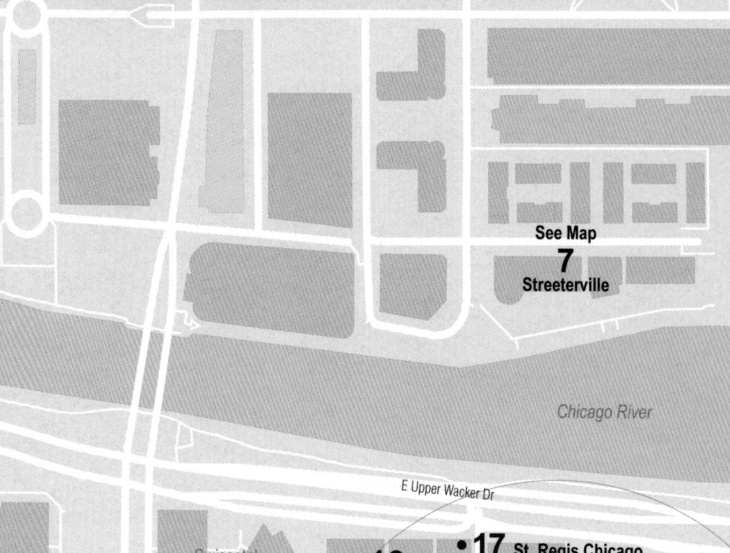
See Map
7
Streeterville
Chicago River
E Upper Wacker Dr
•17 St. Regis Chicago
Swissotel • Chicago
•16 Coast at Lakeshore East
N Field Blvd
•15 GEMS World Academy
E South Water St
•14 Aqua Tower
N Harbor Dr
DuSable Harbor Building •
N Park Dr
•13 The Park at Lakeshore East
N Westshore Dr
1/8-mile radius
N Harbor Service Dr
E Benton Pl
N Columbus Dr
N Lake Shore Dr
N Field Blvd
•11 Blue Cross-Blue Shield Tower
•12 340 On The Park
E Randolph St
See Map
1
Millenium Park

2 Lakeshore East

Just as Millennium Park is built upon Chicago's historical infrastructure, the 28-acre Lakeshore East development occupies land that was once used by the Illinois Central Railroad. The similarities end there though, since Millennium Park is a public amenity built with private funds, while Lakeshore East is a private development geared purely toward profit.

Lakeshore East's site, land at the mouth of the Chicago River, has a varied history. At the time of the city's incorporation in 1837, the Chicago River was not a straight east/west waterway connecting to Lake Michigan. This main stem once turned 90 degrees to the south, creating a hook of land. Eventually, the river was straightened where it meets the lake, and this area, through landfill, turned into a prime spot for grain elevators and, later, a rail yard for the Illinois Central Railroad arriving from the south.

The 20th-century decline of railroad shipping and the movement of the yards south to near Soldier Field led to the creation of several late-20th-century skyscrapers: One Prudential Plaza (completed in 1955, the first tall building in Chicago since the mid-1930s); Aon Center (Standard Oil Building, upon its 1974 completion); and the numerous buildings of Illinois Center (realized starting in the early 1970s). These buildings used air rights—the real estate development practice of selling or renting the empty space above a property to a neighboring site—above the railroad tracks. Decades later, a partially realized Illinois Center had transformed the land north of Randolph Street, east of Michigan Avenue, and west of Columbus Drive from an industrial relic to a neighborhood for living and (primarily) working. But its three-tier system of streets (local traffic above arterial traffic above service vehicles), high-density towers, and uninspired architecture left many Chicagoans wanting something better for this area close to the Loop and Grant Park.

So when it came time for Joel Carlins and James Loewenberg of Magellan Development to "complete" the other half of the planned Illinois Center, they were able to learn from the mistakes of the western half. In 2002, when they unveiled the master plan developed by Skidmore, Owings & Merrill, the residential market was booming, so fourteen of the sixteen proposed towers were residential. The main departure from the plan was the decision not to continue the three-tier system of streets. Instead, Lakeshore East has an at-grade park at its core, with streets circling the development's perimeter at higher elevations: buildings like the Village Market along the southwestern edge make the approximately fifty-foot transition from low to high.

To date, Magellan has realized the majority of its planned construction, with the most glaring gap occurring in the northeast corner overlooking Lake Shore Drive; a 2018 proposal, with Australia's Lendlease, is filling those lots with three residential towers (40, 50, and 80 stories) designed by bKL Architecture and landscaping designed by Claude Cormier + Associés. Most importantly, the quality of the architecture has improved dramatically from Lakeshore East's early days, a fact admitted by Loewenberg, who was also an architect: "I decided early on that I would do a couple of buildings at Lakeshore East, to get it started, and then we would start bringing in the top architects to try different things."[1]

11

BLUE CROSS-BLUE SHIELD TOWER

Goettsch Partners, 2010
300 East Randolph Street
Train: Brown, Green, Orange, Pink, Purple to Washington/Wabash
Bus: #60 to Randolph Street at Columbus Drive

The headquarters for insurance giant Blue Cross-Blue Shield and its operator, Health Care Service Corporation (HCSC), stands as a rare example of a high-rise project that was planned for future expansion from the start, but was built in two phases thirteen years apart. Overlooking the north end of Grant Park, the 33-story building, designed in 1997 by James Goettsch (when he was at Lohan Associates) included foundations, a structural frame, elevators, shaft space, and other services for a future 57-story tower. In 2006, having outgrown the existing building, HCSC made the decision to move forward with the plan and add 24 stories atop the building, all the while keeping their headquarters and tenant spaces operational during construction. To accommodate this, the contractor, Walsh Construction, converted one of the atria

The glass tower forms part of the streetwall on the north side of Grant Park. (Credit Anne Evans, CAC Archive)

spaces into elevator shafts—as planned from the start—erected two cranes on the north side of the building, and took advantage of the building's plaza on the same side to stage construction materials before lifting them 400 feet into the air.

Even with a thirteen-year timeframe between the completions of the phases, the tower looks like one unified tower, thanks to Goettsch being involved throughout and ensuring that exterior finishes and details matched as closely as possible. Round columns poke through the flat, blue-glass south facade roughly every fifteen floors, giving the impression of the building being stitched together. Three-story gaps in the partially stone-clad east and west ends of the tower subtly express the two phases, marking an occurrence when a client made good on its promise to build again.

A pedestrian bridge sandwiched between the two levels of Randolph connects the building's lower lobby to the parking garage below Maggie Daley Park (**10**). (Credit John Hill)

12

340 ON THE PARK

Solomon Cordwell Buenz (SCB), 2007

340 East Randolph Street

Train: Brown, Green, Orange, Pink, Purple to Washington/Wabash

Bus: #60 to Randolph Street at Columbus Drive

A few years before Blue Cross-Blue Shield Tower (**11**) doubled in height, this 62-story tower with 343 condos rose directly to the east. Called "Chicago's first green residential high-rise"[2] when completed, the building is

The south facade of the residential tower overlooking Grant Park. (Credit © James Steinkamp Photography)

more notable for being an improvement over the Lakeshore East towers that preceded it. Perhaps this leap forward in architectural quality owes to facing then three-year-old Millennium Park. Whatever the case, SCB design principal Martin Wolf subtly differed the two major elevations: to the south, balconies and an aluminum-clad grid bracket a center expanse of glass that is broken about a third of the way up by a multi-height amenity floor. A similar language of glass and grid happens to the north, but with a curving wall that orients the tower toward the center of the Park at Lakeshore East (**13**).

13

THE PARK AT LAKESHORE EAST

The Office of James Burnett with Site Design Group, 2005

450 East Benton Place

Train: Brown, Green, Orange, Pink, Purple to Washington/Wabash

Bus: #60 to Randolph Street at Columbus Drive

If applied to real estate, the saying "build it and they will come" would typically apply to buildings: build the apartments, and people will move into them, so the logic goes. But in the case of Lakeshore East development, the "it" was a park. Skidmore, Owings & Merrill's (SOM) master plan arranged the numerous towers of the 28-acre development around a rectangular five-acre park, and this was the first part completed in the development's ongoing realization. This decision on the part of Magellan Development Group could be ascribed to the "Mil-

One of the curving arcs, as seen from atop the podium of Aqua Tower (**14**) (Credit © James Steinkamp Photography)

lennium Park effect," which quickly spurred new economic development and real estate in the surrounding area. The Park at Lakeshore East, constructed faster than a high-rise, also attracted new commercial and residential development while giving future residents an outdoor space to enjoy.

Like Millennium Park, which evolved from SOM's early neoclassical master plan to a contemporary public space, this design by San Diego's James Burnett ditches the master plan's symmetry and axes in favor of asymmetrical curves and variety in plantings and spaces. Two major arcs with walkways astride fountains interlock and cut the site up into irregular chunks with gardens, a playground, dog run, and grass areas. The only straight line inside the park is a walkway on axis with Field Boulevard, which rises 25 feet from north to south, and whose rhythmic pavers recall the rail yard that occupied the land many decades ago.

DUSABLE HARBOR BUILDING

David Woodhouse Architects, 2009

DuSable Harbor, near Dock C

This 5,000-square-foot building designed by David Woodhouse (now Woodhouse Tinucci Architects) is easy to miss: the architect calls it a "landform." The building, buried under a sloped lawn scattered with a few large rocks, houses a café and restrooms, while an office and locker rooms cater to the boaters from one of the more than 400 slips that the boathouse faces to the east.

(Credit John Hill)

14

AQUA TOWER

Studio Gang with Loewenberg Architects, 2010
225 North Columbus Drive
Bus: #6 to Wacker Drive at Columbus Drive

A few of the residential towers that have risen around the Park at Lakeshore East (**13**) take on nautical themes: The Shoreham, Regatta, and The Tides. But where those bland-to-ordinary towers merely insinuate the development's location next to Lake Michigan and the Chicago River, the Aqua Tower visibly resembles waves of water, justifying the moniker. In architect Jeanne Gang's design, each of the balconies wrapping the 82 floors of the hotel and residential tower differ in shape, gently undulating from one foot to twelve feet and sometimes disappearing to reveal the glass box that sits behind them. The design recalls the rounded balconies of Bertrand Goldberg's Marina City, but where those twin towers elicit the "corn cob" label, the exterior of Aqua Tower invites a variety of associations, from the nautical to the topographical. Gang describes the exterior as "a landscape—an inhabitable cliff."[3]

Seen from the south, the "puddles" stand out across the facade's balconies. (Credit Anne Evans, CAC Archive)

In executing her firm's first high-rise project, Jeanne Gang based the varied undulations on views, solar shading, and the type and size of dwellings—a short film produced by her studio shows a "hill" at one corner giving views of *Cloud Gate* (**2**) around nearby Aon Tower. Gang and her colleagues must have considered the undulating effect from the outside as well, since the tower has an oddly beautiful presence from different angles, particularly from below and the southwest corner of the park, where the dunelike balconies recede into glassy "puddles." Technically, the generous balconies enable thermal bridging, where cold temperatures infiltrate the interior via the continuous concrete slab (an unfortunate but common trait of Chicago's residential high-rises). But that negative is offset in their shading of the clear, low-E glass walls from the summer sun (high-performance, reflective glass is used in the puddle areas) and in the exterior's "visual noise" eliminating the chance of bird strikes.

In addition to the tower, which stacks 63 floors of condo and rental units (plus one mechanical floor) above an 18-story hotel, nine townhouses line the eastern edge of the park to hide the large three-story parking garage. Above the garage is a two-story podium with a ballroom and numerous meeting rooms for the hotel, a two-acre roof garden

The tower's clifflike appearance is most pronounced when seen from below. (Credit Anne Evans, CAC Archive)

The varied balconies invite interaction of residents across different floors. (Credit John Hill)

designed by landscape architect Ted Wolff, and a retail space fronting on Columbus Drive. Access up to street level happens at the south and north ends of the townhouses, the former as switchback stairs snaking between poured-in-place concrete walls, and the latter as steps spiraling around a tree in an opening next to the GEMS World Academy (**15**).

15

GEMS WORLD ACADEMY

bKL Architecture, 2014/2020
350 East South Water Street
Bus: #6 to Wacker Drive at Columbus Drive

From its inception, the Lakeshore East development planned for a school. The master plan from Skidmore, Owings & Merrill (SOM) clearly shows a school in the northeast corner of the development's central park, but it would take nine years for a school to be realized, on a site earmarked for townhouses

The horizontal gap of the Lower School aligns with the roadway elevated five stories above the park's grade. (Credit Darris Lee Harris)

A rendering of the Upper School seen from Wacker Drive. (Credit bKL Architecture)

in SOM's plan. Although not a public school as promised, the GEMS (Global Education Management System) World Academy—the first US school for the company that started in Dubai in 1959—is a welcome addition to a neighborhood where many residents can easily afford the school's $30,000-plus yearly tuition.

The JK-12 school is being realized as two buildings in two phases, both designed by Thomas Kerwin and Lynn Sorkin from bKL Architecture. The aptly named Lower School (serving grades K-5 and entered from the lower level of the park) opened in 2014, the same year the Upper School (serving grades 6–12 from an entrance on Upper Wacker Drive) had its ceremonial groundbreaking (it was set to open in 2020, as this book went to press). Architecturally, the curtain walls unite the 10-story Lower School and 16-story Upper School with glass expanses and beige horizontal bands broken up by vertical strips of color. Additionally, the vertical campuses feature dining terraces expressed as horizontal breaks in their midsections, and semi-enclosed rooftop playgrounds top each building.

16

COAST AT LAKESHORE EAST

bKL Architecture, 2013

345 East Wacker Drive

Bus: #6 to Wacker Drive at Columbus Drive

This 47-story glass tower with 515 rental apartments is the first of three projects that bKL Architecture has led at Lakeshore East. Continuous balconies with glass guardrails cover the south and north elevations, the latter fronting

Glass balconies face north, while a flat glass wall faces west. (Credit Darris Lee Harris)

A detail of the glass guardrails on the continuous balconies that face south and north. (Credit Darris Lee Harris)

on Wacker Drive and overlooking the Chicago River. Glass curtain walls on the east and west ends extend slightly past the balconies, giving these ends a much different appearance; guests at the Harry Weese–designed Swissotel next door might think they are looking at an office tower. Coast takes advantage of the multi-height roadway by putting the 277-car parking garage below the height of Upper Wacker Drive to ensure that the tower rises as glass from sidewalk to sky.

17

ST. REGIS CHICAGO

Studio Gang with bKL Architecture, 2020
363 East Wacker Drive
Bus: #6 to Wacker Drive at Columbus Drive

Just when it seemed that Aqua Tower (**14**) would remain the architectural pinnacle at Lakeshore East for both developer James Loewenberg and architect Jeanne Gang, along came Wanda Vista Tower. That was the name of the 88-story tower when it was unveiled in 2014, with a proposed five-star hotel and hundreds of condos for Magellan Group and China's Dalian Wanda Group. As the design progressed, it grew to 101 stories and nearly 1,200 feet tall, maintaining its mix of uses but bumping up the luxury aspects of the $1 billion development, including indoor and outdoor amenities for residents on the 47th floor.

Toward the end of 2020, Marriott's St. Regis brand took over the hotel component, leading to a change of name for the tower: St. Regis Chicago. The hotel's 191 rooms occupy the base of the stepped tower, while 393 condos, officially The Residences at The St. Regis Chicago, sit above the 47th floor. The luxury hotel brand will provide butler service to the residences, much like the earlier Trump International Hotel & Tower (**52**).

While Gang's Aqua Tower is "written" by horizontal lines—the undulating edges of balconies that circle the glass-box tower—St. Regis Chicago is all about vertical lines. The three stepped volumes resemble a Brancusi sculpture, their exterior walls angling in and out as they ascend. Literally bridging Field Boulevard at the north edge of Lakeshore East, the tower—officially the third-tallest skyscraper in the city, after Willis and Trump towers—provides the development its exclamation point, while the stepped massing and angular profile guarantee that St. Regis Chicago will be a 21st-century architectural icon for Chicago.

Opposite: Twelve-story tapered volumes stack into three stems of 47, 71, and 95 stories to give St. Regis Chicago its distinctive profile. (Credit © Tom Harris)

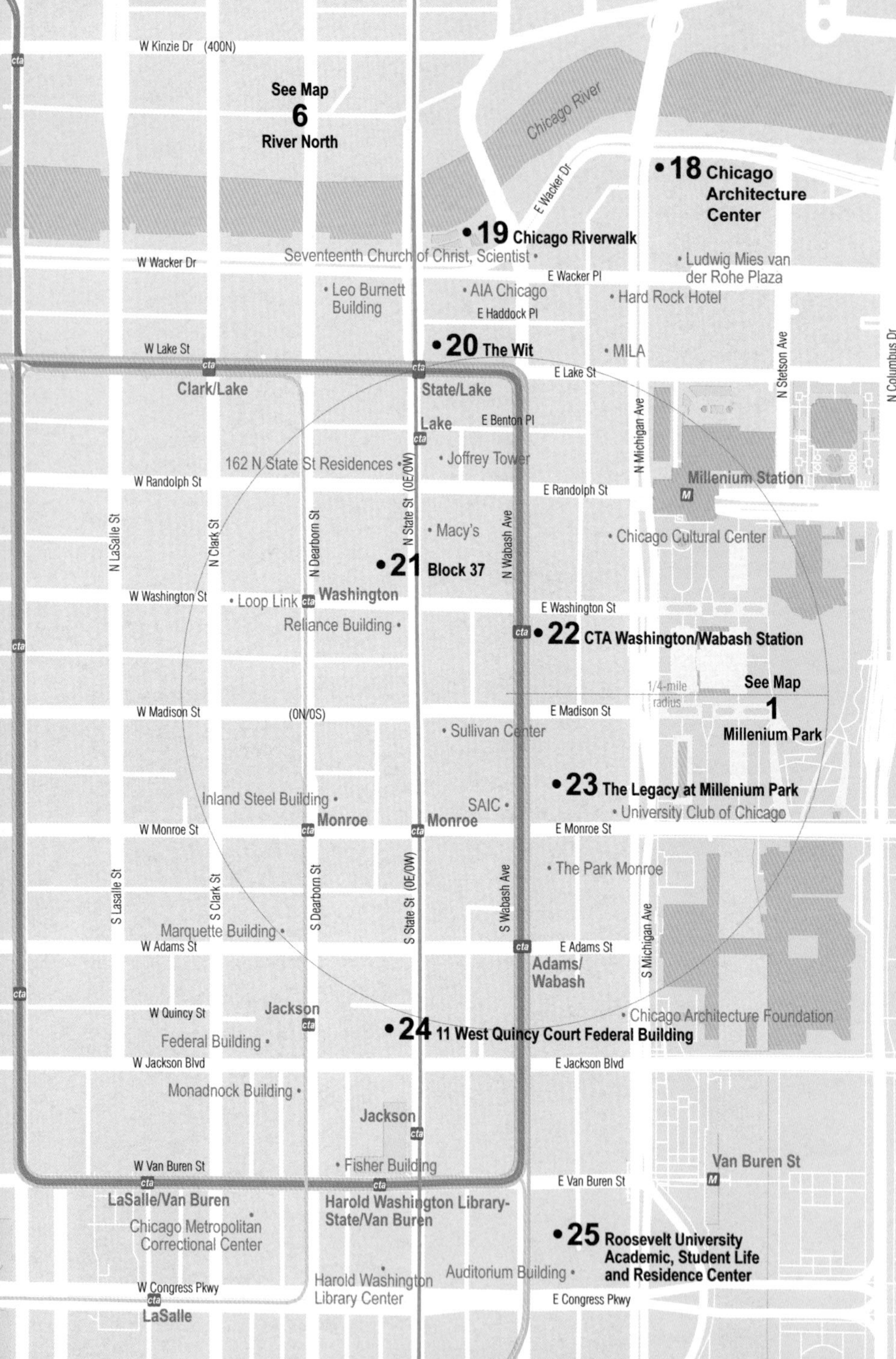

W Kinzie Dr (400N)
See Map
6
River North
Chicago River
E Wacker Dr
18 Chicago Architecture Center
19 Chicago Riverwalk
Seventeenth Church of Christ, Scientist
W Wacker Dr
Ludwig Mies van der Rohe Plaza
E Wacker Pl
Leo Burnett Building
AIA Chicago
Hard Rock Hotel
E Haddock Pl
W Lake St
20 The Wit
MILA
N Stetson Ave
N Columbus Dr
E Lake St
Clark/Lake
State/Lake
Lake
E Benton Pl
N Michigan Ave
162 N State St Residences
Joffrey Tower
Millenium Station
W Randolph St
E Randolph St
N State St (0E/0W)
N LaSalle St
N Clark St
N Dearborn St
N Wabash Ave
Macy's
Chicago Cultural Center
21 Block 37
W Washington St
Loop Link
Washington
E Washington St
Reliance Building
22 CTA Washington/Wabash Station
1/4-mile radius
See Map
1
Millenium Park
W Madison St
(0N/0S)
E Madison St
Sullivan Center
23 The Legacy at Millenium Park
Inland Steel Building
SAIC
University Club of Chicago
Monroe
Monroe
W Monroe St
E Monroe St
The Park Monroe
S Lasalle St
S Clark St
S Dearborn St
S State St (0E/0W)
S Wabash Ave
S Michigan Ave
Marquette Building
W Adams St
E Adams St
Adams/ Wabash
W Quincy St
Jackson
Chicago Architecture Foundation
24 11 West Quincy Court Federal Building
Federal Building
W Jackson Blvd
E Jackson Blvd
Monadnock Building
Jackson
Van Buren St
W Van Buren St
Fisher Building
E Van Buren St
LaSalle/Van Buren
Harold Washington Library-State/Van Buren
Chicago Metropolitan Correctional Center
25 Roosevelt University Academic, Student Life and Residence Center
Harold Washington Library Center
Auditorium Building
W Congress Pkwy
E Congress Pkwy
LaSalle

3 The Loop (East)

For many people, Chicago *is* the Loop. Defined by the elevated tracks that etch a rectangular path around thirty-five downtown blocks (a path set down by streetcars before the 1897 construction of the elevated or "L" lines), Chicago's central business district was built on the "island" formed by the main and south branches of the Chicago River, Lake Michigan (just east of Michigan Avenue in the mid-19th century), and the railroad tracks delivering people and goods into the city from the south. The Loop is home to some of the world's earliest skyscrapers: tall buildings of iron, glass, brick, and terra-cotta by the likes of Adler and Sullivan, Burnham and Root, Holabird and Roche, and William Le Baron Jenney, that began to spring up some fifteen years after the Great Fire of 1871. Progressively taller office buildings of steel and glass were built in the Loop into the middle of the 20th century—most notably by Mies van der Rohe and Skidmore, Owings & Merrill (SOM)—maintaining the city's widespread influence in skyscraper design. But since the late 1960s and early 1970s, the Loop has been transforming itself from a place for business—a nine-to-five, Monday-through-Friday downtown—to a mixed-use, all-hours neighborhood with offices as well as residences, hotels, retail, educational institutions, and cultural venues.

The eastern portion of the Loop has seen a concentrated influx of these noncommercial uses, which can be attributed to the proximity to the lakefront and Grant Park and, more recently, to the construction of Millennium Park and Lakeshore East. This much was evident in 2000, when the city adopted *A Vision for State Street, Wabash Avenue and Michigan Avenue* that stated, "The East Loop is becoming the bustling heart of the city's revitalized historic central area, a thriving mixed-use neighborhood where Chicagoans from all walks of life come to live, work, shop, and learn."[1] Three years later, the city reiterated this shift in *The Chicago Central Area Plan: Preparing the City for the 21st Century*: "East Loop buildings are undergoing profound change as the office market moves on and residential, cultural, and educational uses take its place."[2] Some of the office market's movement was westward, toward the commuter stations between the river and the Kennedy Expressway. (See Chapter 4 for examples.)

State Street is an integral part in the story of the East Loop. In the 1960s and 1970s, suburban malls exploded and high-end retail in the city moved to North Michigan Avenue, so the city responded in 1979 by turning State Street into a pedestrian mall, nearly doubling the width of the sidewalks and limiting the narrowed streets to buses in order to increase foot traffic. The experiment didn't work and "that great street" lost all but two of its department stores the following decade. Less than twenty years later, the city "undid" the pedestrian mall per a 1996 plan by SOM that brought cars back, narrowed the sidewalks, inserted planters and historical lampposts, and redesigned subway entrances. Twenty years later, State Street is a rejuvenated corridor that serves well as the spine of the mixed-use East Loop.

18

CHICAGO ARCHITECTURE CENTER

Adrian Smith + Gordon Gill Architecture, 2018
111 East Wacker Drive
Bus: #121 to Michigan Avenue and Wacker Drive

In September 2017, the Chicago Architecture Center (known as the Chicago Architecture Foundation from 1966 until 2018) announced it would be moving from its 25-year home across the street from the Art Institute of Chicago to a new double-height storefront space in the northwest corner of Illinois Center, adjacent to its popular Chicago Architecture Center River Cruise aboard Chicago's First Lady. The CAC's new home—with a shop, galleries, lecture hall, and design studio—reinforces the importance of the Chicago River's main branch in the life of Chicagoans and visitors to the city this century.

AS+GG's design of the two-story, 20,000-square-foot CAC exhibits the bones of the original building on the first floor, where the concrete waffle slab caps the box office, bookstore, and exhibition spaces, the last done with Gallagher & Associates. Upstairs is a lecture hall and a large exhibition space with views toward the river through 40-foot-tall expanses of glass. The upstairs gal-

CAC's new two-story home announces itself through large signage facing the Chicago River. (Credit © James Steinkamp Photography)

lery has plenty of height, perfect for displaying models of skyscrapers—which is just what the CAC did on opening day in August 2018 and will continue to do well into the future.

LUDWIG MIES VAN DER ROHE PLAZA

Goettsch Partners, Wolff Landscape Architecture, 2015

233 North Michigan Avenue

Above a glass pavilion on East Water Street designed by Goettsch Partners are landscape architect Ted Wolff's amoeboid plantings, which are a soft contrast to the orthogonal geometries of the modern glass towers fronting the raised Illinois Center plaza.

(Credit John Hill)

MILA

bKL Architecture, 2016

201 N. Garland Court

This glassy 41-story tower, on the same block as the former Carbide and Carbon Building (now St. Jane Hotel), adds 402 luxury residences to a stretch of Michigan Avenue not known for having them.

(Credit Jon Miller © Hedrich Blessing)

19

CHICAGO RIVERWALK

Ross Barney Architects, 2009 (Phase 1), 2015 (Phase 2), 2016 (Phase 3)

South bank of Chicago River from Michigan Avenue to Lake Street

Train: Red, Brown, Green, Orange, Pink, Purple to Lake/State

Bus: #146 to State Street at Lake Street

For most of the city's past, the Chicago River was a workhorse, its banks the site of industry rather than recreation. Today, this industrial past is a distant memory on the river's main branch, which was officially earmarked as "a major new public amenity comparable to the lakefront"[3] in the city's 2003 Central Area Plan. It recommended "a continuous pedestrian riverwalk along Wacker Drive on the Main Branch from Lake Street to the lakefront."[4] Before the 2003 plan, a stretch of riverwalk from Michigan Avenue to the lakefront bicycle path, via an SOM-designed walkway under Lake Shore Drive, was already in place

The River Theater portion of phase 2 features an accessible path that winds its way through the steps and planters. (Credit Eric Allix Rogers, CAC Archive)

Reflective canopies under the bridges connect each of the riverwalk's "rooms." (Credit Eric Allix Rogers, CAC Archive)

The Vietnam Veteran's Memorial Plaza, as seen from across the river. (Credit Kate Joyce, Hedrich Blessing Photographers)

and used for amenities like the popular Chicago Architecture Center River Cruise aboard Chicago's First Lady.

The new stretch of riverwalk, designed by Ross Barney Architects, with Boston's Sasaki Associates, was realized in three phases. The first, completed in 2009 with Jacobs/Ryan Associates, stretches from the iconic bridge houses at Michigan Avenue to State Street, encompassing Ross Barney's earlier Vietnam Veterans Memorial Plaza (2005) just west of Wabash Street. The second phase, completed in 2015 with Sasaki Associates, extends the riverwalk three more blocks to the west, as far as LaSalle Street, with each block-long "room" themed for different uses and experiences: Marina Plaza, the Cove, and the River Theater, from east to west. Ross Barney and Sasaki's third phase includes a Water Plaza, Jetty, and Boardwalk terminating at Lake Street, bringing the total length of the riverwalk to 1.3 miles.

20

THE WIT

KOO, 2009

201 North State Street

Train: Red, Brown, Green, Orange, Pink, Purple to Lake/State

Bus: #146 to State Street at Lake Street

Two glaringly different approaches to designing for sites next to the Loop's elevated tracks stand at the corner of State and Lake Streets. To the north are two hotels, both 27 stories, one with close to 600 rooms and one with half as many. The larger hotel is the Renaissance from 1992, which spans the full length of the block, from a drop-off on Wacker Drive to a largely blank wall set back from the "L" tracks. The Wit, which extends only halfway down the block and must therefore confront the "L" directly, is in many ways the opposite—it is a design that embraces the Loop's defining piece of infrastructure through its massing, elevation, and lobby.

The Wit is the first project for architect Jackie Koo and her namesake firm, designed for developer Scott Greenberg of ECD Company and run as a DoubleTree by Hilton. The 298-room hotel—with restaurants, conference space, a spa, and a rooftop lounge—rises from a small footprint of less than 10,000 square feet, but the tower's separation into the three parts makes it look even

The lightning bolt of green glass rises from the lobby to the popular rooftop bar. (Credit John Hill)

smaller. To the north and east of the corner are painted concrete sections that act like background buildings for the glass corner, which is highlighted by a zigzag of chartreuse glass facing down State Street, a gesture that holds its own against the iconic Chicago Theater marquee one block south. Inside the corner is the double-height lobby, which puts the "L" on display and invites those standing on the elevated platform to peer inside a hotel that is clearly proud of its location.

JOFFREY TOWER
Booth Hansen, 2008
8 East Randolph Street

The most interesting part of Booth Hansen's design for this 32-story condominium tower happens below the condos: The Joffrey Ballet occupies the third and fourth floors, giving the project its name and adding to the "street ballet" of State Street with its ballet studios behind floor-to-ceiling glass walls. Also of note is the way the condos are lifted on "legs" that create a unique, urban-size "window" (best seen from Randolph a few steps west of State).

(Credit Eric Allix Rogers, CAC Archive)

21

BLOCK 37

Gensler, Perkins and Will, Solomon Cordwell Buenz (SCB), 2008–2016
108 North State Street
Train: Red to Lake/State
Bus: #146 to State Street at Randolph Street, northbound; to State Street at Washington Street, southbound

The Block Thirty-Seven mall in the foreground with the block's office tower in the background. (Credit Eric Allix Rogers, CAC Archive)

Ross Miller, author of the book-length biography of Block 37, *Here's the Deal: The Buying and Selling of a Great American City*, has written, "To know Block 37 is to know Chicago."[5] Harking back to James Thompson's 1830 platting of the city's original 58 blocks in its numerical designation, the block rose with numerous buildings before and after the Great Fire of 1871, seeing 16 buildings at its peak by the middle of the 20th century. People around the country flocked to the suburbs starting in the 1950s, and, in Chicago, retail headed up to North Michigan Avenue and office space shifted toward the West Loop. As a result, Block 37 was officially designated as "blighted" in 1979, with all of its buildings (minus a ComEd substation on Dearborn) demolished ten years later when Richard M. Daley started his first term as mayor. But recession followed, rather than the hoped-for commercial development, and the site remained vacant despite the numerous developers vying to build there.

Block 37 was used as a skating rink in the winter and a student art gallery in the summer from 1991 until 2006, when work finally commenced on the office and retail components. Two years later, the first piece of the block, 22 West Washington, was completed. Designed by Perkins and Will, it is a glassy, 16-story office building that overlooks Daley Plaza. Wrapping the rest of the block is a four-story retail base—glass and undulating metal outside, a multistory mall inside—that was designed by Gensler and opened in 2010. Taking the name Block Thirty-Seven, the mall (connected to the city's underground pedway system) has the usual stores found in any city or suburb, but it is also home to the one-of-a-kind Chicago Design Museum. Originally planned as a hotel, the third element in the Block 37 puzzle—a 34-story, 700-unit apartment tower designed by SCB sitting atop the retail base along Randolph Street—started construction in 2014 and wrapped up two years later. It's taken almost twenty years to fill Block 37's void in the Loop, and it might very well take another quarter-century to realize, if at all, the planned and partially constructed underground railway Chicago Transit Authority (CTA) station that would speedily connect the Loop to the city's two airports.

162 NORTH STATE STREET RESIDENCES

Booth Hansen, 2000

162 North State Street

This neo-traditional, 17-story building housing student residences for the School of the Art Institute of Chicago made a lot more sense before Block 37 (**21**) was filled in, since the GFRC panels and Chicago-style windows clearly mirrored Daniel H. Burnham's 1895 Reliance Building (now Hotel Burnham) across the infamous void that sat empty for almost 20 years in the middle of the Loop.

(Credit Lynn Becker)

22

CTA WASHINGTON/WABASH STATION

exp, 2017

Wabash Avenue at Washington Street

Train: Brown, Green, Orange, Pink, Purple to Washington/Wabash

The steel ribs extend past the glass canopy to accentuate the design's rippling lines. (Credit John Hill)

Riders on any of the five lines that stop at the Washington/Wabash Station are encouraged to look out the front window of the first car: that vantage point best reveals on approach the undulating lines of the canopy in silhouette against the sky. From the station's platforms, the glass canopy's steel ribs, which recall the skeletal designs of Spanish architect/engineer Santiago Calatrava, are still eye-catching, but their undulating lines are confused by the backdrop of adjacent Loop buildings. The first new CTA station to be built in the Loop in twenty years replaces two adjacent stations along Wabash Avenue, both of which were demolished after more than a century of service. The new station designed by the architects at exp (formerly Teng + Associates) finally brings a portion of the Loop's "L" into the 21st century.

SULLIVAN CENTER

Harboe Associates, 2010

1 South State Street

The Sullivan Center complex consists of nine historic buildings skillfully restored by über-preservationist Gunny Harboe, but the piece de resistance is still Louis Sullivan's 1904 masterpiece—built as the Schlesinger and Mayer Department Store, later occupied by Carson Pirie Scott, and now home to Target—with its rounded corner elegantly marking the zero, zero point of Chicago's street numbering system.

(Credit Anne Evans, CAC Archive)

23

THE LEGACY AT MILLENNIUM PARK

Solomon Cordwell Buenz (SCB), 2010

60 East Monroe Street

Train: Red to Monroe/State

Bus: #146 to State Street at Monroe Street, southbound; to State Street at Adams Street, northbound

One side effect of the Historic Michigan Boulevard District designation in 2002, which maintains the character of the streetwall facing Grant Park, is that a number of tall buildings have sprouted up just one block to the west, along Wabash Avenue. The tallest of them is the Legacy, an 822-foot-high glass tower with 356 condos on 72 floors. When the designation was proposed in

The slender all-glass building features a "zipper" of balconies facing Millennium Park to the east. (Credit Dave Burk © Hedrich Blessing)

2002, the city contended that "tall and thin [was] better for the urban form,"[6] so tall and thin are what SCB delivered, with stepped profiles on the north and south and a plan that tapers toward Grant Park. The tower sits behind the preserved facades of historic buildings on Wabash, including the oldest surviving design by Adler and Sullivan. Behind these facades are classrooms for the School of the Art Institute of Chicago, which sold the land to Monroe-Wabash Development, parking, and squash courts for the University Club of Chicago. Legacy residents enter on Monroe Street, just across the alley from the University Club, which faces Michigan Avenue; look up in the gap between the buildings to see a glass bridge cantilevering from the Legacy's 13th floor to the exclusive private club.

THE PARK MONROE
Pappageorge Haymes Partners, 2007
65 East Monroe Street

A vertical expansion of Alfred Shaw and Associates' Mid-Continental Plaza from 1972 added ten floors and 219 luxury condos to the now-50-story Park Monroe. Pappageorge Haymes, with architect of record Goettsch Partners and structural engineer Klein and Hoffman, removed every other column at the facade to create larger bays for windows and residential balconies, resulting in a subtly odd office/residential hybrid.

(Credit Pappageorge Haymes Partners)

24

11 WEST QUINCY COURT FEDERAL BUILDING

4240 Architecture, 2012
11 West Quincy Street
Train: Red to Jackson/State
Bus: #146 to State Street at Jackson Boulevard, southbound; to State Street at Adams Street, northbound

Just east of the Federal Center—Mies van der Rohe's iconic three-building complex straddling Dearborn Street between Adams and Jackson Streets—is Quincy Court, a formerly grungy alley that the US government cleaned up in 2009 as a pedestrian walk with benches, tables, and leaflike canopies designed by Los Angeles's Rios Clementi Hale Studios. The reason was the purchase of the building at the northwest corner of State and Jackson Streets for the GSA (General Services Administration), which moved three years later into offices designed by 4240 Architecture. Formerly windowless expanses of exterior wall are now glassy, the most eye-catching one found above the entrance facing Quincy Court, which flares out at the top and bottom. The glass panes are etched with tightly spaced lines in homage to Sol LeWitt's *Lines in Four Directions* (1985) around the corner.

A glass wall above the entrance faces the pedestrianized Quincy Court. (Credit Anna Munzesheimer, CAC Archive)

25

ROOSEVELT UNIVERSITY ACADEMIC, STUDENT LIFE AND RESIDENCE CENTER

VOA Associates (now Stantec), 2012

425 South Wabash Avenue

Train: Red to Jackson/State

Bus: #146 to State Street at Van Buren Street

Roosevelt University has been a faithful steward of Adler and Sullivan's 1889 Auditorium Building since it purchased the granite and limestone masterpiece in 1946, one year after the school was founded on principles of social justice, academic excellence, and equal opportunity. Hand in hand with these principles, early faculty spent time "cleaning, painting, and repairing the grand old facility,"[7] what is considered the nation's first mixed-use building with the Auditorium Theater, a hotel, and offices in its ten stories. Given that

Tall floor-to-floor heights for the lower half of the building give the 35-story building more height than comparable towers. (Credit Anne Evans, CAC Archive)

The "Brancusi effect" is most pronounced when seen from the base along Wabash Avenue. (Credit John Hill)

the historic building continues to serve as the school's heart, it makes sense that when it came time to expand—to compete with universities that don't share its nonprofit status and to provide a residence hall for freshmen students—the university decided to build a vertical campus next to, and linking with, the Auditorium Building.

From bottom to top, the 35-story, zigzagging, blue-glass tower contains student services, a student union (visible from "L" trains passing by), classrooms, administrative offices, and the 633-bed dormitory, which takes up roughly the top half of the building. The lower floor-to-floor heights of the student residences can be seen in the smaller pieces of glass, whose random pattern of two shades of blue facing south, east, and west gets progressively darker toward the angled top. On the building's north face is the offset core of elevators, stairs, restrooms, and other service spaces that are hidden behind dark walls rising behind the reused facade of Andrew Rebori's 1927 Fine Arts Annex on Wabash Avenue. The tower's profile, per VOA design principal Chris Groesbeck, was inspired by Constantin Brancusi's *Endless Column*, meant to represent transcendence and transformation at the school of learning.

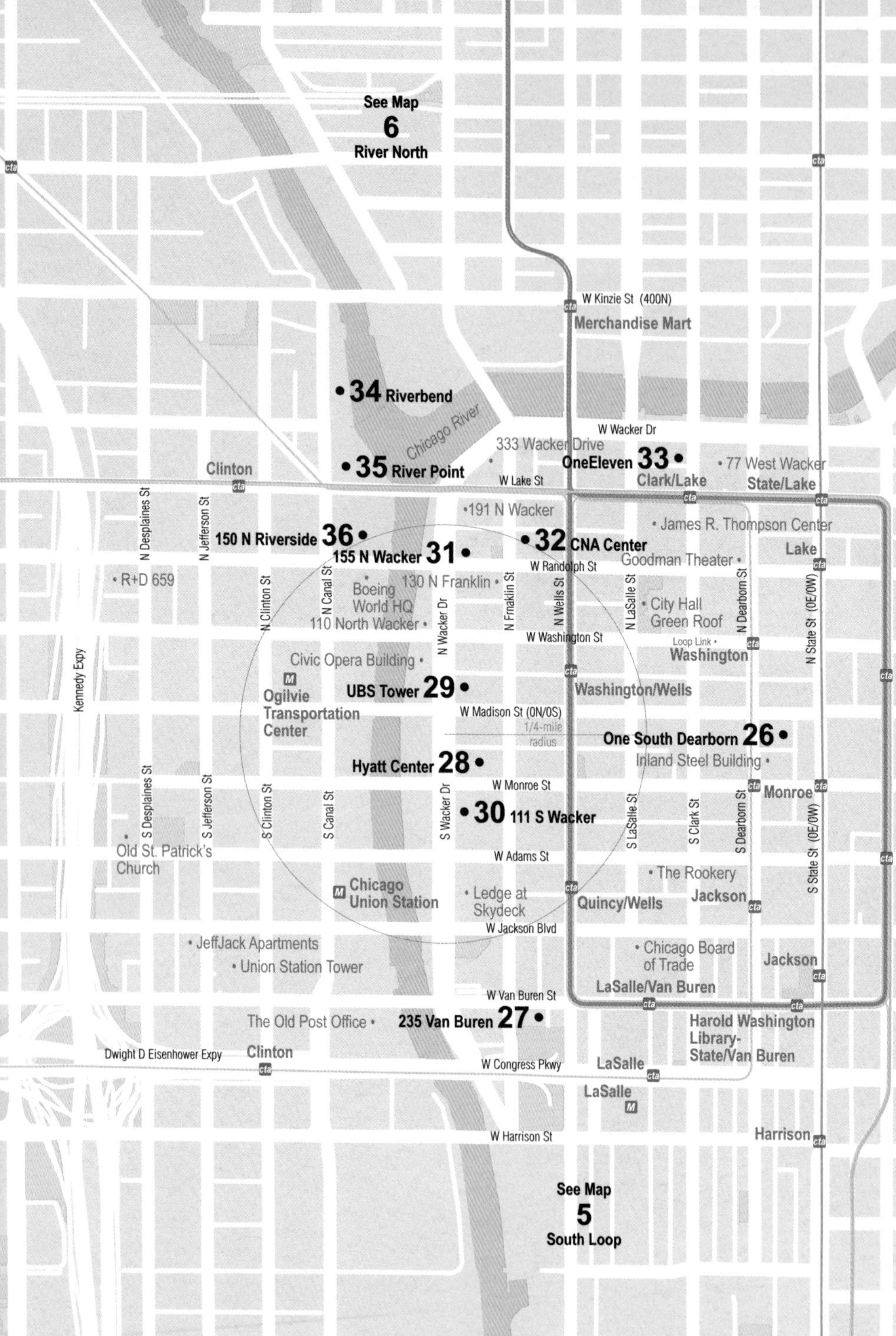

See Map
6
River North
W Kinzie St (400N)
Merchandise Mart
• 34 Riverbend
Chicago River
W Wacker Dr
333 Wacker Drive
• 35 River Point
OneEleven 33 •
• 77 West Wacker
Clinton
W Lake St
Clark/Lake
State/Lake
•191 N Wacker
• James R. Thompson Center
150 N Riverside 36 •
• 32 CNA Center
155 N Wacker 31 •
Lake
Goodman Theater •
W Randolph St
N Desplaines St
N Jefferson St
• R+D 659
N Clinton St
N Canal St
Boeing
World HQ
130 N Franklin •
N Franklin St
N Wells St
N LaSalle St
• City Hall
Green Roof
N Dearborn St
N State St (0E/0W)
110 North Wacker •
N Wacker Dr
W Washington St
Loop Link •
Washington
Civic Opera Building •
Kennedy Expy
Ogilvie
Transportation
Center
UBS Tower 29 •
Washington/Wells
W Madison St (0N/0S)
1/4-mile
radius
One South Dearborn 26 •
Hyatt Center 28 •
Inland Steel Building •
W Monroe St
Monroe
S Desplaines St
S Jefferson St
S Clinton St
S Canal St
S Wacker Dr
• 30 111 S Wacker
S LaSalle St
S Clark St
S Dearborn St
S State St (0E/0W)
Old St. Patrick's
Church
W Adams St
• The Rookery
Chicago
Union Station
• Ledge at
Skydeck
Quincy/Wells
Jackson
W Jackson Blvd
• JeffJack Apartments
• Chicago Board
of Trade
• Union Station Tower
Jackson
W Van Buren St
LaSalle/Van Buren
The Old Post Office •
235 Van Buren 27 •
Harold Washington
Library-
State/Van Buren
Dwight D Eisenhower Expy
Clinton
W Congress Pkwy
LaSalle
LaSalle
W Harrison St
Harrison
See Map
5
South Loop

4 The Loop (West)

Even when the streetcars were circling downtown in the mid-19th century, decades before the elevated trains, the Loop was where businesses located, where the land values were highest, and where buildings reached progressively higher. Some of the most influential office buildings of the late 19th and 20th centuries are located in the thirty-five blocks bounded by downtown's elevated tracks. The early tall buildings that followed in the few decades after the Great Fire of 1871 saw engineers and architects figuring out how to build tall on Chicago's unstable clay soil and how to adorn buildings framed in iron and steel. Structures such as The Rookery by Burnham & Root (with a lobby redesigned by Frank Lloyd Wright), William Le Baron Jenney's Second Leiter Building (now home to Robert Morris University), and Holabird & Roche's Marquette Building stand as examples of the world's earliest skyscrapers.

Holabird & Root's 1930 Chicago Board of Trade was one of the last skyscrapers built in the Loop, thanks to two World Wars, the Great Depression, and the city-imposed height limits that ended partially in the early 1920s and then fully in the mid-1950s. By the time construction on skyscrapers resumed in the mid-20th century, the strong influence of German-born Ludwig Mies van der Rohe could be seen throughout Loop, resuming the city's influential role in commercial architecture. Starting in the 1950s with the Inland Steel Building by Skidmore, Owings & Merrill (SOM), and followed by Mies's own three-building Federal Center complex and SOM's Sears Tower (now Willis Tower, the world's tallest building for twenty-five years) in the 1970s, these buildings espoused structural purity and aesthetic clarity through steel and large expanses of glass. Today's office towers follow the path that Mies and his disciples set, but with all-glass, silicone-glazed (often with no exterior mullions) curtain walls with high-performance glazing for energy efficiency and, increasingly, through frits and special coatings, bird safety.

In the latter half of the 20th century, the Loop had to contend with the suburbs for luring and retaining businesses, particularly large corporations. Sears's move in the mid-1990s from its namesake tower to Hoffman Estates, northwest of O'Hare International Airport, was a blow to the city. So when Mayor Richard M. Daley managed to bring Boeing to the city in 2001, it was seen as a boon to Chicago and the Daley administration's global-city ambitions. Boeing's move to a tower on the west bank of the Chicago River was also in line with a shift of office buildings westward toward the Kennedy Expressway and the commuter train stations west of the river. As the buildings in this chapter reveal, that shift is accompanied by some residential developments, but not nearly to the same degree as the eastern portion of the Loop and other areas close to downtown. It's the south branch of the Chicago River—Wacker Drive to the east, Ogilvie Transportation Center and Union Station to the west (the latter expanding with office, dining, and park components as this book went to press)—that is the spine for new office buildings this century.

26

ONE SOUTH DEARBORN

DeStefano Keating Partners, 2005
1 South Dearborn Street
Train: Blue to Monroe Dearborn
Bus: #20 to Madison Street at State Street, westbound; #22 to Dearborn at Monroe Street, eastbound

The evolution of Chicago's 19th- and 20th-century architecture can be grasped by walking up one street in the Loop: Dearborn. From the load-bearing brick walls of the 16-story Monadnock Building at Jackson Boulevard to the postmodernist granite of Kevin Roche's Leo Burnett Building on Wacker Drive, the street is chockablock with notable buildings from just about every stylistic era. Dearborn is also home to three great plazas in the Loop: the Federal Center, the Exelon Plaza, and the Daley Center. One South Dearborn admirably adds to the street's (and the city's) collection of well-designed buildings and plazas.

The 40-story office building was designed during the short-lived partnership of Richard Keating and James DeStefano, both formerly employed in the Chicago office of Skidmore, Owings & Merrill. SOM's offices were located in the Inland Steel Building during their tenure, so it's no wonder that the taller 2005 tower is pushed to the east to create a plaza that perfectly frames

The large "lantern" atop the tower glows during the day as well as at night. (Credit Anne Evans, CAC Archive)

the north side of the older 19-story building, often considered a masterpiece of modern architecture. The new tower's curtain wall is articulated subtly to match Inland Steel's height, but the best parts of the design are the base and the top. The bright open lobby conceals the parking garage behind backlit stone panels, while the top has city-scaled "lanterns" that glow at night and help the building stand out on the skyline among its taller neighbors.

27

235 VAN BUREN

Perkins and Will, 2009

235 Van Buren Street

Train: Brown, Orange, Pink, Purple to LaSalle/Van Buren

Bus: #151 to Adams Street at Wells Street, westbound

Just about every architect will admit the key to a successful building is a good client—even better when the latter is a repeat client. Such is the case with Ralph Johnson, the design director of the global architecture firm Perkins and Will, and CMK Companies, headed by Colin Kihnke. After first teaming up on the small but widely lauded Contemporaine (**56**) in River North, CMK tapped Perkins and Will for this substantially larger, 714-unit condominium tower on Van Buren just a couple blocks from the south branch of the Chicago River and the Willis Tower. Given that a cooling plant is across Franklin Street, and that Congress Parkway, the thoroughfare leading into downtown from the Eisenhower Expressway, is just one short block to the south, the site is a definite edge condition in the southwest corner of the Loop.

With most of the block taken up by an onramp to westbound Congress (now partially covered by Oscar O. D'Angelo Park), Johnson had no choice

The slablike tower appears slender from the west where the balconies and ribbon are prominent. (Credit John Hill)

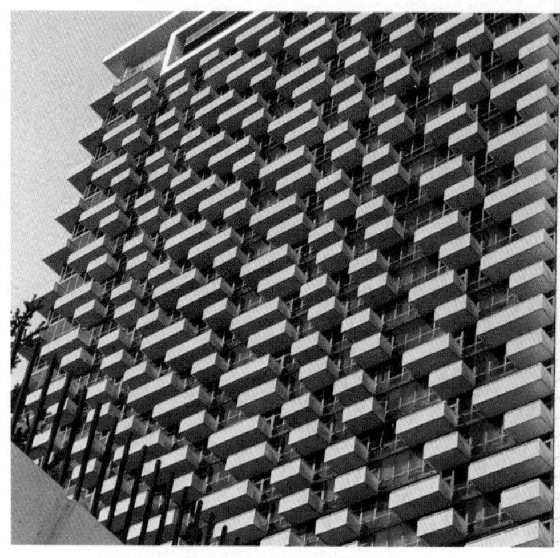

The south-facing balconies resemble abstract art when seen from below. (Credit John Hill)

but to orient the building on an east-west axis tight to Van Buren and lift the residences upon a substantial base of parking. The north-facing Loop side of the tower is flat, with inset terraces, while the more distinctive facade overlooking the park on the south has a Morse codelike pattern of projecting balconies. These balconies are framed by a ribbon of concrete that snakes up, over, and down the building, from the canopy over the corner entrance to the roof and to the top of the parking garage overlooking the park.

THE LEDGE AT SKYDECK

Skidmore, Owings & Merrill, 2009

233 South Wacker Drive

Thirty-five years after its completion, Skidmore, Owings & Merrill (SOM) returned to their iconic Willis (formerly Sears) Tower to add four vertigo-inducing glazed boxes (made from 1.5-inch laminated glass) projecting from the 103rd floor and enjoyed by tourists who stand in midair 1,353 feet above the sidewalk.

28

HYATT CENTER

Pei Cobb Freed & Partners, 2005

71 South Wacker Drive

Train: Brown, Orange, Pink, Purple to Quincy/Wells

Bus: #151 to Jackson Boulevard at Franklin Street, eastbound; to Adams Street at Wacker Drive, westbound

The Pritzker family, owners of the Hyatt Hotels, created the Pritzker Architecture Prize in 1979 as the profession's equivalent of the Nobel Prize. When it came time to build a corporate headquarters in the Loop just after the turn of the century, it made sense that they hired a Pritzker Prize–winning architect as they did in Millennium Park (**3**). The Pritzkers commissioned British architect Norman Foster who had won the prize in 1999. Foster proposed an ambitious tower with an offset core and full-height atrium, similar to his Commerzbank Headquarters in Frankfurt, Germany. But the events of September 11, 2001, derailed the plans and forced the Pritzkers to scale back to something more typical that addressed the heightened safety concerns of tall buildings.

The tower's curving walls on the north and south terminate in angled walls covered in stainless steel. (Credit Anne Evans, CAC Archive)

In place of Foster, they hired New York architect Henry Cobb (partner with 1983 Pritzker laureate I. M. Pei) to design what had become a speculative office building with a central core and deep floor plates. The 48-story tower's lozenge-shaped plan opens up the corners at Wacker Drive and Franklin Street to create plazas, while giving the city a building that contrasts with hard-edged towers like the nearby Willis Tower and more recent 111 South Wacker (**30**) across the street. The amoeboid planters have integral benches, but they also serve safety concerns by protecting the columns and the lobby with its backdrop of bamboo shoots visible through curved glass walls.

29

UBS TOWER

Lohan Associates (now Goettsch Partners), 2001
1 North Wacker Drive
Train: Brown, Orange, Pink, Purple to Washington/Wells
Bus: #20 to Madison Street at Wacker Drive, westbound; to Washington Street at Franklin Street, eastbound

The city's Central Area Plan of 2003 may have predicted that Clinton Street, running north-south between the river and the Kennedy Expressway, would be the spine of the commercial buildings expanding westward in the Loop, but Wacker Drive has become the new backbone of development. No less than five office towers over 35 stories sprouted in the 2000s on a four-block stretch of the roadway's east side, with three of them designed by James Goettsch for the John Buck Company. The first to be completed was the 51-story

A cable-net wall with low-iron glass gives the lobby a high degree of transparency. (Credit Jon Miller © Hedrich Blessing)

UBS Tower, and it set the tone for the two towers to follow (**30**, **31**), namely by focusing on the pedestrian realm. At the base of a fairly mundane stepped tower, a generous plaza—designed by Peter Walker with bulbous-based trees ringed by benches—leads to a large lobby on display behind highly transparent glass walls supported by a then-innovative cable-net structure.

30

111 SOUTH WACKER

Lohan Caprile Goettsch Architects (now Goettsch Partners), 2005
111 South Wacker Drive
Train: Brown, Orange, Pink, Purple to Quincy/Wells
Bus: #151 to Adams Street at Wacker Drive westbound; to Jackson Boulevard at Franklin Street, eastbound

When James Goettsch started his design of the second Wacker Drive tower with John Buck, the first thing he did was lift the office floors twelve stories to gain views over a neighboring building. The space underneath was then filled with a parking garage and a tall lobby behind a curving, cable-net glass wall similar to the earlier UBS Tower (**29**). The most distinctive feature at the base of the building is the ceiling of the lobby, which is the underside of the parking ramp that spirals up clockwise from Monroe Street. Strips of lighting that radiate from the tower's core (these lines are echoed in the paving pattern of the lobby and plaza) accentuate the curling and ascending movement of the ramp. There's more to the design than the lobby: look up at

The highly transparent glass wall puts the radiating ceiling on display. (Credit Anne Evans, CAC Archive)

the walls of the parking garage to see the V-shaped structure transferring four columns on three sides of the 53-story tower to two columns where the building meets the ground.

(Credit courtesy Goettsch Partners)

110 NORTH WACKER

Goettsch Partners, 2020

110 North Wacker Drive

This 56-story tower replaces the low-rise General Growth Building (née Morton Salt building), lifting the office floors 55 feet above a generous riverwalk via exposed diagonal bracing. The west-facing glass facade is serrated to give the tenants multiple corners—facing, incidentally, Goettsch Partners' 150 North Riverside (**36**) across the river.

31

155 NORTH WACKER

Goettsch Partners, 2009

155 North Wacker Drive

Train: Brown, Orange, Pink, Purple to Washington/Wells

Bus: #20 to Madison Street at Wacker Drive, westbound; to Washington Street at Franklin Street, eastbound

The third James Goettsch/John Buck pairing along Wacker Drive continues the pedestrian focus of the earlier towers. Highly transparent, cable-net glass walls are again present at the lobby, which is found behind the elevator cores covered in a striking Italian Rosso Asiago stone. The orientation and size of the 48-story tower is almost the same as the UBS Tower (**29**), but this

The angled pattern in the ceiling reaches out toward the corner and the angled entry. (Credit © Tom Rossiter Photography)

time a generous arcade is found behind a row of large triangular columns, a shape that is echoed in the ceiling and paving. At the east end of the arcade is a small park whose design is not nearly as memorable as the plaza at UBS Tower. A row of trees and a rectangular patch of grass extend the axis of the arcade, begging for its resolution across Franklin Street in the tower (**32**) John Ronan designed for Buck.

32

CNA CENTER

John Ronan Architects with Adamson Associates Architects, 2018

151 North Franklin Street

Train: Brown, Orange, Pink, Purple to Washington/Wells

Bus: #37 to Randolph at Franklin Street, westbound; #20 to Washington Street at Franklin Street, eastbound

The John Buck Company developed this 36-story tower as a speculative office building. In 2018, it took the name of its main tenant, CNA, which moved its employees from 333 South Wabash (the 1970s glass box painted

The three-story "urban room" at the corner is a highlight of this addition to the Loop. (Credit John Ronan Architects; Steve Hall)

the color of the Golden Gate Bridge) to this corner of the Loop. The insurance company and other tenants occupy floors behind the tower's dark-glass exterior walls, but it's best to ignore those surfaces in favor of the "urban room" carved into the base of the building. Supported by a column wrapped in stainless steel that calls attention to itself, the three-story space at the corner of Franklin and Randolph Streets visually terminates the outdoor spaces extending from 155 North Wacker Drive (**31**) and provides a sheltered respite from the rain or a table and chair for a workday lunch. The walls of this "urban room," unlike those of the tower above, exhibit Ronan's careful attention to details and patterns. The south-facing wall extends into the equally spacious and carefully detailed lobby, where stairs lead to a mezzanine and roof terrace, the latter also accessible directly from Randolph Street.

191 NORTH WACKER DRIVE

Kohn Pedersen Fox Associates, 2002
191 North Wacker Drive

One of the highlights of Chicago architecture from the early 1980s is 333 Wacker Drive, a reflective green-glass office tower designed by Kohn Pedersen Fox (KPF) that gracefully follows the bend of the Chicago River. The neighboring 191 North Wacker Drive, also by KPF, is not as memorable but is saved by the glowing white mechanical screen that caps the building and the west facade's cantilever, a response to the widening of Wacker Drive this century.

33

ONEELEVEN

Handel Architects, 2014
111 West Wacker Drive
Train: Blue, Brown, Green, Orange, Pink, Purple to Clark/Lake
Bus: #22 to Dearborn Street at Wacker Drive, northbound; to Clark Street at Wacker Drive, southbound

At 60 stories and packed with 504 rental apartments and nearly as many parking spaces, OneEleven is one of the larger towers on the Wacker Drive streetwall facing the main branch of the Chicago River, nearly as high as Ricardo Bofill's postmodern tower across Clark Street. Yet it was originally planned to be much higher. Architect/developer Teng and Associates (now known as exp) started the project in 2006 as a 1,050-foot-tall luxury condo and hotel tower, but by the time the economy collapsed two years later only 28 of its 90 floors were built. Related Midwest took over the project in 2011, bringing in New York's Handel Architects to redesign and complete the tower (Kara Mann designed the lobby and select amenity spaces). The architects describe their design "as a series of interlocking blocks" with "a cut that runs from the base to the penthouse."[1] Though a tired design trend by 2014, the ribbonlike cut animates an otherwise plain glass box on a prominent site.

The lower horizontal cut aligns with the 1930 Holabird & Root building to the west as well as the 28-story progress of the project's first iteration. (Credit John Hill)

LOOP LINK

AECOM, 2016

West Washington Street at North Clark Street

Across from Daley Plaza is one of the steel-and-glass canopies, designed by AECOM's Ross Wimer, which serves riders of Chicago's first bus rapid transit (BRT) system. Dedicated bus lanes were set aside to whisk people around a nearly two-mile loop along Washington, Madison, Clinton, and Canal streets, linking the Loop to the suburban rail hubs west of the river.

CITY HALL GREEN ROOF

Conservation Design Forum, McDonough + Partners, 2001

121 North LaSalle Avenue

Though not visible from the street or publicly accessible, it is worth pointing out the 21,000-square-foot green roof that covers the western, city half of the full-block County Building and Chicago City Hall, an expression of Mayor Daley's commitment to making Chicago "the greenest city in America." A variety of native prairie plants and sedum ground cover help to reduce the urban heat island effect, absorb water runoff, and provide natural views for the surrounding skyscrapers.

(Credit Eric Allix Rogers, CAC Archive)

GOODMAN THEATRE

KPMB Architects, DLK Architecture, 2000

170 North Dearborn Street

Seventy-five years after the Goodman Theatre opened in Grant Park (on land that is now the Art Institute's Renzo Piano–designed Modern Wing [**8**]), the nonprofit theater company moved into the Loop, renovating the landmark Harris and Selwyn Theaters and placing a glass facade on Randolph Street with colorful LED lights (designed by Lightswitch) illuminating the theater district.

(Credit Eric Allix Rogers, CAC Archive)

34

RIVERBEND

DeStefano Partners, 2002

333 North Canal Street

Train: Green, Pink to Clinton/Lake

Bus: #20 to Madison Street at Clinton Street, westbound; to Washington Street at Canal Street, eastbound

"Site specific" is not a term often dropped in regards to Chicago architecture, which makes sense given the regular grid and flat land that predominates. When irregular conditions violate these norms, such as diagonal streets and waterways, architects have greater opportunities in creating something born from a site's specific circumstances. The curving glass facade of KPF's 333 Wacker Drive is one of the most obvious examples, and a more recent one is the aptly named Riverbend that sits just across the river.

The subtle curve of the east facade can be grasped when seeing the building from the north. (Credit DeStefano Partners)

Designed during the booming residential market of the late 1990s, developer B. J. Spathies's 37-story building places nearly 150 condo units on a narrow trapezoidal site squeezed by the base of the river's north branch on the east and the Metra tracks on the west. The site is so small that a ramp up to the requisite parking garage would not have fit, necessitating the need for car-sized elevators. The architects at DeStefano Partners designed a subtly concave river-facing facade with inset balconies above and townhouses below, while the all-glass west facade kinks in response to the shape of the site. Behind the west-facing glass is a single-loaded corridor that brings light into otherwise windowless bedrooms by "borrowing" light via a transom over the ceiling, a technique previously allowed for in loft conversions but adapted here for new construction. This approach gives east-facing river views to every unit, views that have been eaten away by the three-tower Wolf Point development (**55**) directly to the east.

35

RIVER POINT

Pickard Chilton, Kendall / Heaton Associates, 2017
444 West Lake Street
Train: Green, Pink to Clinton/Lake
Bus: #121 to Canal & Randolph/Washington

Two glass towers rose up simultaneously on either side of Lake Street in the small blocks between Canal Street and the Chicago River. 150 North Riverside (**36**) sits to the south of Lake Street, while the aptly named River Point sits on the north. Designed by Pickard Chilton with executive architect Kendall/Heaton Associates for developer Hines, River Point is located just south of the earlier Riverbend (**34**) residential tower. Although that building squeezed itself between the Metra tracks and the river, the 52-story River Point office tower is set away

The convex tower sits prominently at the west end of the main branch of the Chicago River. (Credit Anna Munzesheimer, CAC Archive)

from the river, tucked between the tracks and Canal Street. This results in a 1.5-acre park on the east that decks over the curving tracks and reaches down to connect to Riverbend's short riverwalk. The most striking aspects of Pickard Chilton's design are found at the base and top, where arches accentuate the tower's subtle convex footprint. A curved tower can happen anywhere, but here it creates a dialogue with KPF's 333 Wacker Drive from 1983 to bookend the river with convex glass walls and curved reflections.

36

150 NORTH RIVERSIDE

Goettsch Partners, 2016

150 North Riverside Plaza

Train: Green, Pink to Clinton/Lake

Bus: #121 to Canal & Randolph/Washington

Many architects have signature moves—recognizable design features they deploy on numerous occasions. For James Goettsch one of those moves is a tower where floors are cantilevered from a central core and tapered near the

The small footprint of the tower led to a "building in the park" effect. (Credit Tom Rossiter Photography)

A dozen liquid mass dampers and the largest steel sections in the world ensure the cantilevered tower's stability. (Credit Tom Rossiter Photography)

base. He executed a quartet of towers in this form in Abu Dhabi in 2012. Back in Chicago, his firm worked with the structural engineering firm Magnusson Klemencic Associates to design a 53-story, core-supported tower as a means of building over the functioning Metra tracks—a task made easier without the perimeter columns so typical of towers.

Precisely, the tower's core touches the ground just east of the tracks such that the cantilever on the east side of the building enables a riverwalk, part of the project's larger 1.5-acre open space. Designed by Wolff Landscape Architecture, the landscape wraps around the south side of the tower and ends at the west, where it sits high upon a small parking garage and where the lobby is found. Here, the tapered underside of the tower is enclosed in walls of highly transparent glass supported with glass fins, reminiscent of Goettsch's earlier towers along Wacker Drive (**29–31**). The architects added some interest to the glass walls on the office floors above through the addition of tapered fins. Their shape echoes the bravura structural engineering and creates a moiré effect when seen while traveling up or down the river on an architectural boat tour.

(Credit Darris Lee Harris)

R+D 659

Brininstool + Lynch, 2009

659 West Randolph Street

This 17-story building with 236 condos overlooks the Kennedy Expressway on the former home of the Catholic Charities of Chicago. One of a handful of midrise condo developments in the downtown area designed by Brininstool + Lynch, R+D 659 departs from the others with a bright-red ribbon that rises up and over the building and a checkerboard of balconies on the south.

JEFFJACK APARTMENTS

Thomas Roszak Architecture, 2015

601 West Jackson Boulevard

Named for the intersection of Jefferson Street and Jackson Boulevard where it sits, this 15-story apartment building should really go by Jeckyl-Hyde, given the different elevations. The east facade has exposed concrete with large windows stacked vertically, while the north face has a curtain wall with bright green fins that are supposed to allude to the grasses of the Illinois prairie.

UNION STATION TOWER

Goettsch Partners, 2022

West Jackson Boulevard between Clinton and Canal Streets

In 2019, Goettsch Partners (GP) wrapped up restoration work on one of Chicago's greatest indoor spaces: the Great Hall at Graham, Anderson, Probst and White's Union Station from 1925. That same year, GP's plans for a fifty-story, 1.5-million-square-foot office tower one block south of Union Station were revealed. Taking the place of an unsightly parking garage, the aptly named Union Station Tower will rise in three tiers from V-shaped angular supports that face a 1.5-acre public park on the west.

(Credit Goettsch Partners)

THE OLD POST OFFICE

Gensler, 2019

433 West Van Buren Street

Graham, Anderson, Probst and White's nine-story, 2.5-million-square-foot Old Chicago Post Office has dominated the southwest corner of the Loop since it was built in 1921 and then greatly expanded in 1932. Its massive floor plates spanning Congress Parkway made redevelopment following the Post Office's 1997 departure for a new building across the street difficult. The building was sold to developer 601W in 2016, who worked with Gensler to successfully transform the postal facility into office space, with the lobby doubling as an event space. The renovation also includes a huge roof deck and other amenities for tenants as well as a riverfront plaza not yet completed when tenants moved in in fall 2019.

Millenium Station
See Map
1
Millenium Park
W Madison St (0N/0S)
See Map
4
The Loop (West)
Burnham
Harbor
Van Buren St
39 Spertus Institute
40 618 S Michigan Ave Facade
Clinton
W Congress Pkwy
Greyhound Bus Terminal
LaSalle
W Harrison St
37 Cook County Circuit Courthouse
38 William Jones College Prepartory High School
Columbia College Chicago Student Center
W Polk St
41 Student Life Center for East - West University
Dan Ryan Expy
S Jefferson St
S Clinton St
S Canal St
River City
Dearborn
Park
Riverline
Southbank
S Wells St
W Taylor St
Pillar of Fire
1000M
Museum Campus/11th St
Lake
Michigan
Roosevelt Collection
Roosevelt
W Roosevelt Rd (1200S)
NEMA Chicago 42
One Museum Park
Shedd Aquarium
Adler Planetarium
The Field
Museum
S Clark St
S State St (0E/0W)
S Wabash Ave
S Michigan Ave
S Indiana Ave
S Lakeshore Dr
Chicago River South Branch
1401 South State
1/2-mile
radius
W 14th Pl
Pacific
Garden
Mission
Northerly Island 44
Soldier Field Expansion 43
W 16th St (1600S)
45 Columbia College Chicago
Media Production Center
49 Ping Tom Memorial
Boathouse & Fieldhouse
Glessner House Museum
W 18th St
18th St
S Canalport Ave
46 Perspectives Charter School
Rodney D. Joslin Campus
Hilliard Towers Apartments
Chinese American 50
Service League
Kam L. Liu Building
51 Chinatown Branch Library
Lakeside Center
at McCormick Place
Cermak-
Chinatown
Wintrust Arena
Marriott Marquis
W Cermak Rd (2200S)
CTA 47
Cermak-McCormick
Place Station
48 McCormick Place West
S Archer Ave
McCormick
Place
Motor Row
Stevenson Expy
W 26th St (2600S)
See Map
19
Bridgeport, etc.

5 South Loop & Chinatown

The story of the South Loop, also referred to as the Near South Side, is a multifaceted one of abandonment and transformation, a process that has resulted in one of the most varied parts of the city. Defined here by four of the city's expressways—Stevenson on the south, Dan Ryan on the west, Eisenhower/Congress Parkway on the north, and Lake Shore Drive (and beyond it Lake Michigan) on the east—the four corners of this rectangle could not be more different from each other: the Jane Byrne Interchange (originally the Circle Interchange) in the northwest, Grant Park and the Museum Campus in the northeast, McCormick Place convention center in the southeast, and Chinatown in the southwest. In the nineteenth century, the area saw two of the city's most dramatic events: the Fort Dearborn Massacre of 1812 and the starting point of the Great Fire of 1871, events that are marked respectively by the Battle of Fort Dearborn Park at the corner of 18th Street and Calumet Avenue and the *Pillar of Fire* statue next to, fittingly, the Chicago Fire Academy at the corner of Taylor and Jefferson Streets.

Historically, much of the land in the South Loop, particularly toward the river, was given over to the railroads for yards and access to their stations at the south end of the Loop. The consolidation of the railroads and the abandonment of their yards in the mid-20th century led to, first, a plan by Mayor Richard J. Daley in 1958 to build a Chicago campus for the University of Illinois, which was built west of the Loop the following decade instead. The 1973 Chicago 21: Plan for the Central Area Communities proposed a South Loop New Town: apartments for over 30,000 people in high-rise towers resting on eight-story bases connected by overhead walkways. What actually ended up being built—the two phases of Dearborn Park—are urban renewal enclaves consisting of eighteen city blocks of predominantly low-rise residential buildings with limited access from the surrounding streets. Dearborn Park laid down a template for the transformation of the former Illinois Central rail yards into Central Station, made up of townhouses and taller residential buildings in primarily neo-traditional garb.

Smaller residential developments have pushed gentrification in the area southward, inching toward Chinatown, the steadfast bastion of Chinese immigrants since 1912 when they moved en masse into Armour Square after rent hikes forced them out of the Loop. Current developments are also moving close to the river as well, as in the oddly introverted Roosevelt Collection, the Riverline and Southbank developments on the east bank of the river, and The 78, a 62-acre mixed-use development so large its developer (Related Midwest) asserts it will become Chicago's 78th neighborhood (the name refers to the city's 77 "community areas").

To the east of Central Station is Museum Campus, created in the mid-1990s by moving the northbound lanes of Lake Shore Drive to the west, thereby consolidating the Adler Planetarium, the Field Museum, and the Shedd Aquarium on one stretch of parkland along the lakefront, accessible to Grant Park via a new pedestrian tunnel. (The railroad tracks between Central Station and Museum Campus have been eyed by developers as a prime, if pricey *tabula rasa* site for residential towers; most recent was in early 2019 by developer Bob Dunn, though it's too early to say if his plans will succeed or fail like the others before him.) To the south, McCormick Place was originally created to the east of Lake Shore Drive in the 1960s, defying the "forever free and clear" mandate for lakefront land. The complex expanded westward in the ensuing decades to become the largest convention center in North America and make its owner, the Metropolitan Pier and Exposition Authority (MPEA, which also owns Navy Pier) the area's most powerful player.

37

COOK COUNTY CIRCUIT COURTHOUSE

Booth Hansen, 2005

555 West Harrison Street

Train: Blue to Clinton

Bus: #60 to Harrison Street at Jefferson Street

The "peninsula" formed by the Dan Ryan and Eisenhower Expressways and the south branch of the Chicago River is home to the city's massive main post office facility, the Greyhound bus terminal, the site of the start of the Great Fire of 1871, and not much else. So if you find yourself in this area, it

Vertical trusses support the new glass and terra-cotta wall. (Credit John Hill)

might be for an unfortunate court date. Thankfully, the courthouse is a bright and welcoming building with a new north facade added by Booth Hansen to a four-story masonry building from the early 20th century. The entry was moved from the south to the north, through the 60-foot-high, 300-foot-long space formed by the terra-cotta rainscreen wall positioned 16 feet in front of the old building. The new section is slightly taller than the old, so light enters the narrow space via clerestory windows and a curved ceiling of wood panels.

RIVERLINE, SOUTHBANK

Perkins and Will, *Estimated completion in 2026*

East side of Chicago River, between Harrison Street and Roosevelt Road

In 2016, developers CMK Companies and Lendlease broke ground on the 14-acre Riverline project, extending from Harrison Street south to Roosevelt Avenue. Jump ahead two years and the $2 billion project split into two large residential developments: CMK's Riverline south of Bertrand Goldberg's sinuous River City and Lendlease's Southbank to the north. Perkins and Will developed the masterplan for both (with Hoerr Schaudt designing park space and a river walk) and designed the eight towers that will add more than 3,000 residential units to the Near South Side by 2026.

(Credit © Tom Harris)

COLUMBIA COLLEGE CHICAGO STUDENT CENTER

Gensler, 2018

754 South Wabash Street

In designing Columbia College's first-ever student center—and only second ever newly constructed building since the institution's founding in 1890 (see also **45**)—Gensler envisioned the five-story building as an atrium turned inside-out, positioning stairs and flexible spaces for students directly behind a patchwork of clear and translucent glass facades.

38

WILLIAM JONES COLLEGE PREPARATORY HIGH SCHOOL

Perkins and Will, 2013

700 South State Street

Train: Red to Harrison

Bus: #146 to State Street at Harrison Street, southbound; to State Street at Balbo Avenue, northbound

Perkins and Will's expertise in designing schools for grades K-12 extends all the way back to 1940, when they designed the highly influential Crow Island Elementary school in suburban Winnetka in collaboration with Eliel and Eero Saarinen. The firm has been responsible for dozens of schools around the United States since, including the 1967 home of Jones College Prep, a concrete building that resembles an office building more than a school. The resemblance was intentional, since in those days the Jones Commercial High School trained students for office work after they graduated. Yet by 1998, when the school adopted its current curriculum with selective enrollment, the emphasis had shifted to readying students for college rather than work.

Designed by the firm's Global Design Director Ralph Johnson and placed just south of the 1967 building, the new building serving 1,200 students is a true vertical campus on a long and narrow site. Classrooms, cafeteria, gymnasium, natatorium, and auditorium fit compactly into seven stories above an

The brick-colored precast concrete wraps around to the south and west side of the building. (Credit © James Steinkamp Photography)

The entrance is on axis with Balbo Drive. (Credit © James Steinkamp Photography)

underground parking garage. The architecture expresses the stacking of functions in its elevation facing State Street, where bands of glass, recessed terraces, brick, and brick-colored precast concrete are stitched together by round concrete columns. The auditorium is behind the brick expanse on the first two floors to the north, while the gym occupies the top floor above it and the pool sits at the top on the southern end. Central stairs provide the main circulation spine for the students, and in the middle of it all is a three-story lobby that is the nexus of the prestigious public school.

39

SPERTUS INSTITUTE

Krueck Sexton Partners with VOA Associates (now Stantec), 2007
610 South Michigan Avenue
Train: Red to Harrison
Bus: #3 to Michigan Avenue at Balbo Drive

In early 2002, the City of Chicago designated a strip of Michigan Avenue, from Randolph Street down to 11th Street, a landmark district, calling it "an incomparable backdrop to Grant Park and Lake Michigan" and "the most enduring image of the Chicago skyline."[1] The streetwall of late-19th- and early-20th-century buildings is often called Chicago's version of New York's Fifth Avenue bordering Central Park. The Spertus Institute is the first new building realized in what is officially named the Historic Michigan Boulevard District (the avenue was a boulevard in the pre-fire decades). Founded in 1924, the Spertus Institute (made up of the Asher Library, Spertus College, and the Spertus Museum) previously occupied the building at 618 South Michigan Avenue (**40**) before buying up the land directly north for its new home. The approval, in 2004, by the city's landmarks commission of architects Ron Krueck and Mark Sexton's design reveals that a contemporary expression and materiality can be a good fit in a landmark district.

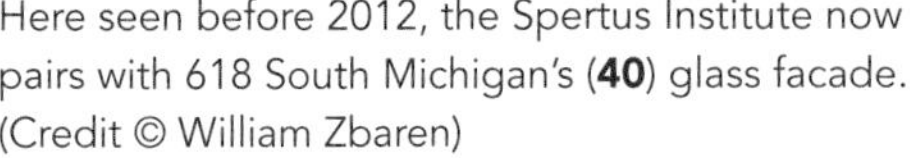

Here seen before 2012, the Spertus Institute now pairs with 618 South Michigan's (**40**) glass facade. (Credit © William Zbaren)

The three-dimensional nature of the faceted facade is best appreciated from below. (Credit John Hill)

Before the landmark designation—even before Krueck and Sexton were selected over the then more well-known finalists Polshek Partnership Architects, Tod Williams Billie Tsien Architects, and Pelli Clarke Pelli Architects in the design competition—Spertus president Dr. Howard A. Sulkin wanted a modern building, "an emblem for his institution distinguishing it from every other building."[2] KSP's design provides this distinction through a faceted curtain wall rising ten stories to an asymmetrical "top" (without cornice) that expresses the Jewish notion of a lifetime of learning, of learning without end. The building is illuminated at night through the milky glass that features a frit pattern of small white dots, a further means of standing out among its masonry neighbors. The building's height—slightly taller than its previous home to the south and a couple stories lower than the building to the north—is in keeping with the other buildings up and down Michigan Avenue, making it an integral part of the streetwall.

But the architecture is more than just a faceted curtain wall made up of 726 panes of glass in 556 different shapes. Inside, past the flared "skirt" of the facade that acts as a canopy, is a light-filled, three-story atrium whose solid rear wall is also faceted, shielding the 400-seat theater beyond. At the top of the building, where the Asher Library (open to the public) is located, is another atrium that receives daylight from a skylight along the north wall. Originally, the two atriums were one that extended through the whole building. Even though they are now disconnected—the space between filled with floors for offices and the like—the building remains a powerful statement of Jewish culture, inside and out, and one of the best Chicago buildings this century.

40

618 SOUTH MICHIGAN AVENUE FACADE

Gensler, 2012

618 South Michigan Avenue

Train: Red to Harrison

Bus: #3 to Michigan Avenue at Balbo Drive

The clear glass facade accentuates the layering of new and old. (Credit Steve Hall © Hall+Merrick)

Columbia College Chicago calls itself "the South Loop neighborhood's largest landowner,"[3] with seventeen buildings south of Congress Parkway. Three of them are old buildings clustered around the Spertus Institute (**39**) on Michigan Avenue just south of Harrison Street. The ten-story building at 618 South Michigan Avenue was previously home to the Spertus Institute and, before that, the IBM Corporation, which replaced the terra-cotta facade designed by Zimmerman, Saxe & McBride in 1913 with a curtain wall typical of the late

1950s. Gensler merged old and new by printing a ghosted image of the original facade on the curtain wall replacement, a skin-deep retracing of a past only visible in historic photos. Look closely to see how each dot is made up of a bird graphic of varying size, alluding to the "bird-friendly" design of the transparent facade.

The ghostly image is accentuated when shadows cast it upon the wall behind it. (Credit Steve Hall © Hall+Merrick)

41

STUDENT LIFE CENTER FOR EAST-WEST UNIVERSITY

Holabird & Root, 2013

829 South Wabash Avenue

Train: Red to Harrison

Bus: #146 to State Street at 9th Street

The Loop and South Loop are home to a large number of colleges and universities: 22 higher education institutions with nearly 60,000 students.[4] This increase in student population led to the construction of the large but bland University Center at Congress Parkway and State Street in 2004 (the building includes dorms for four local universities) but also architecturally ambitious buildings like Gensler's student center for Columbia College

A view of the "Vertical Quad" at the heart of the educational building. (Credit Eric Allix Rogers, CAC Archive)

Chicago and VOA's vertical campus for Roosevelt University (**25**). Falling into the latter camp is this 17-story building with café, bookstore, food court, classrooms, offices, gymnasium, auditorium, library, and dorms for East-West University students. A "glass column" pulled out from the building's corner rises next to a random pattern of solid and void covering the west facade, while inside a 100-foot-high atrium, what the architects call a "vertical quad,"[5] unites the various functions below the residences.

1000M
JAHN, *Estimated completion in 2022*
1000 South Michigan Avenue

In spring 2016, the Chicago Plan Commission approved Helmut Jahn's elegant, glassy design for this 73-story, 832-foot-tall apartment and condo tower at the south end of the Historic Michigan Boulevard District. The project for Time Equities and JK Equities fills the last gap in the streetwall, on a site that served as a surface parking lot for far too long.

ONE MUSEUM PARK
Pappageorge Haymes Partners, 2009
1211 South Prairie Avenue

Central Station was the original name of a large residential development built on land and the air rights of Illinois Central's former rail yards south of Roosevelt Road and west of Lake Shore Drive. As part of that development, new towers along Roosevelt create a southern streetwall of sorts for Grant Park. Most notable of these is One Museum Park, which tiers up through a number of elliptical masses to a height of 62 floors.

Generous balconies alternate with glass walls across NEMA's narrow northern facade overlooking Grant Park. (Credit courtesy of Crescent Heights®)

42

NEMA CHICAGO

Rafael Viñoly Architects, 2019
1200 South Indiana Avenue
Train: Green, Orange, and Red to Roosevelt
Bus: #12, #146 to Roosevelt & Michigan/Indiana

With a developer from Miami, its architect and interior architect both from New York City, and its structural engineer from Seattle, NEMA Chicago is truly an outsider development. No wonder the 76-story tower's massing looks like a residential version of Willis Tower, an instantly recognizable symbol of Chicago. NEMA Chicago is more than an homage though, since its form is the result of the same bundled-tube structure—here designed by Magnusson Klemencic Associates and done in concrete rather than steel.

Developer Crescent Heights unveiled the project in 2015 as two near-twin residential towers that would fill the last empty lots along the south edge of Grant Park. Construction of the shorter, east tower commenced first, wrapping up in 2019. Designed by the firm of Rafael Viñoly with interiors by the Rockwell Group, the tower starts as a rectangular base that sheds structural bays as it rises to a square tower with roof terraces topping setbacks that spiral in a counterclockwise motion about the central core. Although diagrammatic in its geometries, the tower is a satisfying piece of closure at this end of Grant Park—but one that eagerly awaits its sibling.

43

SOLDIER FIELD AND NORTH BURNHAM PARK REDEVELOPMENT

Wood + Zapata with Lohan Caprile Goettsch Architects (now Goettsch Partners), 2003

1410 Museum Campus Drive

Bus: #146 to Museum Campus Drive at McFetridge Drive

It is no coincidence that the most controversial piece of architecture in Chicago so far this century is located along the lakefront. The land along the lake is prized for the public beaches, boat slips, bicycle paths, and other uses that follow from the 1836 decree to keep it "forever open, clear, and free of any buildings." Champions like Aaron Montgomery Ward and Daniel H. Burnham in the late 1800s and early 1900s and *Chicago Tribune* architecture critic

Soldier Field seen from Northerly Island. (Credit Angie McMonigal Photography)

Wood + Zapata's design is a striking contemporary juxtaposition with the neoclassical colonnades. (Credit © Doug Fogelson)

The park above the parking garage can be seen in the approach from the north. (Credit © Doug Fogelson)

Blair Kamin and the nonprofit Friends of the Parks in recent years, have fought attempts at building structures next to the lake. Yet, one look at the stretch of lakefront from Roosevelt Avenue to the Stevenson Expressway—from the Museum Campus's trio of early-20th-century buildings to McCormick Place's 1971 Lakeside Center—makes clear that buildings have managed to skirt this original vision.

Between Museum Campus and McCormick Place sits Soldier Field, designed by Holabird & Roche and built in 1924 as a 75,000-seat stadium for sports and other events—everything from soccer and boxing to stock car races and rock concerts. The Bears moved from Wrigley Field to Soldier Field in 1971, subsequently remodeling the stadium to make it more amenable as an NFL venue. Those changes had little effect on the stadium's signature colonnades and other neoclassical features, but the plans unveiled in 2000 for inserting modern seating and other amenities (for fans and the football team alike) within the original did the opposite, landing inside the stone-clad stadium that some have likened to a glass-and-steel spaceship.

Many people will experience Soldier Field only while driving by on Lake Shore Drive, but this is the least flattering view of the addition designed by

Ben Wood and Carlos Zapata; the underside of the upper-deck seats sharply angles up and over the west-facing colonnade. Seen from the east—from the paths along Burnham Harbor or from Northerly Island (**44**)—the addition is more pleasing, if still a jarring juxtaposition, thanks to a shorter glass facade that conceals the luxury suites and ends in two large cantilevered video monitors. In addition to the seating bowl, the project reconfigured 98 acres of the surrounding Burnham Park, even creating a 2,500-car underground parking garage between the stadium and the Field Museum. Landscape architect Peter Lindsay Schaudt's design (following a plan by Dirk Lohan) includes an entrance to the stadium, but also a children's garden and a sledding hill that add some recreational amenities *outside* of the colonnades.

44

NORTHERLY ISLAND

Studio Gang, SmithGroupJJR, 2015 (Phase 1)
1521 South Linn White Drive
Bus: #146 to Solidarity Drive at Lynn White Drive

In the middle of the night of March 30, 2003, and under police escort, bulldozers carved large "X"s into the sole runway of Meigs Field, debilitating the small airport for private planes that had occupied Northerly Island since 1948. Mayor Daley cited threats of terrorism for his order, but frustration over failed O'Hare expansion plans (plans that would have kept Meigs open until 2026) and the desire to turn the 91-acre manmade peninsula near his home into a park are the more likely reasons. Whatever the case may be, more than fifteen years later the peninsula is well on its way to becoming a multifaceted outdoor amenity for the public and a habitat for birds, fish, and other creatures.

Approach to the lagoon at the southern end of Northerly Island. (Credit Eric Allix Rogers, CAC Archives)

Northerly Island offers generous views of Chicago's iconic skyline. (Credit John Hill)

Envisioned by Daniel H. Burnham and Edward H. Bennett in their 1909 *Plan of Chicago* as the northernmost in a chain of islands stretching to Jackson Park, Northerly Island was the only one realized, created for the 1933 Century of Progress International Exposition. Today, in the hands of Jeanne Gang's firm and the landscape architects at SmithGroupJJR, and officially called the *Northerly Island Framework Plan*, the island is split into two halves. The southern forty acres includes remediated land with a pond, prairie, savanna, wetland, and woodland with trails, boardwalk, and space for camping. The northern section will be developed in the second phase, anchored by an outdoor amphitheater with underground parking close to the Museum Campus and retail fronting a boardwalk overlooking Burnham Harbor. A later phase would include a reef and lagoon reaching further into Lake Michigan, which could serve as a template for sustainably treating the shoreline for habitat and rising waters due to climate change.

(Credit Steve Hall © Hedrich Blessing)

1401 SOUTH STATE
Valerio Dewalt Train Associates, 2008
1401 South State Street

Located across State Street from the main entrance to the low-rise second phase of Dearborn Park, this 22-story building with 278 apartments is a striking contrast to the earlier development in height but also in its contemporary manipulation of glass, balconies, and concrete structure.

45

COLUMBIA COLLEGE CHICAGO MEDIA PRODUCTION CENTER

Studio Gang, 2010
1600 South State Street
Train: Red, Green, Orange to Roosevelt
Bus: #29 to State Street at 16th Street

The southernmost building on Columbia College Chicago's South Loop "campus" is also its first newly constructed building. Most of the school's facilities are housed in existing, repurposed buildings, but as outlined in a 2010 master plan by Valerio Dewalt Train Associates, the Media Production Center (MPC) would require a new facility for the sizable sound stages. The MPC's location, at the corner of 16th Street and State Street, is surrounded by elevated and at-grade railroad tracks, which, combined with a low budget and short schedule, dictated a bare-bones design by Jeanne Gang's firm that partly resembles some of the few industrial buildings remaining in the area.

The east-facing facade on State Street resembles color test patterns. (Credit Steve Hall © Hall+Merrick)

The one-story building is arranged roughly in two halves, with sound stages on the west and classrooms, storage, offices, and support spaces on the east. The tall walls of the sound stages are made from two layers of precast concrete sandwiched with insulation for eliminating the sounds and vibrations of passing trains (aided by the green roof that covers the stages). Along State Street, the precast concrete is overlapped with glass, the latter made up of colorful strips inspired by the color bar test pattern used in TV and film. Behind the glazed corner is a two-story entry/lounge with a salvaged archway from a nearby building that once housed the Famous Players-Lasky Corporation (a silent-era film studio) and a wide stair that leads to a rooftop terrace; the ceiling is cut with an illuminated test pattern that reiterates the building's purpose.

The colored glass enlivens the two-story lounge at the corner. (Credit Steve Hall © Hall+Merrick)

46

PERSPECTIVES CHARTER SCHOOL RODNEY D. JOSLIN CAMPUS

Perkins and Will, 2004

1930 South Archer Avenue

Train: Red to Cermak/Chinatown; Green to Cermak/McCormick Place

Bus: #29 to State Street at Cullerton Street

Perspectives Charter Schools, started by Kim Day and Diana Shulla-Cose, two former Chicago Public School teachers, became one of the first charter schools in Illinois in 1997. They functioned as a "school within a school" on the city's South Side until opening this ground-up building on a triangular site at Archer Avenue and State Street, just north of Bertrand Goldberg's Hilliard Towers. The long, tapered shape of the site (like the tip of a pencil) could have been a potential liability, but architect Ralph Johnson of Perkins and Will exploited the triangular shape by letting the building reach almost to its eastern tip, stopping the enclosed building short but extending the roof to the corner, propped upon a trellis for climbing plants.

The composition of the materials and surfaces at the western end belies the economy of the project. (Credit John Hill)

The entrance is located on the western end of the building, adjacent to a small parking lot. Outside of the eastern tip, the entry is the only part of the building where Johnson goes beyond the simple and inexpensive exterior materials: horizontal ribbon windows set in corrugated metal siding, sitting on a roughly three-foot brick base. At the entrance, the roofline slopes up from the one corner to cover some rooftop mechanical equipment, meeting a tall portion of wall that wraps into the canopy at the other corner. Johnson uses these humble materials to his advantage, resisting the mundane brick-and-stone neo-traditionalism of nearby condos in favor of a gritty neo-industrial aesthetic that in some ways mirrors the area's formerly tough times.

47

CTA CERMAK-McCORMICK PLACE STATION

Ross Barney Architects, 2015
12 East Cermak Road
Train: Green to Cermak/McCormick Place
Bus: #3 to Michigan Avenue at Cermak Road

From 1978 until 2014, riders on the Green Line could not detrain for three miles between Roosevelt Avenue (1200 South) and 35th-Bronzeville-IIT (3500 South). The rough midpoint between these stops coincides with Cermak Road, the major east-west thoroughfare leading to McCormick Place, the nation's largest convention center, so it was only a matter of time that a new

Polycarbonate tops the tube shading passengers waiting for Green Line trains. (Credit John Hill)

station was built. Carol Ross Barney took the material palette from the earlier Morgan Street Station (**125**) and executed it here to a much different effect, wrapping the platform in an arching tube of polycarbonate and perforated stainless steel that shades those waiting for trains. Driven by the need to keep the station open during construction, the cover is propped upon concrete legs that sit outside the structure of the elevated tracks. The tubular form recalls OMA's McCormick Tribune Campus Center (**137**), which is visible in the distance from the platform.

48

McCORMICK PLACE WEST

Mc4 West, 2007

Cermak Road and Martin Luther King, Jr. Drive

Train: Green to Cermak/McCormick Place

Bus: #3 to Cermak Road at Prairie Avenue

McCormick Place, owned by the Metropolitan Pier and Exposition Authority (MPEA, also owner of Navy Pier [**66**]), is comprised of four interconnected buildings that add up to 2.67 million square feet of exhibition halls, making it

A roof overhang reaches to the north while columns form a gateway along Indiana Avenue. (Credit Eric Allix Rogers, CAC Archive)

the largest convention center in North America. Lakeside Center opened in 1971 (the original building east of Lake Shore Drive opened in 1960, but a fire destroyed it seven years later), followed by the North Building in 1986, the South Building in 1997, and the West Building ten years later. Carried out by Mc4 West, a design/build joint venture with Atlanta's tvsdesign and Chicago's Epstein, the West Building brings gargantuan McCormick Place as far west as Indiana Avenue, near the Motor Row Historic District. While more exhibition space is hardly an imminent need, MPEA is continuing its expansion with construction of a data center, as well as a hotel and event center as part of a $400 million entertainment district.

MARRIOTT MARQUIS
Gensler, 2017
Corner of Cermak Road and Prairie Avenue

(Credit © Isaac Maiselman)

Although McCormick Place is the largest convention center in North America, it is served by only one hotel, the 1,258-room Hyatt Regency, a quantity roughly doubled with the new 51-story Marriott Marquis located between the new arena and data center.

WINTRUST ARENA
Pelli Clarke Pelli Architects, 2017
Corner of Cermak Road and Indiana Avenue

McPier is building a venue for conventions, meetings, concerts, and the new home of the DePaul University Blue Demons basketball team, with 10,000 seats underneath a swelling roof with curved skylights.

49

PING TOM MEMORIAL PARK BOATHOUSE & FIELDHOUSE

Johnson & Lee, Site Design Group, Wight & Company, 2013

300 West 19th Street, 1700 South Wentworth

Train: Red to Cermak/Chinatown

Bus: #24 to Clark Street at 18th Street

Ping Tom Memorial Park sits on a former Chicago and Western Indiana rail yard along the east bank of the Chicago River's south branch, stretching just over a half mile on both sides of the 18th Street Bridge. The southern half opened in 1999 per a design by Site Design Group that includes a playground, bamboo gardens, a traditional-style pagoda near the water's edge,

The boathouse's palette of red, white, and black faces the south branch of the river. (Credit BalloggPhoto.com)

The fieldhouse's large canopy shades a roof deck. (Credit BalloggPhoto.com)

and a bust of Ping Tom, the Chinatown businessman who had earlier developed Chinatown Square (designed by Harry Weese) on another former rail yard and who is credited as the leading force behind this riverfront park. The park is accessed via a walkway at the end of 19th Street, one block west of Wentworth Street.

The northern half was completed more than a dozen years later with the second phase of Site Design Group's landscape, highlighted by a zigzag boardwalk with red guardrails, a boathouse designed by Johnson & Lee and a fieldhouse designed by Wight & Company. The boathouse, which houses kayaks for launching into the river, was the first of four planned by Mayor Rahm Emmanuel (see also **96**). It sits on land contiguous with the park's first phase, while the fieldhouse (with pool, gymnasium, fitness center, and community rooms) is to the east of the tracks, accessed from 18th Street. The buildings share a similar *parti* of simple boxes accompanied by larger roof elements. More interesting is the boathouse, which exhibits a wider variety in materials and surfaces, and benefits from proximity to the water and the rest of the park.

50

CHINESE AMERICAN SERVICE LEAGUE KAM L. LIU BUILDING

Studio Gang/O'Donnell (now Studio Gang), 2004

2141 South Tan Court

Train: Red to Cermak/Chinatown

Bus: #62 to Archer Avenue at Cermak/Princeton

CASL serves to bridge the gap for Chinese-American immigrants in Chicago by providing child and elder services, housing and financial education, employment training, and family counseling, as well as hosting special programs and events for the Chinatown community. The architecture responds accordingly, by bridging traditional Chinese motifs with a modern architectural

The lattice on the west facade sits in front of a double-height community space. (Credit Eric Allix Rogers, CAC Archive)

expression suited to Chicago. Most overt is the lattice sunscreen on the west facade that shades the double-height community room. More subtle are the variegated titanium panels that are turned 45 degrees and overlap like shingles to differentiate the boxy three-story building from its neighbors.

51

CHINATOWN BRANCH LIBRARY

Skidmore, Owings & Merrill with Wight & Co., 2015

2100 South Wentworth Avenue

Train: Red to Cermak/Chinatown

Bus: #62 to Archer Avenue at Red Line Station, northbound; to Archer Avenue at Wentworth Avenue, southbound

Reversing Chicago's decades-long trend of building libraries and other public buildings based on prototype designs, the new Chinatown branch of the Chicago Public Library is a one-of-a-kind building that the neighborhood can take pride in. Previously, the Chinatown branch, which started in 1972, was housed a few blocks south of the new location in a storefront on Wentworth Avenue. Carried out as a design/build project with Wight & Company, the design by Skidmore, Owings & Merrill (SOM) partner Brian Lee responds to the triangular site at Archer Avenue with a two-story, tri-oval-shaped building covered in glass and shaded with the design's signature element: vertical aluminum fins. The form of the 16,000-square-foot building on the triangular site allows for the creation of a small plaza to the south and some trees overlooking the intersection to the northeast.

The bronze-colored aluminum fins extend above the edge of the library's glass walls to give the building a unique profile against the skyline. (Credit John Hill)

An emphasis on curves continues inside, where a two-story atrium with rounded corners is topped by an oculus that brings plenty of light to the center of the lower level. Here, the open center is ringed by the children's area and community meeting rooms, befitting the library's desire to be a cultural and information center for Chinatown. Upstairs, stacks are arrayed along the east side of the opening, but lounge areas are grouped to the north, taking advantage of Loop views. Not visible from inside nor the plaza is the green roof that caps the building—this sustainable surface can be seen from the nearby Cermak/Chinatown "L" platform.

PACIFIC GARDEN MISSION

Tigerman McCurry Architects, 2007

1458 South Canal Street

This unassuming brick and concrete structure may look like an existing building renovated by architect Stanley Tigerman as the homeless shelter's new home (its previous building was located on the site of the Jones College Prep expansion [**38**]), but it is new construction, fitting into its industrial context yet with a courtyard "sanctuary" at its core.

North Side

See Map
8
Near North
Chicago
W Chicago Ave (800N)
156 West Superior 59
W Superior St
747 N Clark
Chicago
One Chicago Square
Poetry Foundation 61
N Larrabee St
N Kingsbury St
N Hudson Ave
N Sedgwick St
Richard H. Driehaus Museum
W Huron St
The Godfrey Hotel 60
Ikram
58 Erie on the Park
W Erie St
640 North Wells
58 Kingsbury on the Park
W Ontario St
Bloomingdale Home Store
Tree Studios
McDonald's Chicago Flagship 57
1/4-mile radius
W Ohio St
N Orleans St
N Franklin St
N Wells St
N LaSalle St
N Clark St
N Dearborn St
N State St (0E/0W)
N Wabash Ave
W Grand Ave
Grand
Contemporaine 56
Anti-Cruelty Society
W Illinois St
111 West Illinois
Courthouse Place
W Hubbard St
Museum of Broadcast Communications
W Kinzie St (400N)
53
River Cottages
Merchandise Mart
EnV Chicago
52
Merchandise Mart
300 North LaSalle 54
Trump International Hotel & Tower
55 Wolf Point
Reid-Murdoch Center
W Wacker Dr
W Lake St
Clark/Lake
State/Lake
See Map
4
The Loop (West)
See Map
3
The Loop (East)

6 River North

Imagine being magically dropped onto any intersection within River North—the area bounded by the Chicago River on the south and west, Michigan Avenue on the east and Chicago Avenue on the north. The area is a panoply of galleries, shops, restaurants, hotels, residences, offices, and parking lots—just about everything but parks—so the corners facing the intersection would be as likely to have a parking lot, a theme restaurant, a formerly industrial loft building, or a new residential tower. This 21st-century condition is born from an uneven past to one of the city's oldest neighborhoods.

Kinzie Street, one block north of the river, was the northern boundary of the city when it was platted in 1830, around the time of the city's first bar and hotel on Wolf Point. Twenty years later, trains followed Kinzie eastward across the north branch of the river to a station at Wells Street adjacent to the river ports, which led to a flourishing of industry in the area. Even though the Great Fire of 1871 wiped out everything in what is now known as River North, industry speedily resumed by the end of the 19th century, which earned it the moniker "Smokey Hollow," due to the factory smoke blotting out the sun. But relocation of the ports from the 1920s up to the 1960s led to the neighborhood's descent into one of the city's most notorious slums (where even cops wouldn't respond to calls) and its red-light district.

Things started to change for the better in the 1960s, with the construction of Marina City, and the 1970s when developers, most notably Albert Friedman who coined the area as River North, started to transform old industrial buildings for offices, galleries, and, to a lesser degree, residences. Design-related offices clustered to the south, near the Merchandise Mart, while galleries gravitated toward Chicago Avenue astride the "L" tracks running up Franklin Street. The area between evolved into an odd assortment of theme restaurants, such as Ed Debevics and the Rock N Roll McDonald's (both gone), among a sea of parking lots. Further east, hotels and stores were and have been more prevalent, taking advantage of proximity to the Magnificent Mile of North Michigan Avenue. Developments this century have focused predominantly on multifamily residential towers, first in the form of the "bland concrete hulks" that Richard M. Daley abhorred, but more recently as glass boxes, with several gems highlighted here.

52

TRUMP INTERNATIONAL HOTEL & TOWER

Skidmore, Owings & Merrill, 2009

401 North Wabash Avenue

Train: Green, Brown, Pink, Orange, Purple, to State/Lake

Bus: #151 to Michigan Avenue at Hubbard Street

Since 1974, when the Willis Tower (formerly Sears Tower) was completed in the Loop, the Chicago skyline had been punctuated by three "supertall" buildings over 984 feet (300 meters): Willis Tower, Aon Center, and 875 N. Michigan Avenue (formerly John Hancock Center). This situation changed in 2009 when Donald Trump inserted a 1,389-foot-tall tower designed by Skidmore Owings & Merrill's (SOM) Adrian Smith roughly at the midpoint of an imaginary line in the city skyline connecting the Willis and Hancock towers (both also designed by SOM). This brought a supertall to the banks of the Chicago River on a site that previously housed the squat Chicago Sun-Times building. The first Windy City project of Big Apple developer Donald Trump,

The stepped tower occupies a prominent site next to the Wrigley Building. (Credit Alvesgaspar)

The base of the tower is given over to a multilevel walkway facing the river. (Credit John Hill)

his namesake tower was planned initially to rise even higher, but the events of September 11, 2001, put a damper on his quest for the world's tallest building.

As built, the 98-story, 2.6-million-square-foot tower stacks a lobby and retail base, 10-story parking garage (its glass-enclosed ramp placed to the north of the entrance on Wabash Avenue), 339 hotel rooms on 11 floors, and 60 floors of residential condominiums. These uses partly coincide with the tower's three setbacks, which are devoted to mechanical services and whose heights reference neighboring buildings along the north bank of the river: the Wrigley Building, Marina City, and IBM Plaza (now AMA Plaza), from short to tall. Formally, the tower's glass skin rises with flat facades on the north and south sides. The east and west sides, where the setbacks occur, are rounded to create a distinctive appearance from any direction and to channel winds around the tower. Viewed from west- and north-side neighborhoods at sunset, the tower elegantly reflects the light, making the skin glow orange. East of the tower is a multilevel plaza that meets up with the Wrigley Building's breezeway and Trump's own riverwalk, whose three levels sit below the tower and extend to Wabash.

Five years after completion (two years before he successfully ran for president), Trump returned to Chicago, emblazoning his name in 20-foot-high stainless steel letters silhouetted with LED lights facing the river. The move led Mayor Rahm Emmanuel to propose a special sign district "to ensure that the riverfront is protected from signage that negatively impacts the visual environment."[1] The signage did not involve Smith, who created a tasteful tower that shows deference to its neighbors including the Wrigley Building. The installation of the sign picks up on the increasing popularity of the river as a site of leisure and recreation, on the riverwalks (**19**) or even in the water.

53

MUSEUM OF BROADCAST COMMUNICATIONS

Eckenhoff Saunders Architects with Helen Kessler, 2012

360 North State Street

Train: Green, Brown, Pink, Orange, Purple to State/Lake

Bus: #151 to Michigan Avenue at Hubbard Street

If any city deserves to play host to a museum of television (and its stepsister radio, to a lesser degree), it is Chicago; site of the Great Debate between Kennedy and Nixon in 1960, Siskel and Ebert's weekly film reviews, and Oprah Winfrey's long-running talk show. It also makes sense that the museum has a visible presence in the city, something it lacked at the Chicago Cultural Center or its earlier home in Bertrand Goldberg's River City south of the Loop. The museum planned to move in 2005 into a renovated and expanded parking garage behind another Goldberg project, Marina City, but a corrupt governor and fund-raising problems delayed the project for seven years. Metal mesh sits in front of the old parking garage windows on the north elevation, while an angled curtain wall on the east defines the double-height lobby with its grand stair. Above this piece is a fourth-floor roof terrace covered by a generous roof overhang.

The metal-and-glass museum renovates an old parking garage behind Marina City. (Credit Lynn Becker)

54

300 NORTH LASALLE

Pickard Chilton with Kendall / Heaton Associates, 2009
300 North LaSalle Street
Train: Brown, Purple to Merchandise Mart
Bus: #22 to Clark Street at Kinzie Street, southbound; to Dearborn Street at Hubbard Street, northbound

Before the 108-story Willis Tower was sold in early 2015 for $1.3 billion, this 60-story tower at 300 North LaSalle Street had the honor of being the most expensive office building sold in Chicago. Although the $850-million-dollar price tag in 2014 was far less than the former Sears Tower, it is a substantially higher per-square-foot price ($654/sf versus $285/sf), due in part to its prime location overlooking the Chicago River. The river views for tenants in the office floors, as well as the public's exterior viewpoint of the building, are helped by its corner lot and its lower-scaled neighbors, such as the 1914 Reid-Murdoch Center to the east with its distinctive clock. The LEED platinum-certified tower takes advantage of its south-facing riverfront site with a generous tiered plaza—designed with landscape architect Ted Wolff—that extends from street level down to a river walk at dock level.

The 60-story tower subtly steps as it rises above the Reid-Murdoch Center. (Credit Lynn Becker)

ENV CHICAGO

Valerio Dewalt Train Associates, 2010

161 West Kinzie Street

This 29-story, 249-unit apartment building is located across the street from the Merchandise Mart, a site that would give any architect goose bumps. Standing next to the elevated tracks across from the Merchandise Mart, the requisite parking requirements lift the 29-story apartment building's 249 units seven stories up, above the level of the tracks. Texas's Lynd Development Partners developed the tower, their first (and so far only) foray into Chicago.

(Credit John Hill)

55

WOLF POINT

Pelli Clarke Pelli Architects, bKL Architecture, Wolff Landscape Architecture, 2016 (west tower); *estimated completion of 2020 for east tower and 2023 for south tower*

343 West Wolf Point Plaza

Train: Brown to Merchandise Mart

Bus: #37, #125 to Orleans and Merchandise Mart

Historically, Wolf Point was an early-nineteenth-century settlement at the Y-shaped confluence of the three branches of the Chicago River, with a little bit of land on each bank and a ferry operating between the taverns, hotel, and factory that served early Chicagoans. Today, the name Wolf Point refers to the small peninsula on the north side of the fork, a prime development site just south of the hulking Apparel Center from the 1970s. The triangular plot was a parking lot for more than forty years, until the Kennedy family (yes, *that* Ken-

Wolf Point West, completed in 2016, is a slender tower when seen from the south. (Credit Jon Miller © Hedrich Blessing)

nedy family) moved forward in 2012 with plans for a mixed-use development on the land they owned. Architect Cesar Pelli master-planned the project with three towers—two office and one residential—amid park space, but eventually the mix changed to two rental apartment towers and one office tower.

Wolf Point West, the first to be built, was designed by bKL Architecture as a slender apartment tower composed of a series of layered planes. At 46 stories and 485 feet tall, it is the shortest of the three towers. Wolf Point East, designed by Pelli Clarke Pelli, topped out in 2019 as a 668-foot-tall tower with nearly 700 rentals. Wolf Point South, the third and last phase, also designed by Pelli Clarke Pelli, will house offices and ascend to approximately 813 feet. Tying the towers together is Wolff Landscape Architecture's park and promenades, which skillfully covers the parking below the towers and gives the city another riverwalk.

56

CONTEMPORAINE

Perkins and Will, 2004

516 North Wells Street

Train: Brown, Purple to Merchandise Mart

Bus: #22 to Clark Street at Grand Avenue, southbound; to Dearborn Street at Grand Avenue, northbound

In the waning years of the 20th century, Chicago's River North was littered with high-rise apartment buildings that shared one unfortunate characteristic: painted concrete exteriors. (The title of Lynn Becker's January 2003 article in the *Chicago Reader*, "Stop the Blandness!" summed up the situation pretty well.) The inexpensive and poorly crafted (hence the paint) buildings were also formally unimaginative: parking garages and retail podiums filled their sites, above which smaller residential floor plates were plopped and extruded to sometimes-sculpted tops.

Seen from the northeast, the building is a complex interlocking of concrete and glass surfaces. (Credit © Steinkamp/Ballogg Photography)

Into this context sprang CMK Companies' Contemporaine, which followed the rules of development (storefront retail and indoor parking below residential units) but departed from them dramatically in its highly refined, unfinished concrete, well-sculpted massing, transparent parking ramps, and midrise profile—quality over quantity. Calling the Contemporaine, designed

A penthouse-level terrace with bold poured concrete forms. (Credit © Steinkamp/Ballogg Photography)

by Perkins and Will Global Design Director Ralph Johnson, "sculptural" is hardly hyperbole, since the fifteen-story corner building has a different appearance from each cardinal direction. From the east it is slender, capped by a thin concrete slab at its high point. Balconies project above the glassed-in ramps of the parking garage on the north facade. From the west, tiered glass boxes are separated by a zipper of cantilevered concrete balconies while a wall of glass fronts a taller concrete wall on the south (the concrete wall also serves as a backdrop for the penthouse's traditional Japanese garden designed by Hoichi Kurisu).

But it's at the corner, down on the sidewalk, where everything comes together. A 45-foot-tall round concrete column props up the building (matching an offset one atop the building that supports the roof extension), inviting us to look up and ponder how the various parts fit together. While this isn't the norm in Chicago residential architecture, Contemporaine's use of unfinished concrete and interlocking forms has sparked several other less-inspired residential structures throughout the city.

111 WEST ILLINOIS

Solomon Cordwell Buenz (SCB), 2008

111 West Illinois Street

The Erickson Institute—a graduate school for early childhood development—occupies the western half of this ten-story building, which is easily its most interesting part given the triangular prow that creates a small plaza at the corner and serves as a backdrop for the shorter buildings to the south.

(Credit John Hill)

57

MCDONALD'S CHICAGO FLAGSHIP

Ross Barney Architects, 2018

600 N. Clark Street

Train: Red to Grand/State

Bus: #22 to Clark Street and Grand Avenue, southbound; Dearborn Street at Ontario Street, northbound

In 2005—the 50th anniversary of Ray Kroc's first stand-alone McDonald's in suburban Des Plaines—the fast food company took down its infamously kitschy Rock 'n' Roll McDonald's franchise (a 1983 building adorned with retro murals and musical ephemera) and opened a supersized version of its original 1955 location. The new building featured a pair of 60-foot-tall golden arches piercing an angled, cantilevered roof shading angled glass walls. It was an odd creature, but one that fit into its River North context of frogs, guitars, and

The steel armature supporting the solar panels extends past the footprint of the building to shelter the drive-thru. (Credit Kendall McCaugherty, Hall+Merrick Photographers)

The trees above the "ordering street" make a clear statement about the sustainability of the timber building. (Credit Kendall McCaugherty, Hall+Merrick Photographers)

other oversized signs beckoning tourists to this or that chain restaurant. But just when McDonald's was looking backward with its Rock 'n' Roll replacement, River North was moving forward, shuttering chains and replacing them with condos: swapping out tourists for residents.

With demographic changes swirling around it, McDonald's kept its prime spot, tore down its oversized arches just a dozen years after putting them up, and then built something unexpected: a glass box framed by mass timber and capped by a large roof of photovoltaic panels. The chain's distinctive golden arches are still there, but they're small, positioned at the two street corners, and supported by the steel armature of the PV panels. This is McDonald's for the 21st century: cool, confident, and "green," if a bit self-conscious.

The generous roof, which extends past the footprint of both the glass-box seating area and the precast-concrete kitchen area (a reused part of its predecessor), is propped up on slender steel columns, drawing comparisons to Renzo Piano's Modern Wing at the Art Institute (**8**). But here, the roof is infrastructural, its 1,062 PV panels meeting about half of the building's energy needs. The solar panels are missing in the middle of the roof to bring sunlight to the trees planted on the concrete box and in a terrarium hung from the roof over the "ordering street" (this flagship, like other McDonald's, does not have cashiers). The suspended birch trees also divide the main space into two: the larger dining area on the west and the smaller "McCafé" on the east.

The dining area, with 27-foot ceilings, is generous and full of light. The carbon-sequestering CLT (cross-laminated timber) overhead adds warmth to the space and signals a "green" direction for McDonald's, courtesy of Ross Barney Architects. Mass timber in a contemporary Chicago building is an anomaly: harking to the industrial lofts of the nineteenth century rather than the steel and concrete structures of the modern age. Hopefully, it will set a precedent for larger buildings in the city framed with mass timber—which can be seen as the best way for buildings to keep carbon out of the atmosphere.

58

ERIE ON THE PARK, KINGSBURY ON THE PARK

Lucien Lagrange Studio, 2002, 2003

510 West Erie Street, 653 North Kingsbury Street

Train: Brown, Purple to Chicago/Franklin

Bus: #65 to Grand & Kingsbury; #66 to Chicago & Larrabee

Chevron-shaped cross bracing rises up the middle of the Erie tower. (Credit William Zbaren)

Lucien Lagrange is an architect known for buildings, such as Park Tower (**70**), for example, that are more historical than modern, as if they were from another time or even another place, like Lagrange's native home outside Paris. But on two sites overlooking a three-acre park along the Chicago River (designed by Berkeley, California's Peter Walker with Chicago's Ted Wolff and christened A. Montgomery Ward Park in 2010, in honor of the retail king cum open space advocate), the unlikely firm designed two residential towers that are in the tradition of Chicago's mid-20th-century modern architecture, with glass curtain walls and the expression of their steel structures. The two buildings arrived in the early 2000s, when most residential developments in River North had painted concrete exteriors and were bland to their core; this pair pointed in a direction that valued modern expression over economy.

Erie on the Park, a 24-story tower on the north edge of the park, was completed first, one year before Kingsbury on the Park, which is one story higher; both buildings have around 125 condos each.

Balcony cages sit in front of loftlike exteriors on the Kingsbury tower. (Credit William Zbaren)

Of the two, the earlier building is more interesting. It is angled 45 degrees to the city grid, rising asymmetrically and informally through a series of setbacks, with cross bracing exposed on its northeast- and southwest-facing elevations. Kingsbury on the Park, on the other hand, has steel, cagelike balconies appended to a fairly straightforward glass box. Together, they make a mismatched pair that is unmistakably Chicago, if surprisingly Lucien Lagrange.

640 NORTH WELLS

Hartshorne Plunkard Architecture, 2017

640 North Wells Street

River North's low-scale landscape of parking lots and gimmicky restaurants has been slowly giving way to hotels and residential developments and, as part of the neighborhood's transformation, mainstay Ed Debevic's closed in 2015 to make way for this 22-story apartment tower with a glass skin and floor plates shifting every few floors.

(Credit John K. Zacherle)

59

156 WEST SUPERIOR

The Miller Hull Partnership with Studio Dwell, 2006

156 West Superior Street

Train: Brown, Purple to Chicago/Franklin

Bus: #66 to Chicago Avenue at Wells Street

Despite Chicago's cold winters keeping folks inside for a good chunk of the year, just about every condo and apartment tower in the late 1990s and early

Room-sized terraces cantilever next to glass walls with Hancock-esque X-bracing. (Credit John K. Zacherle)

2000s included a balcony (a trend that continues to this day). This amenity allows developers to notch up prices, but often they are too small to be of much more use than a smoking perch. An excellent precedent for highly usable outdoor space can be found in this nine-story building with its room-sized, 12-foot-by-7-foot balconies that face the street. Yet, aside from the commendable attention given to this aspect of the design, the whole building is a skillful assemblage of glass and steel, highlighted by "X"-shaped tensile rods climbing the front and rear elevations in reference to the nearby 875 N. Michigan Avenue (formerly John Hancock Center). Seattle's Miller Hull and Chicago's Ranquist Development followed up this first effort with further condos in River North and Bucktown, each exhibiting an understanding of amenities and good modern design.

747 NORTH CLARK

The Miller Hull Partnership, 2014
747 North Clark Street

Miller Hull and Ranquist teamed up again on a luxury condo development located right around the corner from their earlier project at 156 West Superior (**59**), this time taking over a project stalled by the recession and turning it into a modern expression of glass and steel, the latter exposed proudly at the seventh-floor terrace.

60

THE GODFREY HOTEL

Valerio Dewalt Train Associates, 2014
127 West Huron Street
Train: Red to Chicago/State
Bus: #22 to Clark Street at Erie Street, southbound; to Dearborn Street at Huron Street, northbound

Architectural Record's May 2004 issue devoted to Chicago architecture, timed to the American Institute of Architects national convention the city hosted, featured an early rendering of what was called Miglin Properties Hotel.[2] Ten years, two developers, and one "Great Recession" later, the hotel finally opened under a new name, christened by *Chicago Tribune* architecture critic Blair Kamin as "the miracle on LaSalle Street"[3] and described in other places as one of the city's newest architectural landmarks. Designed by Joe Valerio's firm as an extended-stay hotel for developer Duke Miglin, construction commenced in 2007, but shortly after topping out the following year construction stopped. Its steel frame sat draped in tarp (locals called it "the Mummy") until 2011, when Oxford Capital Group took over the project as a boutique hotel.

What didn't change in the ten years from design to completion was the building's 16-story height and its structure, a staggered truss

The staggered steel trusses are visible behind the glass walls facing west. (Credit John Hill)

system (story-high steel trusses spanning the building's width alternate column pairs as they rise) developed by Structural Affiliates International for the original client. Selected for its economy and, ironically, speed, in Valerio's hands the system enabled sizable cantilevers that push and pull on the exterior at will, an architectural expression of the structural maneuvering happening inside. Thankfully, the trusses are displayed at the glassy east and west walls, the former facing a narrow alley but the latter proudly fronting LaSalle Street. The elevations facing north and south are covered in metal panels with small, square windows, flat and bland if not for the building's offsets. To get a better look at one of these facades, head up to the fourth-floor roof terrace, which sits atop the wider parking garage; but to see one of the trusses up close you'll have to get a room.

Cantilevers enliven the north side's otherwise flat facade of metal and small square windows. (Credit John Hill)

61

POETRY FOUNDATION

John Ronan Architects, 2011

61 West Superior Street

Train: Red to Chicago/State

Bus: #22 to Clark Street at Huron Street, southbound; to Dearborn Street at Huron Street, northbound

Although the Poetry Foundation dates back only to 2003—its establishment aided by the generosity of philanthropist Ruth Lilly—its roots go back much further: to 1941, when the Modern Poetry Association, out of which it evolved, was founded, and even to 1912. That year, *Poetry* magazine, founded by Harriet Monroe (biographer and sister-in-law of architect John

The zinc panels are carved away at the corner to provide entry to the courtyard and building. (Credit John Hill)

Wellborn Root) printed its first issue; the foundation publishes it to this day. The organization's mission to "discover and celebrate the best poetry and to place it before the largest possible audience"[4] is now accomplished through the exceptional building designed by John Ronan Architects.

A black corrugated metal wrapper (made of oxidized zinc, to be precise) enables the two-story Poetry Foundation to stand out in the midst of residential high-rises, many of them not worthy of this newer neighbor. Some of the zinc panels are solid, but most of them are perforated, offering glimpses of the building and courtyard inside. A cutaway at the corner reveals more of the glass-and-wood building inside, yet the

Glass walls face the courtyard behind the perforated zinc panels. (Credit John Hill)

The double-height library is one of the spaces overlooking the courtyard. (Credit John Hill)

entrance to the building is not here; it is out of sight, located off the garden, reminiscent of the way Frank Lloyd Wright would hide the front door in the houses he designed.

This garden, which was designed with Reed Hilderbrand and sits behind the long, north-facing expanse of perforated metal, is accessible even when the building is closed. Moving along the metal wall from the corner, the glass walls opposite reveal the spaces behind them: a performance space along the narrow path, a double-height library that terminates the gaze at the far west side, and a colorful mural of *Poetry* magazine covers behind the glass wall next to the entry. Turning to the right, the city is seen through the perforated zinc—a gauzy glimpse that borders on the poetic. Ronan has instilled some control to this entry sequence (even as nearby high-rises seem to peer over the walls into the garden), creating a transitional space—a space of urban decompression—that readies one for a visit to the foundation.

Public spaces inside the building are limited to a few on the first floor: performance space, small gallery, and library. As mentioned, each one of these spaces faces onto the garden through full-height glass walls, in effect making the outdoor space the most important part of the project. As the trees mature, the character of the interior spaces will soften, as will the hard edges of the building. The bamboo shooting up through the open stair that connects the public spaces to the offices upstairs hints at this effect. Even when visiting on a cold autumn day well after the trees have lost their leaves, the presence of nature in the garden is an important one, both for this softening and for offering up juxtapositions—natural vs. artificial, a garden in the city—that are potentially poetic and surely enriching.

(Credit John Hill)

IKRAM

Mario Aranda, 2012
15 East Huron Street

The can't-miss, Ferrari-red boutique of Ikram Goldman (the unofficial outfitter of Michelle Obama) is a three-story fashion funhouse with showroom, café, art gallery, and even a play space for the children of Ikram and her husband Josh, who helped designer Mario Aranda on this 16,000-square-foot project.

ONE CHICAGO

Goettsch Partners and Hartshorne Plunkard Architecture, *estimated completion in 2022*
State Street and Chicago Avenue

Ground broke in early 2019 for this two-tower development across the street from Holy Name Cathedral. The taller tower, at 76 stories and more than 1,000 feet, would face east with a stepped profile reminiscent of New York's 30 Rockefeller Center and Chicago's more recent NBC Tower, while the shorter tower, at 49 stories, would sit along Chicago Avenue.

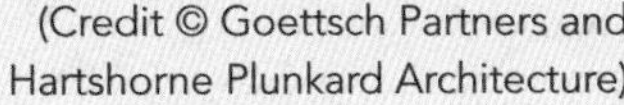

(Credit © Goettsch Partners and Hartshorne Plunkard Architecture)

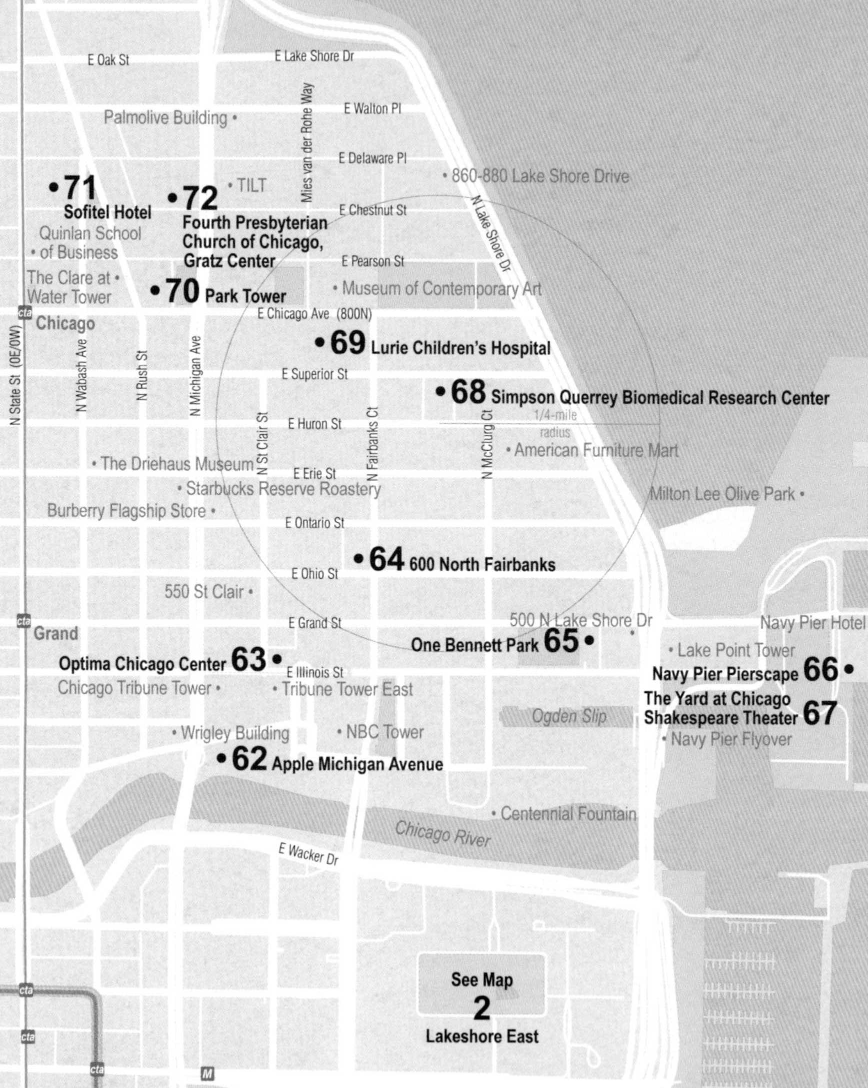

E Division St (1200N)
Lake Michigan
E Oak St
E Lake Shore Dr
Mies van der Rohe Way
E Walton Pl
Palmolive Building
E Delaware Pl
860-880 Lake Shore Drive
71 Sofitel Hotel
72 Fourth Presbyterian Church of Chicago, Gratz Center
TILT
E Chestnut St
N Lake Shore Dr
Quinlan School of Business
The Clare at Water Tower
E Pearson St
70 Park Tower
Museum of Contemporary Art
Chicago
E Chicago Ave (800N)
69 Lurie Children's Hospital
N State St (0E/0W)
N Wabash Ave
N Rush St
N Michigan Ave
E Superior St
68 Simpson Querrey Biomedical Research Center
1/4-mile radius
N St Clair St
E Huron St
N Fairbanks Ct
N McClurg Ct
American Furniture Mart
The Driehaus Museum
E Erie St
Starbucks Reserve Roastery
Milton Lee Olive Park
Burberry Flagship Store
E Ontario St
64 600 North Fairbanks
E Ohio St
550 St Clair
Grand
E Grand St
500 N Lake Shore Dr
Navy Pier Hotel
One Bennett Park 65
Lake Point Tower
Optima Chicago Center 63
E Illinois St
Navy Pier Pierscape 66
Chicago Tribune Tower
Tribune Tower East
The Yard at Chicago Shakespeare Theater 67
Ogden Slip
Wrigley Building
NBC Tower
Navy Pier Flyover
62 Apple Michigan Avenue
Centennial Fountain
Chicago River
E Wacker Dr
See Map 2 Lakeshore East

7 Streeterville

That the area east of Michigan Avenue and north of the Chicago River doesn't take its name from a piece of infrastructure (The Loop) or a waterway (River North, Lakeshore East) should be an indication that it has a colorful past. Streeterville is named for George Wellington "Cap" Streeter, a circus promoter from Michigan who captained a sailing ship into a sandbar just east of the mansions along Michigan Avenue in 1886. Not being able to move the ship, he and his family first took up residence within it, and then built a shack where 875 N. Michigan Avenue (formerly the John Hancock Center) now sits. The land Streeter claimed lay beyond an 1821 shoreline survey, so he conveniently called it the "District of Lake Michigan" and spent the rest of his life defending it as free from city and state control. He invited contractors to dump rubble on the sandbar to increase the land to 168 acres, sold off parcels to gullible investors, and raised the ire of the City of Chicago. During World War I, Mayor "Big Bill" Thompson ordered a raid on Streeter's shack and finally evicted him for selling liquor on Sundays. Even though Streeter was despised in his day and his claims are highly questionable in the eyes of historians, the city pays homage to the man in the name of the neighborhood that has some of the most valuable real estate in Chicago.

Streeter died in 1921, one year after the double-deck Michigan Avenue Bridge opened. As envisioned by Burnham and Bennett in their 1909 *Plan of Chicago*, the formerly residential Pine Street was widened and renamed North Michigan Avenue, flooding the north side of the river with wealth. Galleries and shops opened in the ensuing decade. The Wrigley Building, the Chicago Tribune Tower, and the Allerton House with its Tip Top Tap, among others inched toward, and crowded, the Water Tower and Pumping Station, two of the few downtown buildings that survived the Great Fire of 1871. Coined the "Magnificent Mile" in the 1940s by developer Arthur Rubloff in reference to the "Splendid Mile" of State Street in the Loop, North Michigan Avenue evolved into the undisputed king of the city's commercial thoroughfares, even as galleries and shops were replaced by suburban-style malls sitting at the bottom of architecturally insignificant residential towers set back from the street, beginning with Water Tower Place in 1979 and followed by the Shops at North Bridge in 2000. With smaller lots remaining, the Magnificent Mile is playing host this century to flagship stores by global brands looking for the exposure the busy thoroughfare affords.

The blocks from Michigan Avenue to Lake Michigan are roughly split into thirds. A mix of offices, hotels, and residences in primarily tall buildings occupies the southern section from the river to Ontario Street, encompassing Navy Pier and the Jardine Water Purification Plant jutting into the lake. The middle section is devoted largely to Northwestern Memorial Hospital and Northwestern University's Chicago Campus. North of Chicago Avenue are luxury residences that can be seen as an extension of the Gold Coast from the other side of Michigan Avenue (an area included in this chapter). Uniting them all are the high rents that make it clear Streeter knew he was on to something all those years ago.

62

APPLE MICHIGAN AVENUE

Foster + Partners with Ross Barney Architects, 2017
401 North Michigan Avenue
Train: Red to Grand/State
Bus: #151 to Michigan Avenue at Hubbard Street

Just as with its products, Apple is constantly streamlining its stores, renovating them in some cases or phasing them out with new stores. The latter applies to their Chicago flagship, which sat at the corner of Michigan Avenue and Huron Avenue from 2003 until 2017, when it moved into a new building sited at Pioneer Court overlooking the Chicago River. The earlier store, an old Gap store renovated by Bohlin Cywinski Jackson (BCJ, architect of many Apple stores, including the one at North and Clybourn in Chapter 8), was one of fewer than 60 such stores, all in the US. But with British architect Norman Foster's new flagship, that number increased to 500—*in 22 countries*. Apple's widespread expansion has been accompanied by an ever-increasing architectural ambition, much of it culminating with Foster's design of the spaceship-like Apple Campus 2 in Cupertino, California.

Apple's flagship Chicago store seen from the walkway along the river with the Wrigley Building reflected in the innovative glass wall. (Credit Eric Allix Rogers, CAC Archive)

The entrance draws attention to the floating roof and the ceiling sheathed in wood. (Credit Eric Allix Rogers, CAC Archive)

The ultra-clear glass walls seamlessly blend inside and outside. (Credit Eric Allix Rogers, CAC Archive)

Foster transfers at least one technology from Cupertino to Chicago: huge pieces of laminated, ultra-clear glass, curved at the corners of the large room that cascades down the steps from plaza to riverwalk. These glass walls sit below a slender roof made from lightweight carbon fiber. Although the roof is primarily supported by four columns—two encased in steel, two in stone—the five layers of glass, some as tall as 32 feet, actually provide some secondary structural support to the wood-lined cantilever overhead. The roof, walls, and steps inside and outside the store cohere into a dramatic minimalism, or an architecture of nothingness.

The shift in character and quality of Chicago's two Apple flagships can be gleaned from architecture critic Blair Kamin's reviews of each: BCJ's store was "a decent neighbor,"[1] while he calls Foster's building "a gem," its walls "a wow," and its presence "a boon to the city's riverfront."[2]

TRIBUNE TOWER EAST

Adrian Smith + Gordon Gill Architecture with Solomon Cordwell Buenz (SCB), estimated completion in 2022
North Cityfront Plaza Drive at East Illinois Street

In 2016, the Chicago Tribune sold its namesake building designed by Howells & Hood in 1923 to CIM Group and Golub & Company, which converted the 36-story landmark into residential condominiums. Two years later the development team unveiled plans for a supertall skyscraper on the lot just east of Tribune Tower, its 1,422 pinnacle more than tripling the height of the original's neo-Gothic crown. Tribune Tower East's 113 floors will contain 564 rental and condo apartments, a hotel, and retail. AS+GG's elegant design has narrow, glass-and-metal striped elevations on the east and west, and wider all-glass facades facing north and south. The tower profile tapers toward the top, with the north and south facades dramatically extending above the roof toward each other, but not to the point of meeting.

63

OPTIMA CHICAGO CENTER

Optima, 2013
200 East Illinois Street
Train: Red to Grand/State
Bus: #151 to Michigan Avenue at Illinois/Grand Streets

Optima is a rarity in the world of architecture: the Glencoe-based company founded by architect David Hovey develops, designs, builds, and also manages their primarily residential projects. After successful developments in the north suburbs around their home base—and in Arizona, where their

Looking from the edge of Pioneer Court toward the northwest, the tower is an abstraction in glass. (Credit Eric Allix Rogers, CAC Archive)

second office is located—Optima finally got their feet wet in the city with this project one block east of Michigan Avenue. Codeveloped with DeBartolo Development, the 42-story tower stacks 325 apartments atop a 235-space parking garage, with a fitness center occupying the recessed floor between the two. Closer to the top of the building is another recessed floor, this one given over to a terrace that wraps part of the way around the tower. These "cuts" in the super-flat glass skin (black-translucent at the parking garage, silver-metallic on the residential floors) express the communal amenities that are incorporated into the development. Striving for simplicity, Hovey removed the standard residential amenity of individual balconies or terraces in lieu of these high-end common spaces.

550 ST. CLAIR
Brininstool + Lynch, 2008
550 North St. Clair Street

This 18-story condo building peers over a narrow four-story building and a limestone-clad commercial building designed by Stanley Tigerman to the Magnificent Mile. Continuous balconies with clear glass face west; units on the east side are given small corner balconies with translucent glass guardrails; they all sit atop a parking garage covered in a metal mesh, an improvement over the ugly parking garage that formerly occupied the corner site.

(Credit Darris Lee Harris)

64

600 NORTH FAIRBANKS

Murphy/Jahn (now JAHN), 2007

600 North Fairbanks Court

Train: Red to Grand/State

Bus: #151 to Michigan Avenue at Ohio/Ontario Streets

Looking north, the curved corner gives the residential tower a unique presence. (Credit John Hill)

Helmut Jahn has something for curves. His James R. Thompson Center and 55 West Monroe Street tower, both 1980s buildings in the Loop, curve in plan. Farther afield, Jahn's State Street Village Dormitories (**138**) and Schiff Residences (**76**) curve in section like streamlined train cars. This 41-story condo tower diagonally opposite Harry Weese's Time and Life Building is most akin to Jahn's office building at Monroe and Dearborn, since both are rounded at their corners and angled at their sides. The curved corner here is an expression of the requisite parking garage that occupies eleven floors, while it gives the residential units above sweeping panoramas from their living rooms.

This Streeterville tower cantilevers out to gain some extra square footage above its neighbor to the north, though it was originally proposed to be built boldly over that building. Columns of tiny inset terraces run up the north and south elevations, getting larger and more functional at the penthouses and amenity floor atop the tower. But the exterior wall of the parking garage is the building's highlight: a layered facade of glass and aluminum screens the parked cars, gives the glass tower the base it deserves, and sets a precedent for later residential towers like Optima Chicago Center (**63**).

65

ONE BENNETT PARK

Robert A. M. Stern Architects with GREC Architects and Michael Van Valkenburg Associates, 2019
451 East Grand Avenue
Train: Red to Grand/State
Bus: #29 to Illinois & Peshtigo, Eastbound; #29 to Grand & Peshtigo, Westbound

The first Chicago tower for the famed neo-traditional New York architect who designed Chicago's bus shelters is a stone-clad 70-story tower with a mix of more than 60 condos and nearly 280 rental apartments for Related Midwest. The tower sits along Grand Avenue at the short, one-block-long Peshtigo Court, and includes a two-story volume that extends to Illinois Street; this low piece has access for below-grade parking and a roof terrace with pergola as an extension of the residential amenities tucked in the base of the tower. The residences in the tower have generous views of Lake Michigan,

One Bennett Park's location across the street from the old North Pier warehouse building ensures perpetual sunlight. (Credit Peter Aaron/Otto for Robert A. M. Stern Architects)

Amenities for tower residents sit adjacent to the new park. (Credit Peter Aaron/Otto for Robert A. M. Stern Architects)

but they also look down to a nearly two-acre park built by Related and designed by Michael Van Valkenburgh Associates, who was responsible for the nearby Maggie Daley Park (**10**). The tower rises straight from this adjacent publicly accessible, limited-access park but steps back on the east side, giving the tower an asymmetrical profile on the Chicago skyline.

500 LAKE SHORE DRIVE

Solomon Cordwell Buenz (SCB), 2013
500 North Lake Shore Drive

Occupying its own small block next to Lake Shore Drive and across from Lake Point Tower, this 45-story, 500-unit apartment tower is clad in clear glass punctuated by alternating stripes of gray and blue on its east and west facades; the adjacent parking base is covered in translucent glass.

(Credit Steve Hall © Hedrich Blessing)

NAVY PIER FLYOVER

Muller+Muller, 2020
East of Lake Shore Drive from DuSable Park to Jane Addams Park

Chicago's Lakefront Trail is 18-1/2 miles long, but on summer days it could seem like all of the bicyclists and pedestrians using it converged near Navy Pier. To alleviate congestion along this heavily trafficked stretch, the Chicago Department of Transportation started construction of the Navy Pier Flyover in 2014. The branch leading to Navy Pier was completed as part of the first phase, but the three-phase project didn't wrap up until spring 2020. Each phase has a steel spinelike structure supporting an elevated 16-foot-wide deck running just east of Lake Shore Drive.

66

NAVY PIER PIERSCAPE

James Corner Field Operations with nARCHITECTS, 2016
600 East Grand Avenue
Train: Red to Grand/State
Bus: #29 to Navy Pier Terminal

Since it reopened in 1995 as a tourist destination, Navy Pier has been the most visited destination in Chicago, luring around 10 million people annually. With shops, restaurants, an IMAX theater, the Chicago Children's Museum, the Chicago Shakespeare Theater, excursion boat launches, exhibition/convention space, a ballroom, an outdoor stage, and a Ferris wheel, the 3,000-foot-long pier is an odd mix of entertainment and cultural attractions.

New planters and benches make for a pleasing promenade at Navy Pier. (Credit Angie McMonigal Photography)

The "wave wall" faces the promenade along the south side of the pier. (Credit Angie McMonigal Photography)

Long before the tourists arrived, it opened in 1916 as Municipal Pier per Burnham and Bennett's 1909 *Plan of Chicago*. It originally served as a recreational pier and as a dock for Lake Michigan freight traffic and passenger excursion boats bound for Lincoln and Jackson parks. It was renamed in 1927 in honor of the Navy personnel housed there during World War I, which foreshadowed its use during World War II as a naval training base. It then served for two decades as home for the University of Illinois at Chicago, after which the pier steadily deteriorated with spotty recreational use and failed plans for reuse. It took Governor James Thompson's 1990 promise of $150 million (in exchange for combining the pier with McCormick Place and thereby creating McPier) to get things moving. By then the "marketplace" model of places like Boston's Faneuil Hall and New York's South Street Seaport, both designed by Boston architect Benjamin Thompson, was all the rage. It's not surprising then that Thompson's eponymous firm won the competition to redesign Navy Pier, working with VOA Associates to turn it into the tourist mecca it remains to this day.

In 2011, McPier (now MPEA) leased the pier to the nonprofit Navy Pier Inc., which held the "Pierscape" design competition the following year to reimagine the pier's public spaces for its centennial in 2016. A team led by landscape architect James Corner—responsible for the wildly successful High Line park in New York—won the competition with a design envisioning a sequence of distinct spaces ("The Front Porch," "The Magic Room," "The Fun Room," "The Lake Room," and so forth) along the southern edge of the pier. Design features include paving, seating, trees and other plantings, lighting, pavilions, a "wave wall" facing the promenade, and numerous water features, all of which aim at turning the south side of the pier from a kitschy strip geared to commerce to a multifaceted landscape taking advantage of the pier's amazing natural and urban context. A new Ferris wheel, more than 50 feet taller than the former wheel, opened in time for Navy Pier's centennial celebration.

67

THE YARD AT CHICAGO SHAKESPEARE

Adrian Smith + Gordon Gill Architecture, 2017
800 East Grand Avenue
Train: Red to Grand/State
Bus: #29 to Navy Pier Terminal

The Chicago Shakespeare Theater (CST) was founded in 1986 in Lincoln Park, but in 1999 it moved from its spot above a bar to a more suitable, permanent venue at Navy Pier. CST's popularity—more than 600 performances a year seen by over 200,000 people—meant expansion was necessary. With AS+GG and UK theater consultant Charcoalblue, CST built a flexible venue that sits beneath the fabric-roof structure of the former Skyline Stage. A two-

The curved line of glass wall connects the Yard's old and new facilities. (Credit © Adrian Smith + Gordon Gill Architecture; Photography by James Steinkamp Photography)

story, glass-walled lobby curves from the existing theater on the east to the new Yard, which is made up of nine mobile audience "towers" that can be freely arranged as needed for anywhere from 150 to 850 seats. The Yard can accommodate traditional proscenium performances as well as be set up for in-the-round and traverse (two sides facing each other across the stage) configurations. Computer-controlled, electrochromic glass facades allow CST to make the skin as clear or as opaque as desired: blocking out the sun during the day, for instance, or letting in the warm glow of the setting sun.

NAVY PIER HOTEL

KOO, 2020
600 East Grand Avenue

As part of Navy Pier's centennial, First Hospitality Group announced plans in 2016 for a 200-room hotel near the eastern end of the 300-foot-long pier. Jackie Koo's eponymous firm (see **20**) designed the five-story hotel overlooking the promenade with a checkerboard of angled glass walls and balconies.

(Credit John Hill)

BURBERRY FLAGSHIP STORE

Callison Barteluce with Solomon Cordwell Buenz, 2012
633 North Michigan Avenue

The British label's in-house designers, working with the architects at Callison Barteluce (now Callison), took Burberry's signature tartan, scaled it up to five stories, turned it 45 degrees, and rendered it in a mirror-polished and black-tinted stainless steel that glows at night through recessed LED strips. The stairs facing Ontario Street, a highlight of the building, are backed by an installation of acrylic rods and more LED lights in a— you guessed it—diagonal tartan pattern.

68

SIMPSON QUERREY BIOMEDICAL RESEARCH CENTER

Perkins and Will, 2019

303 East Superior Street

Train: Red Line to Chicago

Bus: #66 to Chicago & Fairbanks

Northwestern Medicine's 600,000-square-foot flagship research facility, the Louis A. Simpson and Kimberly K. Querrey Biomedical Center (SQBRC), was designed by Ralph Johnson of Perkins and Will with a curved glass base that recalls the site's predecessor, Bertrand Goldberg's 1975 cloverleaf-shaped Prentice Women's Hospital, which was not as famous as Goldberg's Marina Towers but was beloved by architects. What was completed and dedicated in mid-2019 is just part of the story. The glassy, 13-story building is the base for a future tower that will add 16 floors and bring the total number to 29. The unfolding construction for SQBRC is best seen from East Erie Street across the one-block green space at the heart of Northwestern's multifaceted campus, but be sure to see it from East Superior Street, where Johnson pays homage to Goldberg with the piano curve of the north-facing base.

The north facade, with its piano-curve facade on East Superior Street. (Credit courtesy Northwestern University)

69

LURIE CHILDREN'S HOSPITAL

ZGF Architects, Solomon Cordwell Buenz (SCB), & Anderson Mikos Architects, 2012

225 East Chicago Avenue

Train: Red to Chicago/State

Bus: #151 to Michigan Avenue at Superior/Huron Streets

A grid of windows broken by expanses of glass faces the MCA to the north. (Credit Nick Merrick © Hedrich Blessing)

The arrangement of the historic Pumping Station, the adjacent play-lot, the Museum of Contemporary Art (MCA), and the six-acre Lake Shore Park has created a block-wide open space east of Michigan Avenue with two streetwalls facing each other. Residential towers look south along Pearson Street, while buildings of Northwestern University and Northwestern Memorial Hospital line Chicago Avenue. The latest addition to Chicago Avenue is the 23-story Ann & Robert H. Lurie Children's Hospital of Chicago, sited at the southern terminus of the short Mies van der Rohe Way. Previously located in Lincoln Park and called Children's Memorial Hospital, the $605 million facility (nearly twenty percent paid for through a gift from Ann Lurie) is linked by bridges to a parking garage across Superior Street and the new Prentice Women's Hospital to the east, which enables speedy transport of critically ill newborns. The move also brings the hospital closer

The rippling wood wall and whale sculpture in the lobby. (Credit Nick Merrick © Hedrich Blessing)

to Northwestern's Feinberg School of Medicine with which it is affiliated.

The design, led by ZGF Architects' Los Angeles office, splits the building into lower and upper halves: the former is devoted to emergency care, diagnostics, outpatient clinics, operating rooms, offices, and support spaces, while the latter is devoted to rooms for inpatient care. This split is visible on the exterior in the articulation of the precast concrete grid interrupted by expanses of glass. The double-height lobby's rippling wood wall, sculptural whales, and "diving bell" elevator are a nautical treat, but the highlight is up at the eleventh floor (not open to the public), which separates the building's two halves: a 5,000-square-foot sky garden designed by landscape architect Mikyoung Kim is housed in a double-height glass box that cantilevers off the hospital's southeast corner. With its bamboo plantings, water features, and a multicolored light wall, the garden works with the design of the hospital's other spaces to make stays there more tolerable, if not enjoyable.

70

PARK TOWER

Lucien Lagrange Studio, 2000
800 North Michigan Avenue
Train: Red to Chicago/State
Bus: #151 to Michigan Avenue at Superior/Huron Streets

In a contextual nod to its prominent site, Park Tower goes out of its way to relate directly to its 1869 neighbor, the Chicago Water Tower, a building that Oscar Wilde called "a castellated monstrosity with pepper-boxes stuck all over it." Lucien Lagrange's tower rises sixty-seven stories on a site to the west of the Water Tower, overlooking but also acting as a backdrop to it. Stone clads

The slender tower, seen from the east, rises sixty-seven stories to a mansard roof. (Credit Willliam Zbaren)

the first two floors, which house high-end retail and lobbies for the hotel and condominiums stacked above, but the rest of the tower is covered in precast concrete colored to match the Water Tower's buttery stone.

The separation of Park Tower into its constituent parts is evident in the massing and details facing east. The hotel, punctuated by a cantilevered restaurant (an odd but justifiable design flourish), occupies the lower floors. Condos stacked above have corner balconies, a slightly smaller footprint, and unencumbered views of the lake over the Water Tower, Pumping Station, and the Museum of Contemporary Art (MCA). Six penthouses cap the building below a mansard roof shielding a tuned mass damper, installed to minimize the lateral sway of the slender tower—a piece of new technology hidden inside an otherwise neo-traditional design.

THE CLARE AT WATER TOWER

Perkins and Will, 2009
55 East Pearson Street

Loyola University's Water Tower Campus sits on four blocks to the west of the eponymous landmark, including the 54-story Clare, which houses classrooms in its base and senior living in the tower, which has a curved wall facing northeast as its most distinctive feature.

(Credit Lynn Becker)

QUINLAN SCHOOL OF BUSINESS

Solomon Cordwell Buenz (SCB), 2015
State Street and Pearson Street

Loyola University's new ten-story Schreiber Center organizes classrooms, labs, lecture halls, and other spaces for its business school around a full-height, south-facing atrium, while the parcel to the north, sold to Newcastle Limited in 2012, is a 35-story apartment tower also designed by SCB and paired with the university building as one planned development.

71

SOFITEL HOTEL

Jean-Paul Viguier et Associés with Teng & Associates (now exp), 2002
20 East Chestnut Street
Train: Red to Chicago/State
Bus: #36 to State Street at Delaware Place

Seen from the east, the building appears to cantilever out over the street. (Credit © Nicolas Borel)

When it opened in the summer of 2002, the 478-room Sofitel Hotel designed by the Parisian architect Jean-Paul Viguier raised the question: "Why aren't more contemporary buildings like this?" As Chicago found itself mired with new buildings sporting the typical reactionary garb of brick, stone, and painted concrete, it was refreshing to see the Sofitel's asymmetrical profile rising against the norm. Through its triangular footprint, the tower responds to both its immediate context and Chicago's architectural history.

The hotel is located directly west of the petite Connors Park, which guarantees the hotel a prominent facade on busy Rush Street. The architect extended this visibility further east, to Michigan Avenue, by cantilevering the building to the south as its long east and west elevations taper to meet thirty-two stories overhead. Within the network of Chicago's grid, this prow seems to lean over the street (it actually stops above the intersection of the two property lines,

The glass end of the hotel corridors sticks out of the triangular tower. (Credit © Nicolas Borel)

The restaurant looks out onto the forecourt through a curved, angled wall. (Credit © Nicolas Borel)

just shy of the sidewalk and street) in an effort to be seen, to attract upward-glancing eyes. Packed into the bustle that fills out the rectangular site to the west of the tower are the hotel's amenities: meeting and banquet facilities, a ballroom, a fitness center, a café, a gourmet restaurant, and a street-level bar.

French architect Viguier, who has built surprisingly little in the United States since the warm reception of Sofitel, captured the essence of Chicago through what I'd call "contemporary contextualism," evident primarily in the way he handles the east and west facades. Chicago's early skyscrapers, influenced greatly by Louis Sullivan, expressed themselves through a strong articulation of the vertical structure filled with decorative spandrels between. Later, lighter and glassier skins retained this *parti* of vertical structure and horizontal infill (see SOM's Inland Steel Building for but one example). Viguier extends this evolution through staggered openings of different sizes between the barely perceptible grid of columns that blends with the opaque white panes between windows, as if the structure's concrete frame inspired an abstract composition.

In its triangular form and its random composition of windows, the hotel recalls Harry Weese's 1975 concrete Metropolitan Correctional Center in the Loop, an odd precedent, but if any architect deserved to have influenced Chicago architecture more, it was Harry Weese with his playful modernism. Perhaps the biggest difference in these two buildings, besides the shift from concrete to glass, is the way the curving, embracing base of Viguier's design welcomes people inside the building for dinner, drinks, or a room for the night.

72

FOURTH PRESBYTERIAN CHURCH OF CHICAGO, GRATZ CENTER

Gensler, 2013
126 East Chestnut Street
Train: Red to Chicago/State
Bus: #151 to Michigan at Chestnut Street/Delaware Place

Echoing the Water Tower two blocks to the south, the Fourth Presbyterian Church is a low-scale relic that harks back to Michigan Avenue's previous life as Pine Street. This bit of breathing room across from 875 N. Michigan Avenue (formerly the John Hancock Center) and amid the other towers lining the Magnificent Mile was threatened in 2004 when the church and its affluent congregation approved plans for a 64-story residential tower designed by Lucien Lagrange. That project would have risen just west of the 1914 Gothic Revival church designed by Ralph Adams Cram and the Tudor Style parish buildings designed by Howard Van Doren Shaw one decade later. In 2009, after struggles with neighbors opposed to the plan and finding themselves in

The two-story chapel sits behind the window cut into the south facade. (Credit Eric Allix Rogers, CAC Archive)

The chapel is a contemporary yet clearly ecclesiastical space. (Credit Eric Allix Rogers, CAC Archive)

the grips of the recession, the church scrapped the development plans and decided to move forward with a new church center, which was planned for the base of the tower.

The five-story Genevieve and Wayne Gratz Center houses classrooms, a dining room and kitchen, offices, meeting space, and the 350-person-capacity Buchanan Chapel. Gensler's design, which required the demolition of some of the church's less notable buildings, is a parallelogram in plan, due to the angle of Rush Street and Ernst Court to the west. The long elevations facing west and east are entirely glass, the latter serving as a low but still visible backdrop to the church's stone buildings when seen from Michigan Avenue. The north and south facades are covered in copper sheets that were pre-patinated to a distinctive green color. A tall window is cut into the south elevation facing Chestnut Street next to the main entrance; behind it is the chapel (open to the public), a double-height space with more copper (but no patina), strips of light entering through the west wall, and a labyrinth made of limestone tiles intended as a walking tool for prayer and meditation.

TILT
Thornton Tomasetti, 2014
875 North Michigan Avenue

Not to be outdone by the glass boxes luring people to the 103rd floor of the Willis Tower in the Loop (see Chapter 4), the Montparnasse 56 Group (owners of 360 Chicago, formerly the John Hancock Observatory) worked with the structural engineers at Thornton Tomasetti to install windows in part of the south-facing facade that tilt a third of the way to horizontal, inducing their own brand of vertigo 1,000 feet in the air.

W Armitage Ave (2000N)

See Map
9
Lincoln Park

Lincoln Park

Apple Lincoln Park

North Avenue Bridge

W North Ave (1600N)

North/Clybourn

Sedgwick

SoNo and SoNo East

W Blackhawk St

N Kingsbury St

W Eastman St

78 Blackhawk on Halsted

Graham Foundation

Carl Sandburg Village

Charnley-Persky House (SAH)

N Cleveland Ave

N Sedgwick St

N Cherry Ave

N Clybourn Ave

Mars Global Services

77 Tower House

76 Schiff Residences

Goose Island

Clark/Division

W Division St (1200N)

Parkside of Old Town

W Elm St

74 Viceroy Chicago

N Crosby St

1/2-mile radius

W Hill St

75 Walter Payton College Preparatory High School & Annex

W Oak St

Newberry Library

W Walton St

N Elston Ave

N Halsted St (800W)

N Larrabee St

N Hudson Ave

N Orleans St

N Franklin St

N Wells St

N LaSalle St

N Clark St

N Dearborn St

Marwen

Chicago

Montgomery Ward and Co. Warehouse

73 Jesse White Community Center and Field House

Eight O Five

W Chicago Ave (800N)

Chicago

Kennedy Expy

See Map
6
River North

W Kinzie St (400N)

8 Near North Side

The Near North Side runs the gamut from rich to poor, from mansions to SRO (Single Room Occupancy) housing, big box stores to warehouses. It includes some of the most valuable real estate in the city along the lakefront, while astride the river is once-forgotten or repurposed land that developers are hoping will be an equally valuable part of this century's tech boom. This study in contrasts was visible as early as the 1920s in an account that described it as "an area of highlight and shadows, of vivid contrasts—contrasts not only between the old and the new, but between wealth and poverty, vice and respectability, . . . luxury and toil."[1] For purposes of this book, this area encompasses parts of the Gold Coast, Old Town, and Lincoln Park neighborhoods, and includes Goose Island and the land once devoted to the Cabrini-Green public housing projects.

The easternmost portion of the Near North Side consists of the aptly named Gold Coast, where proximity to the lake and remove from the railroads made it suitable for the mansions of Potter Palmer, Cyrus McCormick, and others who moved from South Prairie Avenue in the decades after the Great Fire of 1871. Although mid-20th-century high-rise apartment buildings along Lake Shore Drive cut off the earlier residences from the lake, it remains one of Chicago's most prized and affluent neighborhoods. The Gold Coast is home to two prized architecture institutions: the Graham Foundation for Advanced Studies in the Fine Arts and the Society of Architectural Historians, the latter inside the Charnley-Persky House designed by Louis Sullivan in 1892 with a 25-year-old Frank Lloyd Wright.

West of the Gold Coast is Old Town, which although now an affluent area was traditionally a working-class and liberal area at odds with the neighborhood to the east; the Carl Sandburg Village urban renewal project was built in phases beginning in the late 1960s and functioned as a buffer between the wealthy Gold Coast and struggling working-class neighborhoods to the north and west. Even further at odds was Cabrini-Green, a public housing project with over 3,600 units (less than ten percent of the units in the city's numerous projects, most on the south and west sides) in a mix of rowhouses and high-rise buildings constructed in phases from the 1940s to the 1960s on twenty-three acres roughly north of Chicago Avenue and east of Orleans Street. In recent years, the Chicago Housing Authority replaced many of its midcentury high-rise projects with low-scale, mixed-used developments. Cabrini-Green's island of low-income, predominantly African American residents close to downtown was particularly vulnerable for redevelopment, and in 1997, the city sealed its fate, approving the 340-acre Near North TIF aimed at "the transformation of the Cabrini-Green public housing complex and adjacent blighted properties into a healthy, mixed-income community."[2] The TIF area stretches to the North Branch Canal in some spots, traditionally a zone of industry, but one that has seen, in places like Goose Island, manufacturing uses close in favor of office developments catering to tech firms and other businesses.

73

JESSE WHITE COMMUNITY CENTER AND FIELD HOUSE

Ghafari Associates, 2014

410 West Chicago Avenue

Train: Brown, Purple to Chicago/Franklin

Bus: #66 to Chicago Avenue at Hudson Street

Jesse White, the Illinois Secretary of State since taking office in 1999 (making him the first African American in that role) and a gymnastics coach in his days before politics, founded the Jesse White Tumbling Team in 1959 as a juvenile delinquency prevention program for children residing in Chicago's inner-city public housing projects. The new building that serves as the headquarters of the Chicago Park District's gymnastics program and as the home of the Tumblers is located on the site of the southernmost of twenty-three high-rise towers that made up the housing project, all of them demolished (to the west are the Frances Cabrini rowhouses from the 1940s, being redeveloped as a mixed-income housing). The 30,000-square-foot, two-story building houses a gymnasium, a gymnastics center, fitness rooms, locker rooms, administrative offices, meeting rooms, and a computer/learning lab to offer programs geared to physical fitness *and* education.

The orange volume houses the new home of the Jesse White Tumblers. (Credit Lynn Becker)

Based on the design by Ghafari's Joseph Gonzalez, the gymnastics center is the most important part of the project; it is located just beyond the lobby and its roofline angling up to the east—gaining light through narrow windows on that side—is the tallest part of the building. It is clad in brown-orange metal panels, as is the gymnasium to the west. The other functions are found behind contrasting gray metal walls with plenty of glass facing Chicago Avenue, making it a welcoming building in a neighborhood in transition.

MARWEN
Wheeler Kearns Architects, 2015
833 North Orleans Street

Fifteen years after first renovating the Near North facility of the nonprofit arts-based foundation, Wheeler Kearns doubled Marwen's footprint to 30,000 square feet with a new entrance, loggia space, and studios, earning a 2016 SEED Award for Excellence in Public Interest Design in the process.

EIGHT O FIVE

Berkelhamer Architects with Antunovich Architects, 2015

805 North LaSalle Drive

Smithfield Properties and architect Adam Berkelhamer, the team from Sono East, also in this chapter, reunited for this 33-story tower that has a similar glass exterior wall expression from bottom to top, aided by the placement of the parking garage to the north, which acts as a base for townhouses.

(Credit Lynn Becker)

74

VICEROY CHICAGO

Goettsch Partners, 2017

1118 North State Street

Train: Red to Clark/Division

Bus: #36 to State Street at Bellevue Place, northbound; State Street at Division Street, southbound

Sited prominently at the west end of East Cedar Street, the 18-story Viceroy Hotel sits behind and occupies a portion of a historic four-story brick building from the 1920s. This predecessor was the Cedar Hotel, which now serves as Viceroy's lobby, restaurant, and lounge, and the base for a sizable roof terrace. The new tower contrasts dramatically with this old brick and terracotta building, but with a serrated curtain wall facing east it is different than just about every building around it—for the better. The folded glass facade is a standout, more memorable than 99 percent of glass skins produced this century. The glass wraps the corner on the south, engaging with a projected brick volume with windows, while it turns the corner on the north just slightly, stopping just short of the core; this side recalls the way vernacular Chicago buildings spend more money on the front than on the sides and rear. In this case, the money was spent by Chicago developer Convexity Properties; the

The new glass facade oriented east is a strong counterpoint to the masonry Cedar Hotel. (Credit James Steinkamp Photography)

180-room hotel is operated by the Viceroy Hotel Group, a Los Angeles–based chain of boutique hotels. Together with Goettsch Partners, Viceroy has made a stunning entrance with its first Chicago hotel.

75

WALTER PAYTON COLLEGE PREPARATORY HIGH SCHOOL & ANNEX

DeStefano Partners with Mann Gin Dubin & Frazier, 2000; KOO, 2016

1034 North Wells Street

Train: Red to Clark/Division

Bus: #22 on Clark Street at Maple Street

Following U.S. Department of Education findings in the mid-1990s on the aging infrastructure of public schools, the Chicago Public Schools (CPS) went on a spending spree, building new schools and additions throughout the city

The annex on the left, designed by KOO, is linked to the original building by DeStefano Partners. (Credit James Steinkamp Photography)

as part of its $2.5 billion Capital Improvement Program. CPS started with elementary and middle schools and then built its first high school since the late 1970s with the 1999 Northside College Preparatory High School designed by OWP/P (now part of CannonDesign). This was followed one year later by the Payton College Prep designed by DeStefano Partners, the firm that served as the managing architect for CPS's K-8 schools at the time. Though named for the Chicago Bears' famous wide receiver, the selective-enrollment high school is focused on math, science, and language. A greenhouse and planetarium on the top floor of the four-story academic wing facing the athletic fields subtly articulates this emphasis, as does the sine wave in the floors of the four-story glass-enclosed atrium that connects the classrooms to the library, gymnasium, auditorium, dining, and administration spaces along Hill Street on the north.

A three-story annex designed by KOO grows the school's population by half to approximately 1,200, with classrooms, a gym and fitness room, a lounge, and a black box theater, among other spaces. Most distinctive is the third-floor gym atop the building, set at an angle to the rest of the addition in reference to the flared plan of the original building's atrium.

PARKSIDE OF OLD TOWN

Landon Bone Baker Architects, 2016

545 West Division Street

Phase IIB of Parkside of Old Town, part of the Chicago Housing Authority's Plan for Transformation on the former site of Cabrini-Green public housing, is made up of mixed-income residences in a nine-story building that faces townhouses across a green space (designed by McKay Landscape Architects), a big improvement over the first phase and a promising step forward in redeveloping Chicago's failed public housing.

76

SCHIFF RESIDENCES

Murphy/Jahn (now JAHN), 2007

1244 North Clybourn Street

Train: Red to Clark/Division

Bus: #70 to Division Street to Clybourn Avenue

Although Helmut Jahn, in partnership with Charles Murphy, was the biggest name in Chicago architecture in the 1980s since Mies van der Rohe, the controversial James R. Thompson Center across the street from City Hall led to a drought of his working in the city for the better part of the 1990s. Jahn returned with vigor in 2003 with the IIT State Street Village Dormitories (**138**), a long glassy building with metal walls that turn into roofs through an elegant curved profile.

A similar approach happens with the design of the Margot and Harold Schiff Residences designed for Mercy Housing Lakefront, which provides supportive housing for formerly homeless individuals: corrugated metal panels angle out slightly and wrap up and over the building, from the street side to the alley side, giving the impression that the building is a five-story train car or a metal-and-glass loaf of bread. But the shape isn't just a formal flourish: the curves at the roofline help to drive the prevailing winds to a row of wind turbines at the building's peak. Out of sight, but also serving to reduce the ongoing energy costs of the building, is a row of solar panels oriented southwest.

A grid of windows faces the main elevation on Clybourn, with the building's train-car-like glassy end facing south. (Credit Rainer Viertlböck, courtesy of JAHN)

Further, rainwater that hits the roof is collected in a cistern for irrigating the garden that sits on the west side of the building next to a small parking lot.

Inside, the building houses ninety-six individuals in the same number of rooms, common areas on each floor (behind the glass walls above the main entrance on Clybourn), and a community space on the ground floor. The interior features a graywater system, supposedly the first in Chicago, where water from showers and sinks is treated and then used for toilets. Combined with the green features outside, the design expresses that SRO housing is as suitable a typology for sustainable (and sexy) architecture as any.

77

TOWER HOUSE

Frederick Phillips and Associates, 2001
1306 North Cleveland Avenue
Train: Red to Clark/Division
Bus: #70 to Division Street at Clybourn Avenue

Chicago has a strong legacy of residential architecture, from the Prairie Style houses of Frank Lloyd Wright to Mies van der Rohe's nearby Farnsworth House and the midcentury homes of Keck and Keck. Architect Frederick Phillips appears to be more enamored with Mies than the others in this steel-framed house he designed for himself on a small triangular lot just steps from the then-

extant Cabrini-Green housing project. The aptly named Tower House places the bedrooms and living spaces behind large windows and corrugated metal walls on the second and third floors, respectively, situated between the open ground-floor carport and fourth-floor terrace. A concrete-block stair tower, accompanied by an external spiral stair, sits on the west to maintain the views to the east and downtown.

The four-story house's stacking of carport, bedrooms, living space, and terrace as seen from the east. (Credit John K. Zacherle)

78

BLACKHAWK ON HALSTED

Valerio Dewalt Train Associates, 2007

814 West Eastman Street

Train: Red to North/Clybourn

Bus: #72 to North Avenue at Clybourn Avenue/Halsted Street

Ribbons of metal unite the three parts of this full-block, mixed-use development a few blocks south of North and Clybourn. The southernmost portion is home to the British School of Chicago, a private pre-K-12 school that first opened in 2001, moved into this new five-story building six years later, and opened a second location in the South Loop in 2015. The aforementioned metal, corrugated as it is, rises up from the sidewalk above some storefront glazing along Clybourn, where it is punctured by a tall window before it extends along the roof until mid-block when it dips down to call out the school's entrance on Eastman. The rear elevation on Dayton does a similar thing, positioned next to a 550-car parking garage that extends to Blackhawk Street. To the east of it is the development's third element, a retail and medical office building; its metal ribbons undulate up and down along Clybourn, and its high

The southeast corner of the full-block development is anchored by the British School of Chicago. (Credit Anna Munzesheimer, CAC Archive)

point in the middle signals the building's entrance. Take away the ribbons and the block is a forgettable hodgepodge of metal and glass, but with them it is a contemporary expression of what a development can be when it strives for something different.

(Credit Lynn Becker)

SONO WEST/SONO EAST

Booth Hansen/Berkelhamer Architects with Antunovich Associates, 2009/2012

860/840 West Blackhawk Street

The intersection of North and Clybourn is the epicenter of suburban-style retail, where two glass towers south of North Avenue (SoNo) stand out. Built four years apart, with a recession in between, are two towers for Smithfield Properties that sit perpendicular to each other: Booth Hansen's 28-story condo tower parallel to Blackhawk, and the east tower, designed by Adam Berkelhamer (a former principal at Booth Hansen), which is a 22-story rental tower. Although the towers look like duplicates, they differ in details like the balconies, the concrete columns, and the way each tower is capped, slight evidence of the project's evolution over its two phases with two architects.

APPLE LINCOLN PARK

Bohlin Cywinski Jackson, 2010
801 West North Avenue

Apple opened its second store in Chicago—its 319th internationally at the time—on a triangular site at North and Clybourn streets. Glass walls on the north and south ends are bracketed by metal panels, and the building sits beside a plaza with trees, seating, and a fountain designed by Hoerr Schaudt Landscape Architects. This open space is a welcome addition to a part of the city geared more to motorists than pedestrians.

NORTH AVENUE BRIDGE

Muller+Muller, HNTB Corporation, 2007
1200 West North Avenue

Connecting the neighborhoods of Bucktown and Wicker Park on the west with the retail corridor along Clybourn and other places on the east, this bridge spanning the Chicago River at North Avenue replaces a bascule lift bridge from 1907. The new bridge uses a hybrid suspension/cable-stay structural system for the 420-foot-long span. Crossing the bridge by bike or foot on its south side is recommended, in order to take in skyline views of downtown beyond the North Avenue Turning Basin, which is being eyed as the north end of the Wild Mile eco-park.

See Map
10
Lakeview &
North Center
W Belmont Ave (3200N)
Row 2750
Diversey
W Diversey Pkwy (2800N)
Brewster Apartments
N Lincoln Ave
N Clark St
N Lakeview Ave
Lake Michigan
W Wrightwood Ave
N Burling St
87 Wrightwood 659
88 Concrete Townhouse
Peggy Notebaert Nature Museum
Ion Lincoln Park
Fullerton
W Fullerton Pkwy (2400N)
DePaul Art Museum
89 The Theater School
N Lakewood Ave
N Orchard St
W Belden Ave
W Grant Pl
Grant Place
Private Residence 82
83 Chicago Residence
W Webster Ave
1/2-mile radius
N Lake Shore Dr
85
Zoo Visitor Center
Pritzker Family Children's Zoo 86
Oz Park
Lincoln Park
N Clybourn Ave
N Racine Ave (1200W)
N Sheffield Ave
N Daytona St
N Halsted St (800W)
N Larrabee St
N Mohawk St
N Sedgwick St
W Armitage Ave (2000N)
Armitage
Steel and Glass House
84
Nature Boardwalk at Lincoln Park Zoo
Floating World Gallery
W Wisconsin St
80
Seigle House
See Map
13
Bucktown, etc.
Orchard Willow 81
Willow Residence
W Willow St
1737 North Bissell
Steppenwolf
79 Mohawk House
Chicago History Museum
W North Ave (1600N)
North/Clybourn
Sedgwick
See Map
8
Near North
Goose Island
W Division St (1200N)
Clark/Division

9 Lincoln Park

As reflected in the numerous single-family houses in this chapter, the Lincoln Park neighborhood is one of the most desirable places in Chicago to live. Initially oriented around the McCormick Theological Seminary (present-day DePaul University) in the mid-1800s, the neighborhood thrived with German immigrants building large houses near the lake and workers' housing for Irish and Polish populations farther west. With its fabric of primarily two- and three-story brick houses (many with raised first floors to create garden apartments) in a diversity of styles—some of them dating back to the late 1800s (the Great Fire of 1871 wiped out the area up to Fullerton, the northern city limits at the time)—and its proximity to downtown and the beaches along Lake Michigan, Lincoln Park became a magnet for families with means and young, educated professionals.

During the mid-20th century, the prospects of this rosy future were close to nonexistent. Shortly after a 1950 sociological report that forecast "the end of much of Lincoln Park as a residential community," 226 acres in the once-working-class area then considered a "slum" were earmarked for urban renewal.[1] But by the time funds were allocated in the mid-1960s, building owners had already started renovating the post-fire building stock, spearheading gentrification. This fixer-upper trend was the outcome of the efforts of the Lincoln Park Conservation Association that formed in 1954, in turn inspired by the Old Town Triangle Association, which started in 1948 to protect the triangle once formed by North Avenue, Clark Street, and Ogden Avenue. (A walk through the triangle's narrow streets is highly recommended, particularly to see some of the rare wood-frame buildings that were built between 1871 and the city's ban on wood construction three years later.)

As might be obvious but deserves some discussion here, the Lincoln Park neighborhood takes its name from the lakefront park that now stretches six miles from Ohio Street in Streeterville to Ardmore Avenue in Edgewater. Originally called Lake Park, and a far cry from the beautiful spot it is today (portions were a cemetery until the 1870s), it was renamed for the sixteenth president after his 1866 assassination. Subsequently it became a desirable place for the wealthy, as well as for institutions that were founded in the 19th century and remain to this day: Lincoln Park Zoo, Chicago History Museum, and Peggy Notebaert Museum. The most valuable land in Lincoln Park lies toward the lake, while the traditionally working-class immigrant areas reaching westward—beyond DePaul University, the biggest single landholder in the neighborhood—have maintained some level of affordability. Yet the houses in this chapter show a departure from this long-held condition, as the rich combine lots on inland blocks for mansions—increasing the area's desirability but decreasing its affordability and diversity.

(Credit © Adrian Smith + Gordon Gill Architecture)

STEPPENWOLF THEATRE COMPANY
Adrian Smith + Gordon Gill Architecture,
Estimated completion in 2021
1650 North Halsted Street

In March 2019, Steppenwolf Theatre broke ground on a new 400-seat theater-in-the-round between its existing home and parking garage. Like The Yard at Chicago Shakespeare (**67**) AS+GG worked with Charcoalblue on the theater, where the audience will never be more than 20 feet from the stage. Halsted Street will be enlived by the angular glassy facade of the two-story lobby.

79

MOHAWK HOUSE

UrbanLab, 2015
1712 North Mohawk Street
Train: Red to North/Clybourn
Bus: #72 to North Avenue at Cleveland Avenue

If there is a vernacular Chicago architecture, it is most surely made of brick. Although the city was predominately wood before the Great Fire of 1871,

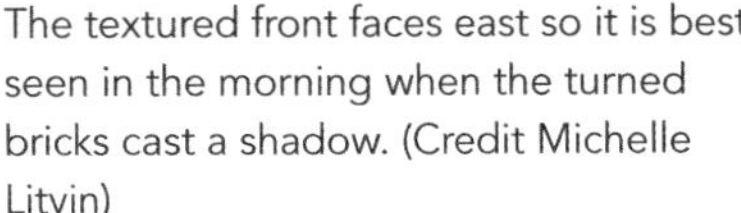

The textured front faces east so it is best seen in the morning when the turned bricks cast a shadow. (Credit Michelle Litvin)

Turning every other brick perpendicularly gives texture to an otherwise flat facade. (Credit John Hill)

the city rebuilt with large areas of masonry construction after the catastrophe. Brick adorns the bungalows, two-flats, and apartment buildings that are found throughout the city. This house designed by the architecture duo of Sarah Dunn and Martin Felsen indicates that brick is still ripe for experimentation. While most exterior walls utilize a running bond pattern, this huge four-story house on two lots has a textured front elevation that is formed by turning every other brick ninety degrees and offsetting each row to create a checkerboard pattern. A random pattern of windows—each with one pane of glass, recessed headers, and short sills—combines with the dark brick to make the house look like an abstract assemblage of solid and void. Also of note is the short brick wall at the front, which has a similar checkerboard pattern, but with openings. Take a peek along the side walkways to glimpse the lawn that cascades above the garage roof off the alley.

80

SEIGLE HOUSE

Lohan Anderson, 2008
1856 North Mohawk Street
Train: Red to North/Clybourn
Bus: #72 to North Avenue at Cleveland Avenue

The mantra of "location, location, location" is especially fitting for this house facing two open spaces: across the street is a small playlot and next door is a pedestrian walkway that connects Mohawk Street to Larrabee Street. These small spaces give the house plenty of sunlight, surround it with trees, and effectively create a corner lot without the extra traffic of two through streets (the pedestrian walkway terminates Wisconsin Street). In their design of this large three-story house on two lots, Dirk Lohan's firm took advantage of the location through large horizontal windows facing the playlot on the east and a four-story-high curtain wall on the north that encloses the stair running from the ground floor to the roof terrace. Limestone walls wrap the base of the house for privacy, while the top floors are covered in a terra cotta rainscreen system that melds the modern house with its brick predecessors. The terracotta is reiterated as horizontal slats at the front fence, letting passersby touch what is otherwise out of reach.

Large horizontal windows face the street and playlot to the east. (Credit Angie McMonigal Photography)

81

ORCHARD WILLOW

Wheeler Kearns Architects, 2012
1840 block of North Orchard Street
Train: Red to North/Clybourn
Bus: #72 to North Avenue at Orchard Street

This relatively small three-story house sits on two lots overlooking the parking lot of Newberry Academy. The unique site condition led architect Jon Heinert from Wheeler Kearns to nearly fill the width of the site at the glass-walled first floor, enclose the generous backyard and narrow side yard with an in situ concrete wall, and place the narrow second and third floors to the north, thereby creating an outdoor zone of privacy and giving the house plenty of sunlight. The most striking aspect of the house's exterior is the copper cladding that covers the top two floors and should patina to purple and then green over time.

A narrow, copper-clad volume sits atop the one-story base. (Credit Angie McMonigal Photography)

1737 NORTH BISSELL

Filoramo Talsma, 2011
1737 North Bissell Street

A one-story building that started its life as a service station is covered in dark metal panels, while the second-floor addition—its stair expressed on the side yard of the triangular site—is covered in a counterpoint of wood shingles.

(Credit John Hill)

WILLOW RESIDENCE

Searl and Associates, 2004

922West Willow Street

A former four-lane bowling alley was renovated by architect Linda Searl (now Searl Lamaster Howe Architects) into a three-story house overlooking a full-lot side yard that allows the metal and glass addition behind the original brick facade to be on display for passersby.

FLOATING WORLD GALLERY

S. Conger Architects, 2009

1925 North Halsted Street

The husband-and-wife team of Bill and Roberta Stein called on architect Susan Conger-Austin to transform a small 1920s factory into what turned into two galleries: a public gallery on the first floor and a private gallery with offices and restoration facilities upstairs. Uniting the two realms is the new front facade of slate tiles, a simple and calming presence that is appropriate to the art inside.

(Credit Angie McMonigal Photography)

82

PRIVATE RESIDENCE

DeStefano Partners, 2005

838 West Webster Avenue

Train: Brown, Purple to Armitage

Bus: #8 to Halsted Street at Webster Avenue

Avram Lothan, a partner at DeStefano Partners (now with Lothan Van Hook DeStefano Architecture), designed this house for himself and his family on a tree-lined street close to Oz Park. A decade previously, Lothan had renovated

Gray metal panels frame large expanses of clear and translucent glass. (Credit Barbara Karant / Karant & Associates)

two buildings for the Alliance Francaise de Chicago, linking the buildings with a glass enclosure overlooking a courtyard; hidden from the street, it nevertheless put the architect on the local radar. Although this house is a new building that seems to lurch forward for the attention of passersby, there is a similar internal focus happening: the two-story volumes at the front and rear, and the three-story volume connecting them on the west side are oriented to a courtyard on the east. This orientation allows the morning sun to infiltrate the courtyard and adjacent double-height living space to the west, while shielding the outdoor space from the warm afternoon sun. Aside from some wood at the front door, the material palette is limited to two materials. Brick is capped at two floors, while metal pops above it and in front of it as a contemporary expression in a context of traditional brick residences.

83

PRIVATE RESIDENCE

Dirk Denison Architects, 2010

2202 North Orchard Street

Train: Red, Brown, Purple to Fullerton

Bus: #8 to Halsted Street at Webster Avenue

In the architect's description of this house for an AIA Chicago awards submission, there is, alongside the boasts of its green features, an element most unexpected: the large, integrated aquariums for the family's extensive fish collection. Designed to fit into, and project from, a wall located near the house's front door, the aquariums could be seen as a parallel for the rest of the house. Given its location overlooking Oz Park, the corner house gets plenty of sunlight but most likely its fair share of glances. And given that many people consider modern glass boxes fishbowls, in which the life inside is put on display for others to see, it's fitting that Denison departed from a simple all-glass exterior and instead articulated the house, particularly its long southern facade, in a manner where solid wood cladding is more prevalent than glass. Further, openings are carved into the three-story, L-shaped volume while windows and small rooms project from it, akin to the aquariums inside. The projections and carvings give the exterior a complexity that makes it concealing yet also an architectural expression of the family's life inside.

The south elevation is a complex, three-dimensional composition of wood and glass. (Credit Michelle Litvin)

GRANT PLACE

Pappageorge Haymes Partners, 2005
432 West Grant Place

This four-story building with seven dwelling units is an unexpectedly modern design from a firm more comfortable designing residences in neo-traditional styles. A recessed ground floor and setback front elevation help the brick-and-concrete building fit well into its smaller-scale context.

(Credit Pappageorge Haymes Partners)

84

NATURE BOARDWALK AT LINCOLN PARK ZOO

Studio Gang, 2010
North Stockton Drive between West LaSalle Drive and West Dickens Avenue
Train: Brown, Purple to Armitage
Bus: #151 to Stockton Drive at Dickens Drive

Like many of Jeanne Gang's post-Aqua (**14**) projects, the Nature Boardwalk at Lincoln Park Zoo received a fair amount of attention when it was completed, much of it centered on the open-air pavilion of wood and fiberglass that sits on the east side of the pond. But the project is much more than the admittedly eye-catching pavilion. As the name suggests, the project focuses on a boardwalk, a path that follows the edge of the zoo's South Pond, from Café Brauer on the north to the Grant Monument and the Farm-in-the-Zoo on the south.

The pond was created around 1870, shortly after the zoo's founding. Over the years, its hard, engineered edges and shallow bed contributed to the unhealthy nature of the oxygen-starved pond. Gang and her team of consultants, including landscape architect WRD Environmental, worked to transform

The softened edge of the pond attracts wildlife—and people as well. (Credit Eric Allix Rogers, CAC Archive)

the fourteen-acre landscape into a native Midwestern ecosystem with plants, trees, naturalized shorelines, and water depths that welcome wildlife. Its softened edges and snaking boardwalk completely changed the character of the place, making it resemble a piece of nature that predated Chicago's buildup rather than a human-made landscape. Walking the boardwalk is a great experience, as it zigzags among the plantings and sometimes juts out over the water. The changes are not just visual; the transformation of the pond has increased the diversity of the

Milkweed pods influenced the pavilion's design. (Credit John Hill)

The wood and fiberglass pavilion sits on axis with 875 N. Michigan Avenue. (Credit Eric Allix Rogers, CAC Archive)

landscape's wildlife; from the fish and turtles that live there, to birds that use it as a migratory stop.

The pond has become a laboratory, a barrier-free zoo exhibit, and a classroom. The last is primarily served by what is officially called the Peoples Gas Education Pavilion. Gang was inspired by the form and related structural strength of milkweed pods, a prairie plant. This inspiration can be seen in the fiberglass domes that shade the classes and other groups within the 17-foot-high structure made from curved strips of laminated wood bolted together; openings at the base of the structure aid in natural ventilation and make it a pleasant place to be. The alienlike presence, which sits on axis with the John Hancock Center (now 875 North Michigan Avenue) to the south, adds an exclamation point to the Nature Boardwalk, but more importantly it provides an excuse to stop for a while and take in the zoo's return to nature.

85

SEARLE VISITOR CENTER

Ross Barney Architects, 2018

2001 North Clark Street (East Gate entrance)

Train: Brown, Purple to Armitage

Bus: #151 to Stockton Drive at Webster Avenue

Lincoln Park Zoo is free and open to the public every day of the year, echoing the "forever open, clear, and free" of the Lake Michigan shoreline it sits just steps away from. Occupying a swath of Lincoln Park between the park's namesake neighborhood and Lake Shore Drive, the zoo can be accessed by public transit from the west or by car from the east via a paid parking lot. The new Searle Visitor Center sits at the East Gate, the main entrance for those driving to the zoo. Housing guest services, an information center, administrative offices, restrooms, and services such as stroller rentals, the 9,500-square-

The new visitor center forms a gateway from the parking lot east of the zoo. (Credit Kendall McCaugherty, Hall+Merrick Photographers)

foot, $10 million building also has the first dedicated space for zoo members. The Center is part of Lincoln Park Zoo's Pride of Chicago campaign, which raised over $125 million to make improvements to the century-and-half-old zoo, most of them focused on animal habitats.

Ross Barney Architects split the Center into two buildings: a stone-clad rectilinear building on the south with restrooms, and a larger glassy building on the north housing most functions. The two buildings are linked by a canopy composed as overlapping planes—what the architects describe as "a delicately stacked card tower"[2]—to create a gateway to the zoo from the east. The canopy's aluminum panels are laser-cut with angular, nature-inspired patterns that filter the sunlight both at the entrance and at the courtyard of the C-shaped building on the north. The pattern of these overhead planes is reiterated in the sliding gate that closes off the zoo at night. The information center, located next to the gate on the north, features sliding walls that enable the space to open to the elements in nice weather—a gesture as welcoming as the design of the whole Searle Visitor Center.

Laser-cut metal panels connect the buildings and provide shade. (Credit Kendall McCaugherty, Hall+Merrick Photographers)

86

PRITZKER FAMILY CHILDREN'S ZOO

EHDD, 2005

2001 North Clark Street

Train: Brown, Purple to Armitage

Bus: #151 to Stockton Drive at Webster Avenue

In 1993, Lincoln Park Zoo launched its $50 million "Heart of the Zoo Campaign" to renovate some of its structures, build new ones, and provide more visitor services. The fund-raising resulted in, among other things, a new pavilion with gift shop and café and, at the tail end of the spending spree, the Pritzker Family Children's Zoo, which replaced the 1959 building that was overhauled in the late 1980s. This zoo-within-a-zoo is accessed from a path next to the main entrance gate from Stockton Drive on the west.

The glass-and-concrete box sits behind a wire grid for vines to climb. (Credit Architecture Is Fun/Doug Snower Photography)

A few steps in and it's clear that the Children's Zoo is as much about landscape as building—one might even wonder if there is a building at all, for in warm months the boxy glass and concrete structure designed by EHDD is hidden behind ivy. The winding paths and dense tree cover, designed with Mesa Landscape Architects, is meant to immerse visitors in the world of the forest as they walk past indoor habitats for wolves, bears, otters, and beavers. Inside the building that defines the western edge of the Children's Zoo is a large space filled with

Architecture Is Fun's climbing tree occupies the space inside the building. (Credit Architecture Is Fun/Doug Snower Photography)

an elaborate treelike construction supported by slanting columns, where children climb within wire mesh nets and rest upon leaves made from plywood. Designed by Architecture Is Fun—a firm that, as the name indicates, specializes in spaces for children—the educational environment turns the Children's Zoo into an experience that kids will enjoy and also learn from.

87

WRIGHTWOOD 659

Tadao Ando Architect & Associates, with Vinci|Hamp Architects & Gensler, 2018

659 West Wrightwood Avenue

Train: Red, Brown, Purple to Fullerton

Bus: #22, #36 to Clark and Deming

Chicago can boast of two firsts in the long career of Tadao Ando. The Pritzker Prize–winning Japanese architect's first commission in the United States was a small gallery at the Art Institute of Chicago: the Gallery for Japanese Screens, completed in 1992. Five years later Ando completed his first house in the United States, an introverted concrete shell arranged around a reflecting pool on three lots of Wrightwood Avenue. Even though the house was visible only as a concrete wall and imposing steel door on the street and a concrete garage and ivy-covered wall on the alley, almost immediately it became a popular destination for visiting and local architects.

The house was commissioned by Fred Eychaner, the philanthropist and activist who, two decades later with architectural historian Dan Whittaker, founded Wrightwood 659 and inserted it into a neighboring, 90-year-old apartment building renovated by Ando. The dynamic of Eychaner and Whittaker

Light coming from the windows hints at the large atrium space behind the old apartment building's brick shell. (Credit William Zbaren)

Ando's signature concrete is found in the atrium's stair. (Credit Anna Munzesheimer, CAC Archive)

On the roof, a walkway allows views of Ando's earlier house next door. (Credit Anna Munzesheimer, CAC Archive)

ensures that Wrightwood 659's exhibitions will alternate between architecture and socially engaged art (it is not a collecting institution). Fittingly, the gallery space opened to the public in October 2018 with an exhibition on Tadao Ando and Le Corbusier, the modern master who greatly influenced Ando.

Although the 38 apartments of 659 West Wrightwood are gone, the brick walls remain, meaning Wrightwood 659 resembles its previous self from the street. But a roof apparently floating above the parapet (best visible from across the street) hints at the dramatic changes inside. Visitors enter from the street into a full-height atrium that reveals how Ando completely gutted the old building and inserted a hefty new concrete-and-steel structure inside the shell. This approach to adaptive reuse is accentuated by the bricks lining the inside of the old walls, surfaces that visitors visually encounter as they ascend the concrete stair that juts into the atrium. Wrightwood 659 consists of three gallery floors inside the old four-story building (the atrium ensures that the new floors don't misalign with the old window openings) as well as a new floor on the roof. From here, beneath the floating roof visible from the street, is a glassed-in corridor that overlooks the earlier Ando house. Terraces on the north and south ends look, respectively, on to the intimacy of Wrightwood Avenue and to the towers of downtown, among which Ando's other Chicago gallery nestles.

88

CONCRETE TOWNHOUSE

John Ronan Architects, 2005
2465 North Burling Street
Train: Red, Brown, Purple to Fullerton
Bus: #8 to Halsted Street at Fullerton/Lincoln Avenues

To get a glimpse at the material that gives this hefty three-story house its name, take a look at the primarily solid wall facing north. Here, overlooking the house's open second lot, is a board-formed reinforced concrete wall that, in Ronan's words, "explores the beauty of imperfection."[3] By using individual wood boards rather than plywood sheets for the formwork, the wall exhibits the varied grain and size of each piece, a process that involved numerous mockups with the contractor. Some precision is evident though in the vertical joints that are aligned with the few windows in the wall. Wood and glass, side-by-side, are found on the front elevation, the former punctured by an entry portal reached from a plinth, both rendered in limestone. And while we can't venture inside, this front elevation tells us clearly that living spaces and bedrooms are on the right, while stairs and other spaces are on the left.

The concrete of the house's name faces the yard to the north. (Credit © Nathan Kirkman 2009)

89

THE THEATRE SCHOOL

Pelli Clarke Pelli Architects with CannonDesign, 2013
2350 North Racine Avenue
Train: Red, Brown, Purple to Fullerton
Bus: #74 to Fullerton Avenue at Racine Avenue

In DePaul University's ambitious 2009–2019 master plan, Antunovich Architects (the firm responsible for many of the school's post-1990 buildings) proposed no less than a dozen new and renovated buildings for the school's Lincoln Park campus. One of the new buildings, The Theatre School, was given a prominent corner site at Fullerton and Racine and therefore was envisioned as a gateway to the campus from the west. In turn, the design by the East Coast firm of Cesar Pelli marks the corner at its highest point with a cantilevered two-story box housing the 100-seat Sondra & Denis Healy Theatre behind a translucent, north-facing glass wall. The massing of the five-story building below, beside, and behind this box serves to accentuate it as a special object propped upon the corner.

The cantilevered Healy Theatre marks the western gateway to the campus. (Credit Eric Allix Rogers, CAC Archive)

Much of the building is covered in limestone panels, interspersed with narrow windows. One large window atop the building gives a subtle glimpse into the theatrical realm and is echoed by a storefront at sidewalk level on Fullerton Avenue that reveals the lobby to the 250-seat Fullerton Stage. (Both theaters were designed with consultants Schuler Shook.) Entry to the building, though, is around the corner on Racine, next to glass-enclosed stairs. Past those, windows at sidewalk level provide views into the theater's costume and prop shops. Inside, the spaces were laid out so theatergoers are given even more behind-the-scenes glimpses, passing rehearsal spaces on the way to the theater on the fourth floor.

ION LINCOLN PARK

Antunovich Associates, 2006
1237 West Fullerton Avenue

When faced with building codes that required the steel structure of his towers to be covered in fireproofing, Mies van der Rohe famously added smaller steel sections to the facades, in effect expressing what was encased in concrete underneath. A similar sentiment can be found here, where five-story steel columns marching along Fullerton Avenue give this 170-room apartment "community" for 580 DePaul University students a contemporary "loft" expression.

(Credit John Hill)

ROW 2750

Hartshorne Plunkard Architects, 2010
2750 North Lakewood Avenue

These modern rowhouses of brick, metal, and wood sit at the northern end of a one-block stretch of unexceptional neo-traditional townhouses on wide lots, facing each other across some of the last remaining street railroad tracks in the city.

W Foster Ave (5200N)
See Map
11
Lincoln Square, etc.
Lake Michigan
W Lawrence Ave (4800N)
Montrose
W Montrose Ave (4400N)
Montrose Harbor
N Lincoln Ave
N Clark St
Graceland Cemetery
N Broadway
N Lake Shore Dr
Irving Park
W Irving Park Rd (4000N)
Sheridan
Immaculata High School
95 Claremont House
W Byron St
Alta Vista Terrace
Center on Halsted 92
W Waveland Ave
Gallagher Way
93 Town Hall Apartments
Addison
W Addison St (3600N)
Lane Tech College Prep High School
Addison
1-mile radius
WMS Gaming
Paulina
Southport
W Roscoe St
96 WMS Boathouse at Clark Park
Yao House
W Belmont Ave (3200N)
Belmont
91 Advocate Illinois Masonic Medical Center
W Barry Ave
Lakeview Residence
Wellington
Lake Shore Dr 90 Residence
W Wellington Ave
94 Lathrop Homes
Presence Center for Advanced Care
W Diversey Pkwy (2800N)
Diversey
Kennedy Expy
N California Ave (2800W)
N Western Ave (2400W)
N Damen Ave (2000W)
N Clybourn Ave
N Ashland Ave (1600W)
N Southport Ave
N Racine Ave (1200W)
N Sheffield Ave
N Halsted St (800W)
N Lakeview Ave
Lincoln Park
W Fullerton Ave (2400N)
Fullerton
Chicago River North Branch
N Lincoln Ave
See Map
13
Bucktown, etc.
W Armitage Ave (2000N)
See Map
9
Lincoln Park
W North Ave (1600N)

10 Lakeview & North Center

Chicago tripled its area in 1889 with the annexation of four townships north and south of the city. One of them was Lake View, which had close to 50,000 people living in the area east of Western Avenue from Fullerton Avenue up to Devon Avenue. This extensive area, which boomed after annexation thanks to the subsequent northward extension of streetcar lines and then the "L," is now home to neighborhoods such as Lincoln Square, North Center, Edgewater, Uptown, Andersonville, and Bowmanville; the last two actually take their name from villages that were part of the township at the time of annexation. Today, the Lakeview (one word) neighborhood is smaller than in the late 19th century but still includes a large area, covering the blocks east of Ravenswood Avenue between Diversey Parkway and Irving Park Road.

East of Halsted Street is often referred to as Lakeview East, where, in the 1850s, the hotel that gave the township its name was founded. Guests at Lake View House, at Grace Street and the lakefront, once had an unimpeded view of Lake Michigan. Halsted Street also came into play around the time of annexation as the western boundary of fire limits in Lake View. This led to the construction of masonry buildings to the east, a condition still apparent in the taller apartment buildings in the neighborhood that took advantage of their proximity to the lake. (The 1893 Brewster Apartments on Diversey is a great example.) Finally, Halsted Street was the site of the township's first public building, the Town Hall, constructed in 1872 on the northwest corner of Addison Avenue.

West of Halsted Street, historically referred to as Old Lake View, did not have restrictions on wood-frame construction, so the area was covered with workers' cottages tied to the industry found along the Ravenswood Corridor and factories along the North Branch of the Chicago River. This late-19th-century housing stock served immigrants from Sweden and Germany; the latter's beer gardens arose from Lake View not being a dry township, unlike the others annexed in 1889. Although the wood-frame houses and beer gardens are long gone, the low-scale fabric of the former continues in the residential two-flats and townhouses infilling the blocks between commercial streets, while the drink and merriment of the latter is concentrated in the blocks around the "Friendly Confines" of Wrigley Field. Appropriately called Wrigleyville, this area south of Graceland Cemetery is anchored by the historical home of the Chicago Cubs, which has remained remarkably intact since 1914 but is at the heart of mixed-use "lifestyle" development this century.

The area west of Ravenswood Avenue includes the neighborhoods North Center, Roscoe Village, and an extension of Lakeview now called West Lakeview, signifying the appeal of the neighborhood to the east and the reach of its gentrification. Ironically, the 19th-century wood-frame cottages in the area sat near the brickyards along the North Branch of the Chicago River, which served the city's insatiable thirst for noncombustible construction after the Great Fire of 1871.

90

LAKE SHORE DRIVE RESIDENCE

Wheeler Kearns Architects, 2011

310 West Wellington Street

Bus: #151 to Sheridan Road at Wellington Avenue

The handful of blocks east of Sheridan Road, from Diversey Parkway to Belmont Avenue, is filled mainly with apartment buildings and medical facilities. But the eastern portion of the block bounded by Wellington Avenue on the south and Barry Avenue on the north is an exception. Since 1913, it has been home to the 16,000-square-foot Meeker Mansion. A developer bought the mansion along Barry and its 1.6-acre lot facing the park in 2005, subsequently cutting up the mansion into condos and tearing down later additions on the site to create parcels for "townhouses, rowhouses and single-family homes built of stone and masonry."[1] In the design of this three-story house by Wheeler Kearns, stone is the material of choice, though executed in a more modern style than must have been anticipated a half-decade earlier. Split-faced limestone is used at the base, raising the house upon a plinth, while the upper floors are clad in smooth limestone. Windows are fairly large but sized and located for privacy from the neighbors in their taller buildings.

The modern manse is set back from the street to preserve as much of the lot as possible. (Credit Angie McMonigal Photography)

PRESENCE CENTER FOR ADVANCED CARE

RTKL (now CallisonRTKL), 2015

North Sheridan Road and West Surf Street

With its dramatic Y-shaped building overlooking Lincoln Park, Presence Saint Joseph Hospital is a distinctive structure. RTKL's hospital addition to the west reiterates the older building's distinctive *parti* of a prominent narrow end-wall bracketed by stone walls, here giving the hospital an identity on Sheridan Road.

91

ADVOCATE ILLINOIS MASONIC MEDICAL CENTER, CENTER FOR ADVANCED CARE

SmithGroupJJR, 2015

West Barry Avenue and North Wilton Avenue

Train: Brown, Purple to Wellington

Bus: #8 to Halsted Street at Clark Street/Barry Avenue

In the 21st century, hospitals have turned into the urban equivalent of universities, growing over time and gobbling up land for more buildings. Previous to the new Center for Advanced Care, Advocate Health Care's Illinois Masonic Medical Center "campus" in Lakeview was made up of a handful of buildings on different blocks linked by bridges (the Lurie Children's Hospital [**69**] in Streeterville is another example). But this new three-story building for cancer care and digestive health connects directly to the main hospital, thereby closing off Nelson Street and creating its own superblock. For those not accessing

The curved glass wall follows the entry drop-off and connects to the main hospital. (Credit Angie McMonigal Photography)

the new Center for Advanced Care from within the hospital, there is a drop-off on Nelson accessed from Sheffield Avenue on the west. Here is the most distinctive part of SmithGroupJJR's design, a glass wall that starts at the existing brick hospital and curls around, wavelike toward the west, inviting people into the hospital and stealing glances from the nearby "L" tracks.

YAO HOUSE
Perimeter Architects, 2010
932 West Fletcher Avenue

The standing seam metal wall facing the "L" tracks 30 feet away wraps up and over the roof, a fitting expression for the renovation of a three-story house where the new walls incorporate spray-in polyurethane insulation to keep the sounds of rumbling trains at bay.

(Credit Anna Munzesheimer, CAC Archive)

LAKEVIEW RESIDENCE
Perimeter Architects, 2009
3028 North Southport Avenue

The triangular lot for this house, only one block from diagonal Lincoln Avenue, is half the size of a typical lot, making it a tight squeeze for the house and the required parking. John Issa of Perimeter Architects raised the top floor of the three-story house on stilts, creating a small yard but also setting an example of how even the most awkward urban spaces can be useful when considered creatively.

(Credit Angie McMonigal Photography)

92

CENTER ON HALSTED

Gensler, 2007

3656 North Halsted Street

Train: Red to Addison

Bus: #8 to Halsted Street at Waveland Avenue

The glassy corner is visible in the foreground, while the 1924 building incorporated into the project is seen in the distance. (Credit Eric Allix Rogers, CAC Archive)

If the twenty-two bronze pylons wrapped in rainbow rings signal that Halsted Street north of Belmont Street serves as the epicenter of the largest LGBTQ community in Chicago, then the Center on Halsted is certainly its heart. The community center's roots extend back to 1973, when Gay Horizons, a volunteer-run meeting place, was started. The organization grew in the ensuing decades and relocated numerous times, eventually buying a property at Halsted Street and Waveland Avenue in 2000 for what would become its permanent home for its diverse programs and services. Gensler's design places the entrance at the corner in a glass box that, in the words of the Center, "proclaim[s] boldly LGBTQ people will no longer reside behind a curtain but will be visible for the world to see."[2] This transparency extends away from the corner until it reaches a 1924 brick-and-terra-cotta building on the south that was incorporated into the project and now houses a grocery store. The Center's second floor is given over to offices and other administrative functions, while the top floor has an auditorium, a gymnasium, and a roof terrace that overlooks Halsted Street.

93

TOWN HALL APARTMENTS

Gensler, 2014
3600 North Halsted Street
Train: Red to Addison
Bus: #8 to Halsted Street at Addison Street

Seven years after the Center on Halsted opened (**92**), an affordable senior housing project devoted to the LGBTQ community was completed right next door. This location for the Town Hall Apartments is logical, given its proximity to the Center (a partner on the project). But the site is also symbolic, as it involves the transformation of the decommissioned 1907 Town Hall police station, where many would-be residents were arrested in the 1970s and 1980s during raids on gay establishments—"From a place of degradation to a place of honor"[3] is how developer Heartland Alliance describes it. Gensler "completes" this block on Halsted Street with a three-part design: six floors of studio and one-bedroom units, a one-story retail "porch" in front of the resi-

The green and blue panels of the new building echo the Town Hall's patinated cornice. (Credit Lynn Becker)

dences (with terraces), and the renovation of the old police station into common spaces for residents and for the Center on Addison, the Center on Halsted's senior program. Architecturally, the most interesting aspect of the design is the residential block's facade, an abstract composition with narrow windows, duotone gray panels, and angled green and blue panels that give the building a shifting appearance depending on one's position, while echoing the copper cornice of the original Town Hall.

GALLAGHER WAY

Stantec (formerly VOA Associates), 2019
1060 West Addison Street

(Credit Angie McMonigal Photography)

Most of the Chicago Cubs' multiphase 1060 Project, as it's also known, consists of the restoration, renovation, and expansion of various features and public amenities within the 1914 "Friendly Confines," but Hickory Street Capital (the real estate arm of the Ricketts family who owns the team) has reached out into the neighborhood with a development along Clark Street that includes a plaza, office building, hotel, and plenty of commercial space for bars.

94 LATHROP HOMES

bKL Architecture, 2019
2000 West Diversey Parkway
Bus: #50 to Damen at Diversey/Clybourn, #76 to Diversey at Damen/Clybourn

The Lathrop Homes, straddling Diversey Parkway between the North Branch of the Chicago River and Damen and Clybourn Avenues, is notable as one of Chicago's first public housing projects (completed in 1938) and for being on the National Register of Historic Places (added in 2012, six years after the CHA announced its intent to raze the project). The latter pointed to preservation rather than demolition for a mixed-income development that renovates existing buildings and adds new ones. It also led to new construc-

The Hoyne building is one of two new buildings designed by bKL to contextualize with the 1930s housing project. (Credit Tom Rossiter)

tion whose designs closely match the existing low-scale buildings with their predominant brickwork. A six-story, 59-unit residential building at 2737 North Hoyne Avenue was designed by bKL Architecture with masonry facades and divided-lite windows that could mistake new for old.

95

CLAREMONT HOUSE

Brininstool + Lynch, 2007
3909 North Claremont Street
Train: Brown to Irving Park
Bus: #80 to Irving Park Road at Oakley Avenue

Architect Brad Lynch tore down his small 1940s bungalow on a North Center street full of other bungalows and two-flats to build a house for his family that is more befitting the regional modernism of the firm he founded with David Brininstool in 1989. There's a lot of glass—the living room's ten-foot-square picture window fronts the house—but it is balanced by brick surfaces, which help the modern house fit with its neighbors, and by unexpected flourishes of zinc on the side walls. The large front window extends down as a clerestory for the bedroom on the lower level, but the bedrooms on the second floor face the side yard to the north, giving them privacy behind the solid street-side wall. This privacy is balanced by the "publicity" of the first floor, which offers views through the open plan and matching rear window to the sunken courtyard when the shades are open—as clear an expression as any of the modern ideals at play in Lynch's architecture.

Large windows enable views completely through the house. (Credit Christopher Barrett)

96

WMS BOATHOUSE AT CLARK PARK

Studio Gang, 2013

3400 North Rockwell Street

Bus: #152 to Addison Street at Rockwell Street

Jeanne Gang and her firm have been infatuated with water for some time now: metaphorically, in the rippling facade of the Aqua Tower (**14**) and directly, in landscape projects at the Lincoln Park Zoo (**84**) and at Northerly Island (**44**), where an old airport was turned into a habitat for fish and other creatures. An addition to these water-related projects is the WMS Boathouse at Clark Park, situated along the Chicago River about eight miles north and west of the Loop. It is the second of four boathouses planned by Mayor Rahm Emanuel for spots on the river's north and south branches; the first to open was at Ping Tom Memorial Park (**49**) in 2013.

Gang and company's design separates the boathouse into two buildings: a two-story fieldhouse on the south and a one-story boat storage on the

The serrated profile of the boat storage building as seen on approach from the east. (Credit Steve Hall © Hedrich Blessing)

From the river, the two-story field house is seen on the right. (Credit Steve Hall © Hedrich Blessing)

The field house stair, as elsewhere, has a ceiling made of plywood. (Credit Steve Hall © Hedrich Blessing)

north; located between is a courtyard that aligns with the access down to the water. Each building has a distinctive serrated roofline seen from the river on the west and the approach on foot from the east. The peaks and valleys are like a solidification of the motion and rhythm of rowing, akin to Eadweard Muybridge's documentation of it with his stop-motion camera. More than eye candy, the alternating roof trusses create a warped surface and clerestory openings that bring southern light into the spaces.

Each building is clad in zinc and slate, dark materials that give them a sense of solidity while also accentuating the interior spaces when artificial lights glow from the inside in the evening. On the interior, plywood is used for the walls and ceilings and exposed concrete on the floors. It all adds up to an inexpensive building ($8.8 million) that hardly looks cheap.

3401 NORTH CALIFORNIA

Solomon Cordwell Buenz (SCB), 2012
3401 North California Street

(Credit John Hill)

Right across the river from the WMS Boathouse at Clark Park (**96**) is the technology campus originally built for WMS Gaming (it left in 2018). The company donated money for the boathouse's construction and then doubled its square footage with this five-story reflective-glass office building that has, appropriately, a roof terrace overlooking the river and the boathouse.

Northtown Apartments and Branch Library
W Pratt Blvd (6800n)
See Map
20
North Suburbs
Warren Park
Lake Michigan
Loyola
Richard J Klarchek Information Commons 101
W Devon Ave (6400N)
Institute of Environmental Sustainability 102
W Granville Ave
Granville
W Peterson Ave (6000N)
Thorndale
W Thorndale Ave
W Ardmore Ave
Periscope House
Rosehill Cemetery
W Ridge Ave
Bryn Mawr
W Bryn Mawr Ave (5600N)
Edgewater Beach Hotel
100 Rogers Park Montessori School
W Balmoral Ave
1-mile radius
Berwyn
N California Ave (2800W)
N Lincoln Ave
N Western Ave (2400W)
N Damen Ave (2000W)
N Ravenswood Ave
N Ashland Ave (1600W)
N Clark St
Myron Bachman House
N Broadway
N Sheridan Rd
N Marine Dr
N Lake Shore Dr
W Foster Ave (5200N)
W Winnemac Ave
99 Doblin Residence
Argyle
W Argyle St
97 Argyle
98 Yannell Net-Zero Energy Residence
W Ainslie St
N Rockwell St
Ravenswood
W Lawrence Ave (4800N)
Lawrence
Rockwell
Western
Damen
Wilson
Krause Music Store
W Wilson Ave
Old Town School of Folk Music
Lycée Français de Chicago
Pensacola Place
Montrose
W Montrose Ave (4400N)
N Lincoln Ave
Graceland Cemetery
See Map
10
Lakeview &
North Center
N Broadway
Irving Park
W Irving Park Rd (4000N)
Sheridan

11 Lincoln Square, Ravenswood, Bowmanville, Edgewater, & Rogers Park

This chapter presents buildings in a handful of neighborhoods that reach from Montrose Avenue on the south to the city limits on the north, where Chicago meets Evanston.

Boundaries between Lincoln Square and Ravenswood are blurry, to the extent that the two monikers are used interchangeably. Generally, Lincoln Square refers to the commercial areas along Lincoln Avenue, centered on the one-way stretch just south of Western Avenue. The area's German past is found in a few remaining bars and occasional festivals that are found along the diagonal thoroughfare. Ravenswood, on the other hand, is the primarily residential area around Lincoln Square extending east to Ravenswood Avenue, which sits astride the Chicago & North Western Railway tracks. While still home to some light industry, the neighborhood now houses arts institutions, and large mixed-use developments front this once industrial corridor, a testament to the area's growing appeal.

To the north of Ravenswood is Bowmanville, in the shadow of Rosehill Cemetery, and, to the east of it, Andersonville, a traditionally Swedish neighborhood centered at Clark Street and Foster Avenue. Bowmanville, one of the lesser known neighborhoods on the north side, has a history that recalls Streeterville (Chapter 7): Jesse Bowman was caught selling plots of land in the middle of the 19th century that he didn't own; he left town after the discovery but the area nevertheless takes his name.

The northernmost neighborhoods along Lake Michigan—Rogers Park and Edgewater—are also respectively the first and seventy-seventh of Chicago's 77 "community areas" as defined by sociologists in the 1920s. Although Edgewater didn't receive this status until 1980, when residents argued for its distinction from Uptown to the south, the land at the northern tip of Lake View Township dates back to the 1880s, when it was founded as a suburban subdivision under the Edgewater name. The area flourished after the city's 1889 annexation of Lake View, aided by the extension of the "L," the suburban character of the area, and its proximity to Lake Michigan. The current northern edge of Edgewater is Devon Avenue. Bordered by Rogers Park, Edgewater was incorporated as a village a decade before its founding and was annexed by Chicago in 1893. The area is best known as the home of Loyola University Chicago; its 30-acre lakefront campus extends into Edgewater to become the largest employer in both neighborhoods.

97

ARGYLE

Wheeler Kearns Architects, 2011
2575 West Argyle Street
Train: Brown to Western
Bus: #11 to Lincoln Avenue at Argyle Street

Northwest of the three-way intersection of Lawrence, Lincoln, and Western avenues that anchors the Lincoln Square neighborhood, a few east-west streets depart slightly from Chicago's grid, due in part to Lincoln Avenue's diagonal path and the parallel North Branch of the Chicago River a couple of blocks to the west. One of these streets, Argyle, jogs to create a one-block section lined primarily with bungalows and two-flats—those vernacular housing types that place the two-story dwelling toward the street, a garage along the alley, and a yard between the two. This modern house by Wheeler Kearns, which replaces an old two-story frame house on a wider-than-normal lot, departs from those types in a number of ways: 1) it is only one story high facing the street; 2) it places most of the living spaces in a

Just visible behind the one-story front facade is a two-story volume in the middle of the lot. (Credit John Hill)

two-story volume in the middle of the lot (visible from across the street); 3) this footprint creates two courtyards, a small one for the entry beyond the stainless steel door and a larger one by the garage; and 4) there's the yard, which is dark mulch instead of grass. It is a study in oppositions, yet one that does not scream for attention.

OLD TOWN SCHOOL OF FOLK MUSIC

VOA Associates (now Stantec), 2012
4545 North Lincoln Avenue

(Credit Frank Hashimoto)

Founded in 1957, the Old Town School of Folk Music expanded into Lincoln Square in 1998, inside the former Hild Library renovated by Wheeler Kearns Architects. The school's success necessitated a new three-story facility directly across the street housing classrooms, a café, and a performance space behind a brick-and-glass facade with ornamented terra-cotta spandrels.

LYCÉE FRANÇAIS DE CHICAGO

STL Architects, 2015
1929 West Wilson Avenue

(Credit Frank Hashimoto)

Located on the site of the old Ravenswood Hospital, this new private, dual-language, pre-k-through-12th-grade school building has four floors of classrooms, a cafeteria, a gymnasium, office, and playing fields. The first floor is all-glass, while the upper floors feature a random smattering of square windows with red frames popping out against the white metal cladding.

98

YANNELL NET-ZERO ENERGY RESIDENCE

Farr Associates, 2009

4895 North Ravenswood Avenue

Train: Brown to Damen

Bus: #81 to Lawrence Avenue at Ravenswood Avenue

Instead of LEED Certification, or even LEED Platinum (the USGBC green rating system's highest level), the next generation of green buildings is striving for net zero, where a building produces as much energy as it consumes over the course of a year. Designing for net-zero involves a combination of active

Solar panels are mounted to the butterfly roofs that capture rainwater for irrigation. (Credit Eric Allix Rogers, CAC Archive)

and passive energy strategies. Jonathan Boyer of Farr Associates, a firm that champions green buildings and sustainable urbanism, designed active energy strategies that include three elements taking advantage of the butterfly roofs: solar panels for electricity, solar thermal panels for hot water and radiant heating, and rainwater recycling for irrigation. In addition, the home includes a geothermal system for heating and cooling and the city's first residential graywater system. Passive energy strategies focus on a southern orientation for maximizing solar heat gain in the winter, while generous overhangs shield the large glass walls from the high summer sun. Splitting the house into two volumes (two stories on the north and one story on the south, connected by an enclosed corridor) maximizes cross-ventilation, creates different zones for more efficient heating and cooling, and results in a courtyard and another yard off the alley. Although not all of the numerous green features have performed as anticipated,[1] Michael Yannell's ambitious house pushes urban dwellings in a new, much needed direction, at the same time giving it an appealing environmental expressionism.

99

DOBLIN RESIDENCE

Valerio Dewalt Train Associates, 2002/2014
5017 North Ravenswood Avenue
Train: Brown to Damen
Bus: #81 to Lawrence Avenue at Ravenswood Avenue

A dozen years after this neo-industrial house was inserted into the brick remains of a 1940s-era factory in the Ravenswood Corridor, the same architects were called upon to design an addition for the expanding family of Bruce Doblin. The first iteration of the house, completed in 2002 when Doblin was a bachelor, presented to the street low walls of galvanized metal with two huge scissor doors (each 24-feet wide and 12-feet high): the one on the left for the garage, the one on the right opening up to the courtyard behind it. These doors remain in the 2014 design, but a section of the wall above the garage door was removed for the addition, which sits above the garage and emphasizes the one-story house's vertical expansion through two tall-and-skinny windows that project from the galvanized metal wall. Like the net-zero house (**98**) one block to the south, the Doblin Residence is visible to Metra riders as they zip by; astute ones are able to catch a glimpse of the steel and glass home that lies behind the galvanized metal.

The addition uses the same galvanized metal but turns it ninety degrees to horizontal. (Credit John Hill)

100

ROGERS PARK MONTESSORI SCHOOL

OWP/P (now CannonDesign), 2006; George Beach and Jeremy Olsen, 2016

1800 West Balmoral Avenue

Bus: #92 to Foster Avenue at Ravenswood Avenue

Although Rogers Park Montessori School (RPMS) is no longer located in Rogers Park, it continues the teaching philosophy established by Maria Montessori in the early 1900s. The nonprofit school moved to the Bowmanville neighborhood, a small triangular area south of Rosehill Cemetery, two years after it bought the land along the Metra tracks. A focus on the classroom environment and independent learning for children age two to fourteen is paramount, finding physical expression in bell-shaped classrooms that create additional, informal spaces in the corridors and on terraces; the latter are visible

A small patch of green is located in front of the green entry wall. (Credit Frank Hashimoto)

as small openings cut into the reddish precast concrete walls facing the Metra tracks on the east and a private road on the west. Complementary green precast concrete walls are found at the front and rear of the two-story school from 2006, respectively signaling the entrance and the gymnasium. The popularity of RPMS's approach is evident in the new wing on the north, added ten years later; the yellow addition is propped upon columns to retain spaces in the school's existing parking lot.

(Credit Frank Hashimoto)

PERISCOPE HOUSE

Nicholas Design Collaborative, 2014

5833 North Magnolia Avenue

This renovation of a 1970s-era house lifts the second-story "periscope," as architect Peter Nicholas calls it, above the existing eight-foot-high wall at the front of the house. The rear elevation is covered in fiber cement panels in primary colors, a nod to the way designers Charles and Ray Eames used ordinary materials in extraordinary ways in 1950s California.

101

RICHARD J. KLARCHEK INFORMATION COMMONS

Solomon Cordwell Buenz (SCB), 2008

6501 North Kenmore Avenue

Train: Red to Loyola

Bus: #147 to Sheridan Road at Kenmore Avenue

Although Loyola University Chicago celebrated its 100th year as a chartered university in 2009, the Jesuit school's origins go back to 1870, when it was established as St. Ignatius College on Chicago's west side. Loyola moved to its Lake Shore Campus, which bridges the Edgewater and Rogers Park neighborhoods, just a few years after it was made a university. Today it is comprised of four campuses: two in Chicago, one in Maywood (just west of Chicago), and one in Rome. A 2004–2009 university-wide strategic plan, timed to its centennial, envisioned for the Lake Shore campus a number of renovations and new buildings, the latter including a library expansion designed by SCB, which worked on the campus master plan (with SmithGroupJJR) and has designed numerous buildings for Loyola over a span of three decades.

Clear glass and open floor plates between the limestone "bookends" ensure transparency through the building. (Credit John Hill)

The east facade overlooks Lake Michigan, here covered in ice. (Credit John Hill)

The three-story Information Commons (IC) sits on a prominent lakefront site between the Cudahy Library on the north and the Madonna della Strada Chapel on the south; the IC is connected to each through enclosed links. Limestone "bookends" with arched windows and hip roofs enclose glass walls facing the lake on the east and a large quad on the west. Much of the design attention appears to have gone into these low-iron glass walls, which have automated windows for natural ventilation, automated shades on the east and blinds on the west for minimizing heat gain, and a striking cable-supported exterior wall on the campus side. Open floor plates combine with the glass walls to prioritize transparency inside and through the building.

102

INSTITUTE OF ENVIRONMENTAL SUSTAINABILITY

Solomon Cordwell Buenz (SCB), 2013

6349 North Kenmore Avenue

Train: Red to Loyola

Bus: #147 to Sheridan Road at Kenmore Avenue

Five years after SCB added the Information Commons (IC) (**101**) to Loyola University Chicago's Lake Shore campus, the architecture firm took on one of the school's most ambitious projects, south and west of Sheridan Road, on the Edgewater side of campus. The Institute of Environmental Sustainability (IES) houses Loyola's sustainability programs as well as research facilities focused on urban agriculture, all geared toward making it one of the most sustainable urban campuses in the United States. The IES is made up of three interconnected buildings—the renovated BVM Hall (purchased from the Sisters of Charity of the Blessed Virgin Mary), a freshman and sophomore dormitory, and the Ecodome/atrium between—that

The greenhouselike curved wall hints at the urban agriculture research going on inside. (Credit John Hill)

Curved steel trusses support the glass enclosing the three-story atrium. (Credit John Hill)

echo SCB's earlier design of the IC, where a central glass wall is bookended between masonry walls, in this case brick.

Like the IC, the west-facing glass wall of the Ecodome gets all of the attention. Starting from the top of the first floor, the glass wall bows out then curves up and over to serve as the roof of the three-story atrium. The roof is designed to catch rainwater, draw air from its low point to its high point for natural ventilation, and function as a greenhouse for the urban farm inside. Curved steel trusses with a triangular cross section (designed with engineers from Halvorson and Partners) support the glass wall, accentuating the space's curved and sloping section. Operable shades sit below the trusses, while plants climb the masonry back wall, where the classrooms, labs, and support spaces of the IES are located.

While the project was nearing completion, Loyola successfully purchased and vacated the 6300 block of North Kenmore Avenue, subsequently turning it into a pedestrian walkway that connects some of the school's numerous buildings, like the IES.

NORTHTOWN APARTMENTS AND BRANCH LIBRARY

Perkins and Will, 2019

6800 North Western Avenue

(Credit © James Steinkamp Photography)

One of three co-located affordable housing/public library projects spearheaded by the city (see also **103** and **133**), the design lifts 44 senior housing apartments in a sinuous two-story volume above the highly transparent library at grade. "V"-shaped concrete columns at the corner of Western Avenue and Pratt Boulevard enable an auditorium beneath the apartments and signal this project—developed by Evergreen Real Estate Group—as something special in West Ridge.

West Side

Kimball
N Elston Ave
N Pulaski Rd (4000W)
N Kimball Ave
N Kedzie Ave (3200W)
N California Ave
N Western Ave (2400W)
N Damen Ave
W Montrose Ave
N Narragansett Ave (6400W)
N Austin Ave
N Central Ave (5600W)
N Laramie Ave
N Cicero Ave (4800W)
W Irving Park Blvd (4000N)
•103 Independence Apartments and Branch Library
Schurz High School
Grayland
Addison
W Addison St
N Milwaukee Ave
•104 Northeastern Illinois University El Centro Campus
105• Intrinsic School
W Belmont Ave (3200N)
Belmont
Kennedy Expy
Belmont Gateway
Harmony House Net Zero No Kill Cat Shelter
W Diversey Pkwy
Flexhouse2 106•
Logan Square
Acero Roberto Clemente Charter School 108
W Fullerton Ave (2400N)
Haas Park Fieldhouse
Healey
California
Flexhouse 106•
"L"
Hanson Park
Gatewood
W Armitage Ave (2000N)
•107 F10 House
Grand/Cicero
North Grand High School
W North Ave (1600N)
3-mile radius
Damen
W Grand Ave
Humboldt Park
•113 Erie Elementary Charter School
Paseo Boricua
W Division St
N Oak Park Ave
N Ridgeland Ave
By the Hand Club for Kids & Moving East Charter School 111
N Kostner Ave
W Chicago Ave (800N)
Garfield Park Conservatory City Garden 112
109 Oak Park Public Library
Christy Webber Landscapes
Kedzie
Western Ave
W Lake St
Cicero
Pulaski
Oak Park
Austin
Laramie
California
Peace Corner Youth Center
Conservatory-Central Park Dr
Breakthrough FamilyPlex and Community Center
W Madison St (0N/0S)
W Jackson Blvd
•110 Christ the King Jesuit College Preparatory School
Dwight D. Eisenhower Expy
Oak Park
Austin
Cicero
Pulaski
Kedzie-Homan
Western
W Roosevelt Rd (1200S)
Douglas Park
54th/Cermak
W Cermak Rd (2200S)

Irving Park, Avondale, Kilbourn Park, Logan Square, Hermosa, Galewood, Oak Park, Austin, Garfield Park, & Humboldt Park

12

The large area covered in this chapter includes neighborhoods that stretch from Western Avenue—the western edge of Chicago from 1851 until 1869 (1889 in parts far north and south)—to the jagged line of today's city limits. These neighborhoods generally date their histories to the years around the time of the Great Fire of 1871. They grew in part because of trolley service and being located outside of the city's fire limits, which enabled cheaper frame construction. These neighborhoods were initially home to immigrant working-class populations—German, Polish, and Scandinavian, primarily—but saw an influx of Latinx and African American populations toward the end of the 20th century, with parts now seeing gentrification.

In the 19th century, Pennsylvania native John Lewis Cochran, who also developed Edgewater, was responsible for developing the village of Avondale, incorporated in 1869. In that year, the Avondale Mine disaster occurred near Plymouth, Pennsylvania, and given Cochran's background it's not surprising that a number of street names in the neighborhood are named after towns in the Keystone State. Avondale extends from the Chicago River to Pulaski Street, between Belmont and Addison streets, but the presence of the Kennedy Expressway, which follows the earlier Union Pacific Northwest railroad tracks, cuts the area into residential and industrial chunks. Polish in its early years, west of Avondale is Kilbourn Park, centered by the namesake park.

South of Avondale is Logan Square, which also has a namesake park at its center, where Logan and Kedzie boulevards meet Milwaukee Avenue. The traditionally immigrant and Hispanic populations are giving way to gentrification, as the west side neighborhood bordering Bucktown on the east is now home to residential developments as well as microbreweries and urban farms. Some of this popularity can be attributed to the boulevards, the "emerald necklace" that links the neighborhood to Humboldt Park and, just recently, The 606 (**114**), a linear park to the south. A good deal of credit should go to block after block of intact residential streets with impressive mansions and three- and four-story "greystones," a number of them uniquely running perpendicular to the diagonal commercial thoroughfare of Milwaukee Avenue.

West of Pulaski Road, the western edge of Logan Square, is Hermosa, a predominantly Hispanic neighborhood that will forever be known as the birthplace of Walt Disney. Further west still is Galewood—sandwiched between the Milwaukee District West railroad tracks and Oak Park—and Austin, a primarily African American neighborhood that also borders the famous suburban home of Frank Lloyd Wright. South of Logan Square are the neighborhoods Humboldt Park and Garfield Park, which reach from Armitage Avenue all the way to the Eisenhower Expressway. As their names imply, they are oriented around two namesake parks that are also part of the three parks in the West Park System (Humboldt, Garfield, and Douglas Parks) laid out in the late 19th century.

103

INDEPENDENCE APARTMENTS AND BRANCH LIBRARY

John Ronan Architects, 2019

4024 North Elston Avenue

Train: Blue to Irving Park

Bus: #80 to Irving Park Road at Elston/Monticello Avenues

In mid-2017, the Chicago Housing Authority and the Chicago Public Library announced a partnership that would lead to the construction of three projects pairing mixed-income housing with public libraries. The three projects, meant to strengthen their communities through the introduction of public space, broke ground in January 2018. The Independence Apartments and Branch Library is one of two (see also **133**) that opened just twelve months later, in January 2019. It's also the most striking. Panels in bright colors frame terraces that spread across the white corrugated metal facades. The white metal wraps all four sides of the apartment floors with rounded corners, softening the tall building's presence in the neighborhood.

The terraces visible along Elston signal some of the 44 subsidized apartments for seniors that are set back and above the two-story branch library that is tight to the sidewalk. Outside, with its gray facade and tinted glass storefront, the library is a dark foil to the bright, colorful apartment block. But

The colorful frames are meant to individualize the apartments, giving their residents a source of personal pride. (Credit John Ronan Architects; James Florio)

A green roof atop the parking garage is visible and accessible from the library's second floor. (Credit John Ronan Architects; James Florio)

With a double-height space along Elston, the branch library is an impressive space that belies its branch status. (Credit John Ronan Architects; James Florio)

inside, the library is full of natural light from glass walls facing the street, a clerestory at the base of the apartments, and a green roof toward the middle of the block.

The Independence Apartments and Branch Library was developed by Evergreen Real Estate Group, which was also responsible for the third colocated affordable housing/library project (see Chapter 11).

104

NORTHEASTERN ILLINOIS UNIVERSITY EL CENTRO CAMPUS

JGMA, 2014

3390 North Avondale Avenue

Train: Blue to Belmont

Bus: #82 to Kimball Avenue at Avondale/Henderson Avenues

As the name of one of Northeastern Illinois University's (NEIU) four locations implies, the El Centro campus is geared to providing education for the Hispanic community. It is located in Avondale, a largely Hispanic population between the Kennedy Expressway and the North Branch of the Chicago River about five-and-a-half miles northwest of the Loop. The site of the school is a difficult one, a one-block "island" between the Union Pacific Northwest railroad tracks and a jog in the Kennedy Expressway. Further, many of the nearby

Drivers on the Kennedy can be seen left of the building, here seen from its entry plaza. (Credit JGMA)

The southwest side of the building also features angled fins of blue and yellow. (Credit Tom Rossiter)

Curving second floor hall behind blue and yellow fins overlooking the Kennedy. (Credit Eric Allix Rogers, CAC Archive)

blocks are devoted to industry and big-box retail, resulting in a surrounding character that is more suburban than urban.

Juan Moreno, principal of JGMA (Juan Gabriel Moreno Architects), responded to this otherwise discouraging site by going with the flow: the three-story building curves like a boomerang to follow the Kennedy and give El Centro a strong identity. Angled two-color aluminum fins projecting from the glass walls provide a shifting impression, with blue surfaces facing east and yellow surfaces facing west—or to put it another way, one sees yellow during the inbound morning commute and blue during the outbound evening commute. While clearly designed to be seen from the expressway, the design includes a generous (if noisy) plaza by the entrance at the building's southeastern prow and a lobby with concrete surfaces and a ceiling that picks up on the pattern of parallel fins outside.

BELMONT GATEWAY

Ross Barney Architects, 2019
3355 West Belmont Avenue

(Credit courtesy Ross Barney Architects)

Yet another CTA station by the firm of Carol Ross Barney (see **47** and **125**), this one caters as much to bus riders as to people entering and exiting the Blue Line subway station. A striking blue canopy, inspired by the long-gone Olson Rug Park and Waterfall in Avondale, shelters people waiting for buses and creates a new neighborhood landmark at the corner of Belmont and Kimball Avenues.

105

INTRINSIC SCHOOL

Wheeler Kearns Architects, 2014

4540 West Belmont Avenue

Bus: #77 to Belmont Avenue at Kilbourn Avenue

The combination of digital technologies and new charter schools has led to a number of alternatives to traditional classrooms in Chicago, but none more daring than Intrinsic School, which was founded in 2013 as "a revolutionary new school model."[1] It purports to be the first school in Chicago designed for blended learning, which replaces some face-to-face instruction with web-based learning. Rather than standard classrooms with students in chairs facing the teacher at the front of the room, students learn in "pods" that are organized into smaller informal learning environments, such as the "Pop-Up Class" and "Genius Bar," which takes its name tellingly from Apple stores. Six pods for grades seven through twelve sit behind the two-story checkerboard that faces Belmont and a drop-off with landscapes designed by Wolff Landscape Architects on the west; at the rear of the school is a gymnasium and playing field. That the school is a composite of new construction and the transformation of an old lumberyard's buildings (the latter with exposed bowstring trusses) is evident on the east side, overlooking the alley.

The school's south and west checkerboard facades mask the industrial renovation underneath. (Credit Don Guss)

106

FLEXHOUSE AND FLEXHOUSE2

ISA (Interface Studio Architects), 2013, 2014

2805 West Shakespeare Avenue; Ridgeway Avenue and Shubert Avenue

Bus: #73 to Armitage Avenue at California Avenue; #76 to Diversey Avenue at Hamlin Avenue

Ranquist Development Group describes their Flexhouse developments as "a new type of home that is tuned to the 'new normal' of the twenty-first century."[2] Even if the fairly standard open plans and custom finishes give owners the flexibility that the name of the development implies, there is something traditional about the two iterations of Flexhouse, namely that they are rowhouses. Yet, outside of anomalies like Alta Vista Terrace near Wrigley Field and the McCormick Row House District near DePaul University, rowhouses are not a very common vernacular housing stock in Chicago, like two-flats and three-flats. But Flexhouse's rowhouse typology makes sense considering that ISA is from Philadelphia, where the firm has executed a number of contemporary updates to the rowhouse typology. Ranquist tapped ISA because of their 100K Houses, conceived as small, sustainable, and affordable dwellings for Philadelphia, built for $100,000.

The striped fiber cement panels and large windows of the first Flexhouse. (Credit John Hill)

ISA worked with architect of record Sullivan, Goulette & Wilson on Flexhouse to create eight dwellings that are served by a shared garage off the alley to the west.

The alternating angled geometries of the second Flexhouse. (Credit Nicholas James Photo)

The front facades are composed of alternated groupings of windows and striped gray fiber cement panels, giving some variation to the repeated houses. Ranquist and ISA (with Osterhaus McCarthy as architect of record this time) took things a bit further with Flexhouse 2, which occupies the majority of a city block. The developer nearly quadrupled the number of units from the first development, while the architect used angled geometries to create an alternating rhythm fronting the street.

(Credit Don Guss)

HARMONY HOUSE NET ZERO ENERGY ADOPTION CENTER

Farr Associates, 2013
2914 North Elston Avenue

White and yellow metal panels give this small building for Harmony House for Cats (the first net-zero commercial building in Chicago) a strong street presence along diagonal Elston Avenue. The LEED-certified platinum building is "C"-shaped, wrapping around a bright central courtyard where yellow panels predominate.

HAAS PARK FIELDHOUSE

Booth Hansen, 2010
2402 North Washtenaw Avenue

For several years, the City of Chicago commissioned prototype designs for many of its neighborhood public buildings, from fire and police stations to schools and libraries. Booth Hansen designed two prototype fieldhouses for the Chicago Park District, with one of the second, smaller iterations built in Logan Square's Haas Park.

"L"

Brininstool + Lynch, 2016
2211 North Milwaukee Avenue

The trend for transit-oriented developments—those providing fewer cars (or close to none, as in 1611 West Division [**122**]) than what the city requires due to proximity to public transit—continues with this six-story building. It accommodates 120 residential units but only about half as many parking spaces.

(Credit Eric Allix Rogers, CAC Archive)

107

F10 HOUSE

EHDD, 2004
1919 North Keeler Avenue
Bus: #73 to Armitage Avenue at Keeler Avenue

In 2000, the City of Chicago held a design competition under its Green Homes for Chicago program, which envisioned sustainable homes that working families could afford; at the time, building green meant higher upfront costs. One of the winners, San Francisco's Esherick Homsey Dodge & Davis (EHDD), called their design F10, (originally Factor10) since it strove to reduce its environmental impact by a factor of ten over the average American house. Built on an infill lot in the Hermosa neighborhood, the house calls attention to itself—if not its green

The red siding conceals a very "green" building. (Credit CAC Archive)

attributes—through its red siding. Made with reconstituted cement and a low-emission stain, the siding is just one of the house's numerous green features. Others are now fairly standard in houses in Chicago and elsewhere: super-insulated exterior walls, high fly-ash concrete, a whole-house fan, and a green roof, among others. Most unique is what sits behind the tall stair volume anchoring the north side of the house: a clerestory window lets south-facing winter sunlight hit a wall of water bottles that absorbs the heat during the day and radiates it back to warm the home at night.

NORTH GRAND HIGH SCHOOL

OWP/P (now CannonDesign), with VOA Associates (now Stantec), 2004
4338 West Wabansia Street

This sprawling high school in the Hermosa neighborhood is organized into two halves with classrooms to the west and the gymnasium and other big spaces to the east. A central corridor starts at the south, where the entry facade leans forward between masonry walls.

108

ACERO ROBERTO CLEMENTE SCHOOL

UrbanWorks, 2012
2050 North Natchez Avenue
Bus: #86 to Narragansett Avenue at Dickens Avenue

Acero Roberto Clemente School is one of fifteen charter schools run by Acero Schools. It is located in Galewood, a relatively little known neighborhood compared to its neighbor to the south: Oak Park, home to Frank Lloyd Wright and a large number of the buildings he designed. Some of the residential charm of Oak Park extends into Galewood, though a small chunk of the neighborhood to the north is cut by large industrial tracts lining the Milwaukee District West railroad tracks. The school straddles these two realms: it faces a residential street while it sits on a formerly industrial site just north of the Metra tracks.

The curved wood wall faces the railroad tracks to the south. (Credit Christopher Barrett)

Inside the southern volume is an impressive space that can be used by the community after school hours. (Credit Christopher Barrett)

The design by UrbanWorks, the firm founded by Patricia Saldaña Natke, responds to this location by splitting the building into two parts: the classrooms are positioned away from the tracks, while a taller volume with library and other common spaces is on the south. The latter is most striking, with all-glass walls facing east and west and wood-resin panels covering the curved wall facing the tracks—like a quarter-pipe for a giant skateboarder. The wood-resin panels also clad the classrooms, which have smaller windows and are framed by precast concrete panels. Still, most inviting is the curved volume whose spaces, sensibly, can be used by neighborhood organizations after school hours.

109

OAK PARK PUBLIC LIBRARY

Nagle Hartray Danker Kagan McKay with Eva Maddox Branded Environments, 2003

834 West Lake Street, Oak Park

Train: Green to Oak Park

Any new building in Oak Park will come under a good deal of scrutiny. This is after all the western suburb that was home to Frank Lloyd Wright and has more of his Prairie School buildings than any other place. This scrutiny was especially pronounced for the main branch of the Oak Park Public Library, which replaces a smaller 1964 library located directly across the street from Wright's Unity Temple. The architects at Nagle Hartray Danker Kagan McKay (now Sheehan Nagle Hartray Architecture) had to navigate approximately 25 public meetings to get a design the community would approve, and their resulting plan takes a smart approach: instead of trying to compete with Wright's concrete masterpiece across Lake Street to the south, the library orients itself to the east and Scoville Park, designed by Jens Jensen in 1913 and redesigned

Folded copper walls face Scoville Park on the east. (Credit John Hill)

Treelike columns hold the jagged roof overlooking the park. (Credit John Hill)

by Altamanu nearly one century later. Most of the library is housed in a straightforward three-story box covered in stone with punched openings, but on the east elevation, the top two floors project forward above a first-floor colonnade. These copper walls are subtly kinked in plan, culminating in a dramatically jagged roofline that gives the library a distinctive presence from the park, like a mountain peak in the prairie.

Interiors were designed with Eva Maddox Branded Environments (now Perkins and Will) and are oriented about a stair that library visitors will want to take: it is capped by a skylight that illuminates the decorative glass lining the stairs. Walk up to the third floor to see the wood beams and treelike wood columns holding up the roof's peaks. With views of the park through the fritted glass, this structure and the resulting building profile make perfect sense.

110

CHRIST THE KING JESUIT COLLEGE PREPARATORY SCHOOL

John Ronan Architects, 2010

5088 West Jackson Boulevard

Bus: #126 to Jackson at Lockwood

John Ronan takes his random-paneled brand—first used at the Gary Comer Youth Center (**170**) on the south side—to the west side, to the Austin neighborhood just east of suburban Oak Park. Here, Ronan aligns the facade's tricolor gray fiber-cement panels with the school's businesslike approach to education (as well as its Catholic mission—the Stations of the Cross are printed on panels facing the courtyard and the existing middle school). The building does not resemble a typical school from the street, but this is appropriate given that the private high school veers from the norm by incorporating the Cristo Rey work-study model: students pay for a portion of their education by working with Chicago companies.

The school's exterior has a businesslike attire of gray fiber-cement panels. (Credit © Nathan Kirkman 2010)

A small budget and accelerated schedule led Ronan to use rainscreen panels on top of a steel structure with precast concrete planks—all economical and quick to erect. The "L"-shaped plan—derived from the Jesuit educational concept of *Corus Personalis*, or care of the whole person—places the gymnasium on the north, while the cafeteria, library, and chapel are found within the three-story classroom wing along Jackson. This last piece, the Chapel of St. Ignatius of Loyola, anchors the east side of the ground floor, where glass block walls wrap three sides to bring gentle light to the space for 200 students, or about one-quarter of the school's enrollment. More light comes from a central skylight that pierces through the corridors above, an architectural gesture melding scholarship and religion.

Inside the Chapel of St. Ignatius Loyola with its glass-block walls and central skylight. (Credit © Nathan Kirkman 2010)

PEACE CORNER YOUTH CENTER
DeStefano Partners, 2011
5022 West Madison Street

This small building provides a place of recreation for children in South Austin, a rough neighborhood lacking in parks. The design by Avram Lothan (now with Lothan Van Hook DeStefano Architecture) places colorful volumes in an open, industrial-like space behind a translucent facade of polycarbonate sheets.

(Credit Lothan VanHook DeStefano Architecture)

111

BY THE HAND CLUB FOR KIDS AND MOVING EVEREST CHARTER SCHOOL

TEAM A, 2013, 2015
415 North Laramie Avenue; 416 North Laramie Avenue
Train: Green to Laramie

TEAM A, founded by Joe Buehler and Andy Leitz in 2009, realized their first two major buildings right across the street from each other in the city's Austin neighborhood. The location is not coincidental, since the two institutions share some facilities, and students from the charter school participate in the club's after-school programs. First to be built was the two-story, 26,300-square-foot

The inexpensive By the Hand Club for Kids building gains interest from a cantilevered glass corner. (Credit Don Guss)

Supergraphics meld with the architecture to make Moving Everest hard to miss. (Credit Don Guss)

building for By the Hand Club for Kids, a religious after-school program that began in 2001 near Cabrini-Green. The building is highlighted by images of children integrated into low-cost corrugated siding on the street facade and a corner window that cantilevers toward the Metra tracks. Two years later the building was joined by Moving Everest Charter School, a K-5 school that follows the blended-learning model, much like the nearby Intrinsic School (**105**). The entrance to the three-story, 53,000-square-foot school is on Laramie, but the most interesting side faces the parking lot and train tracks on the south, where images of children overlap a wall painted bright green.

112

GARFIELD PARK CONSERVATORY CITY GARDEN

Doug Hoerr Landscape Architecture, 2007

300 North Central Park Boulevard

Train: Green to Conservatory-Central Park Drive

Before William LeBaron Jenney designed the pioneering Home Insurance Building in the Loop, built in 1885, the versatile architect and engineer laid out the West Park System, an ensemble of three parks on the west side of the city linked by boulevards. Originally called North, Central, and South Parks, they are now known respectively as Humboldt, Garfield, and Douglas Parks. Garfield Park covers 184 acres in the East Garfield Park neighborhood, and much of its current character can be attributed to the great landscape architect Jens Jensen, who took over in 1905. On a map, the park looks like a sideways "T," with the middle leg devoted to a lagoon and "Gold Dome" fieldhouse. The leg south of Madison Street is home to a bandstand and playing fields, while

An arcing footbridge traverses the lily pool west of the Conservatory. (Credit John Hill)

the area north of the "L" tracks is given over to Jensen's huge Conservatory, which replaced smaller conservatories at each of the three parks.

Cor-ten steel walls hold back the earth of the mound bisected by a walking path. (Credit John Hill)

Doug Hoerr's firm (now Hoerr Schaudt Landscape Architects) worked with the Chicago Park District to turn the area next to the glass conservatory, formerly used as tennis courts, into a landscape for education and leisure. Small gardens where children and grown-ups can learn about urban gardening meld with paths that curl around the site. Highlights include the arcing footbridge across the lily pool, views of the Conservatory from the path around the elliptical lawn, and the path through a tall mound that approaches the height of the nearby elevated tracks.

(Credit Don Guss)

BREAKTHROUGH FAMILYPLEX AND COMMUNITY CENTER

Built Form, 2014
3219 West Carroll Avenue

The nonprofit Breakthrough Urban Ministries has three drop-in homeless shelters for homeless adults in East Garfield Park, all within a few blocks of each other. The FamilyPlex contains a day-care center as well as a community center, medical clinic, library, after-school classrooms, and fitness center. The project incorporates an adjacent building, but architecturally the focus is on the new construction, where walls clad in gray metal panels sit above a transparent first floor, and the second floor over the entrance is propped upon bent steel columns.

(Credit Eric Allix Rogers, CAC Archive)

CHRISTY WEBBER LANDSCAPES

Farr Associates, 2004
2900 West Ferdinand Street

This office building for a landscaping firm is part of the 12.5-acre Ranch Verde eco-industrial park tucked between two rail yards in East Garfield Park. Farr Associates, which also designed the park's Center for Green Technology (it unfortunately closed in 2014), expresses the building's green technology in a lean-to wall with solar panels at the entrance.

113

ERIE ELEMENTARY CHARTER SCHOOL

John Ronan Architects, 2013

1405 North Washtenaw Avenue

Train: Blue to Western

Erie Neighborhood House's charter school for kindergarten through eighth grade opened in a former Humboldt Park Catholic school in 2005, one year after Mayor Richard M. Daley launched the Renaissance 2010 initiative focused on creating one hundred new schools in the city. Lacking a gymnasium and other facilities, the school tore down the convent next door on the corner and erected this four-story addition. Ronan's design places classrooms, library, and computer lab on the first two floors so the community can use the spaces after hours. The gymnasium is upstairs next to a rooftop playground that can be seen through an opening in the exterior wall at the corner, one of eight large openings on the addition's three sides. The addition's character derives from the facade's huge precast concrete panels in shades of beige and gray, with ground and polished finishes that are, respectively, rough and smooth to the touch. Be sure to take a peek at the alley side, where the fourth floor mechanical space is shielded by a panel perforated with a mysterious pattern of dots.

The double-height entrance is tucked behind the large window facing Washtenaw Avenue. (Credit Steve Hall © Hedrich Blessing, 2013)

W Fullerton Pkwy (2400n)
116 Finfrock House
Chicago River North Branch
W Webster Ave
Kennedy Expy
W Armitage Ave (2000N)
N Winchester Ave
N Wolcott Ave
N Wood St
N Paulina St
Clybourn
Western
W Cortland St
St Mary of the Angels
Leavitt Residence 115
120 Chicago Townhouse
W Bloomingdale Ave
The 606 114
1748 North Winchester
119 Wood House
W Wabansia Ave
1713 North Wood
2136-2150
West North Avenue
118 1617 North Wolcott
121 Fletcher Jones Mercedes-Benz of Chicago
W North Ave (1600N)
Damen
117 Urban Sandbox
1/2-mile radius
Wicker Park
N Milwaukee Ave
N Western Ave (2400W)
N Leavitt St
N Damen Ave (2000W)
N Ashland Ave (1600W)
Division
St Mary of Nazarene Hospital
W Division St
1611 West Division 122
Holy Trinity Russian Orthodox Cathedral
W Augusta Blvd
N Hoyne Ave
N Wolcott Ave
N Wood St
N Paulina St
N Noble St
W Chicago Ave (800N)
Volume Gallery
W Huron St
C3 Prefab v1.1
2002 West Ohio
W Ohio St
C3 Prefab v1.0
Pfanner House
123 Brick-Weave House
Upton's Naturals 124
W Grand Ave
N Ogden Ave
Western Ave

13 Bucktown, Wicker Park, & West Town

The neighborhoods in this chapter are located directly west of the Kennedy Expressway. (East of the Kennedy is the Industrial Corridor, a good chunk of it being transformed into Lincoln Yards, a mixed-use development in the works since 2018.) It's not the Kennedy's diagonal path, paralleling the nearby Chicago River, that gives these neighborhoods their character, though—it is Milwaukee Avenue, which also cuts a northwesterly path across the west side. Much as it was as an Indian trail, then a plank road bringing farm products into the city, and then as the "Polish Corridor" extending from Division Street all the way up to Avondale, Milwaukee Avenue remains the commercial and transportation spine of these neighborhoods. The density of commercial activity, and therefore of impressive commercial buildings historically, happens where this diagonal thoroughfare intersects major east-west streets, particularly Division Street and North Avenue. These main arteries have seen an influx of new condominium buildings, while the residential streets lined with 19th-century cottages and brick two- and three-flats have been either torn down or are being joined by the contemporary equivalent: houses and condos in neo-traditional garb.

North Avenue is one of the major east-west spines in the area that defines the edge of two popular neighborhoods. North of North Avenue is Bucktown, whose name subtly references the Polish immigrants that settled in the area shortly after Chicago was incorporated as a city in 1837—the area was nicknamed "goat prairie" in its early days. South of North Avenue is Wicker Park, whose namesake park is located on Damen Avenue a couple blocks south of North Avenue. Their shared intersection of Damen, Milwaukee, and North avenues is a busy commercial hub that was an epicenter of the arts community that first arose in the last decades of the 20th century and thrives today. As sociologists such as Sharon Zukin have explored at length,[1] artists in search of affordable rent and large spaces have inadvertently paved the way for gentrification, much to the chagrin of local residents and the artists who are eventually priced out in the process. Bucktown and Wicker Park are Chicago's most overt example of this phenomenon, as the traditional immigrant populations, Latinx residents, and trailblazing artists have given way to young professionals and families, many of the latter building million-dollar homes in Bucktown that now sit astride The 606 (**114**), a park and bike corridor built atop the old Bloomingdale Trail and a sure sign of the area's gentrification.

Wicker Park is technically part of West Town, a community area that also consists of a few smaller neighborhoods south of Division Street: East Village, Noble Square, and Ukrainian Village. The intersection of Milwaukee and Division is the Polish Triangle, which marks the traditional downtown of the Polish population, but parts south and west were predominantly home to immigrants from the Ukraine. Although Ukrainians are still concentrated in these parts of West Town, gentrification can be seen in the various modern houses found in this chapter.

114

THE 606

Michael Van Valkenburgh Associates, 2008–2014

Along Bloomingdale Avenue from Ashland to Ridgeway Avenues

Train: Blue to Damen

Named for the three digits that prefix all Chicago zip codes, the 606 is a linear park built atop the unused, elevated rail line along Bloomingdale Avenue that ceased operations in 2001. Two years later, the Friends of the Bloomingdale Trail formed and started its slow process of advocating for transformation. In its reuse of an old urban freight line that was elevated after being built at grade, the 606 immediately recalls New York's High Line, a raised linear park on Manhattan's west side that has been a widely popular destination and a magnet for development. But the two parks are completely different, due to their locations, lengths, uses, and designs.

While the 1.5-mile-long High Line floats three stories above the street, cutting through dense neighborhoods, the 2.7-mile-long 606 is about half of that height, elevating people seventeen feet in the air. This may not sound very high, but the surrounding buildings are fairly low and not very dense, so the effect is nevertheless dramatic. Further, the High Line is a pedestrian-only park (no bicycles, no pets) whose length is conducive to strolling. Since the City of

Ten feet wide with walking/running strips along the edges, the 606 cuts a scenic bike route between Bucktown and Humboldt Park. (Credit Eric Allix Rogers, CAC Archive)

Chicago used federal funds targeted for alternative transportation, a major element of the 606 is a bicycle lane; so here pedestrians share the elevated way with bicyclists, joggers, and dogs on leashes.

Perhaps the most significant difference between the two linear parks is the way the 606 connects street-level parks along its length. Some of these parks existed beforehand and some are new. Several are immediately adjacent to the elevated trail and serve as access points to it, while some are located a few blocks away. This postindustrial "emerald necklace" reinforces the elevated park's function as a conduit for moving people, in this case to the much-needed parks for residents of Wicker Park, Bucktown, Humboldt Park, and Logan Square.

The team led by New York landscape architect Michael Van Valkenburgh developed a design that is fairly inexpensive and long-lasting—planting beds are positioned alongside the concrete path, a fairly plain design compared to the overly complex "combing" of the plants and precast planks at the High Line. With a narrow width predominating, highlights of The 606 occur where the trail expands, creating places to sit, to get off and head to a park, or to look at public art by Frances Whitehead, who created a number of en-

The Western Trailhead is adjacent to some of the industry once served by the Bloomingdale Line. (Credit Dennis O'Neil)

vironmental pieces along the trail, including an observatory on the western terminus. And while much of the emphasis is on the landscape, a new bridge arches over Milwaukee Avenue, a bit of engineering bravado that harks to the elevated park's former industrial days.

115

LEAVITT RESIDENCE

The Miller Hull Partnership with Studio Dwell Architects, 2007

1804 North Leavitt Street

Train: Blue to Western

Located on a triangular lot across the street from The 606 (**114**) and one of its new parks, this house is similarly a renovation of an old piece of 20th-century industry—a 1920s warehouse to be precise. Commissioned by developers Bob and Karen Ranquist—Miller Hull's client on multifamily buildings in River North (**59**) and elsewhere in Bucktown (**117**)—the house selectively preserves the original building's brick walls and timber structure to make it a layered assemblage of old and new. This layering is most pronounced on the elevation facing Leavitt, where corrugated metal covers part of the second floor, and at the southern tip of the triangle. This corner overlooks the alley and is given over to a light court with a tree, with the new walls of metal and glass set back from the brick walls and its enlarged openings. The three-story house has a roof terrace but also a sizable yard on the west, next to the entrance facing Wilmot Avenue to the north.

A tree is visible behind the enlarged opening at the corner facing the 606. (Credit John K. Zacherle)

116

FINFROCK HOUSE

Curt Finfrock, 2008

2318 North Oakley Avenue

Bus: #74 to Fullerton Avenue at Oakley Avenue

Take a quick glance at this house architect Curt Finfrock designed for himself and his family in Bucktown, and the exterior panels are the most prominent feature. Made of fiber cement that is finished with hand-troweled cement, the panels are set in a pronounced running bond pattern of varying heights. Small and big windows—the latter boldly wrapping corners—fit into this coursing to create a contemporary box with a singular expression. But take a longer look and what comes to the fore is the house appearing to

The house wrapped in fiber cement panels appears to hover above the sidewalk. (Credit John K. Zacherle)

float a couple feet above the sidewalk. At this level, Finfrock, who served as contractor on the house as well, placed a ribbon of windows—set back from the facade that is supported by short round columns—for the basement level of the four-story corner house. This narrow, horizontal slot is reiterated at the entrance, which is a vertical gap between the fiber-cement panels wrapping three sides and one freestanding wall of it facing the neighbor to the side.

2136–2150 WEST NORTH AVENUE
UrbanLab with Norsman Architects, 2008
2136–50 West North Avenue

Some brick experimentation recalling UrbanLab's Mohawk House (**79**) is found on the exterior of this mixed-use assemblage next to the late-19th-century Association House. Three new buildings are set back from the street in respect to the 100-year-old building on the west that was renovated as part of the project.

(Credit John K. Zacherle)

1748 NORTH WINCHESTER

Studio Dwell Architects, 2005

1748 North Winchester Avenue

This four-story modern townhouse has a pretty straightforward design facing the street, but the most interesting aspect is on the side alley: dark brick walls angle in toward concrete-block walls at the front and the rear to create narrow slots for windows in the otherwise solid elevation.

117

URBAN SANDBOX

The Miller Hull Partnership with Osterhause McCarthy Architects, 2009

1615 North Wolcott Avenue

Bus: #72 to North Avenue at Wolcott Avenue

The block of Wolcott Avenue just north of North Avenue has a density of modern residential architecture that is impressive even for Bucktown, which has arguably seen more new modern houses than any other part of the city. This is mainly due to Ranquist Development, which embraces modern design and works with a few select architects, one of them The Miller Hull Partnership from Seattle. Their contribution to Ranquist's Urban Sandbox development, which includes the single-family houses to the north (**118**), is a four-story building that consists of eight condominium units and commercial space. A four-by-

A grid of steel faces the street while the residential entrance is tucked behind the solid wall in the foreground. (Credit John K. Zacherle)

four grid of square openings created by steel beams and paired steel columns faces the street. This technique gives the units generous outdoor spaces akin to Miller Hull's 156 West Superior Street (**59**), while layering the facade in a way that is rational yet very appealing.

118

1617 NORTH WOLCOTT

Studio Dwell Architects, 2009

1617 North Wolcott Avenue

Bus: #72 to North Avenue at Wolcott Avenue

This four-story townhouse is one element of Urban Sandbox, an almost full-block development by Ranquist Development just north of North Avenue. Studio Dwell, led by architect Mark Peters, has worked with Ranquist on numerous projects, and here the developers were responsible for this and a few other townhouses on the north side of the condo building designed by The Miller Hull Partnership (**117**). Immediately north of that project is 1617 North Wolcott, a custom residence that places an office space on the ground floor (shared with the garage off the rear alley) and the living spaces upstairs. Peters calls the house a light box, though this might seem like a misnomer given the primar-

The central courtyard bringing light to the townhouse is just visible past the predominantly solid front. (Credit John K. Zacherle)

ily solid front facade of white brick and cedar above a dark brick base. But the rectangular box is carved in the middle to bring plenty of light into the house. This light well can be seen from the setback side entrance to the Miller Hull building.

119

WOOD HOUSE

Brininstool + Lynch, 2013
1736 North Wood Street
Train: Blue to Damen
Bus: #50 to Damen Avenue at Wabansia Avenue

Privacy and modern architecture are often difficult bedfellows, since the former wants small windows while the latter prefers large walls of glass. This house, which occupies three lots on a quiet residential street in Bucktown, is

The primarily solid front elevation of brick and copper is all about privacy. (Credit Christopher Barrett)

all about privacy, a mandate of the client. From the sidewalk, this translates into primarily solid, brick walls, a perforated copper screen, and glass walls partially hidden behind a Cor-Ten steel fence with angled pickets. Combined with the trees, the front elevation is a well-composed assemblage of reds, browns, and greens. Glances can be had through the pickets of the living space located about three feet below sidewalk level, but most of the glass is oriented to a private south-facing courtyard created by the three-story, L-shaped house and the garage at the rear alley.

1713 NORTH WOOD

The Miller Hull Partnership with Osterhaus McCarthy Architects, 2010
1713 North Wood Street

Just across the street and a half-block down from the Wood House (**119**) is this three-story house on an infill lot next to a side alley. The architects took advantage of the site to bring in plenty of south light through horizontal clerestory windows. Head to the back to see the bridge connecting the house to the deck atop the garage.

120

CHICAGO TOWNHOUSE

Alexander Gorlin Architects, 2004
1808 North Paulina Street
Bus: #73 to Cortland Avenue at Hermitage Avenue

New York architect Alexander Gorlin knows a thing or two about townhouses, having written *The New American Townhouse* book in 2000 and a follow-up five years later. In the earlier book, he describes townhouses as "a typology of enormous restrictions, and therefore a laboratory of creative possibilities."[2] For this three-story Bucktown townhouse, his only Chicago project, Gorlin was faced with the restrictions of a 25-foot-wide lot and a limit of 25 feet to the bottom of the roof joists. This led him to create a low ground floor and two floors above it that project toward the street, expressing what

The double-height living room projects toward the street and paved forecourt. (Credit John K. Zacherle)

is happening behind the large front window. The exterior steps land in the middle of the open living space on the first floor, which is fronted by a double-height space expressed in the tall window facing the street. A departure from the Chicago townhouse norm can be seen in the alley, where the garage is set back, eliminating a yard between the garage and house, but linking the house directly to the deck atop the garage.

121

FLETCHER JONES AUDI

CDR Studio Architects with Gensler, 2017

1523 West North Avenue

Just as car dealerships cluster together along strips like Western and Cicero avenues, two Fletcher Jones showrooms sit astride North Avenue facing the

The northeast corner of the 2017 building that overlooks the Kennedy. (Credit John Muggenborg)

Kennedy Expressway. In 2009, Gensler completed Fletcher Jones Mercedes-Benz, with its angled metal wall facing the Kennedy, and, in 2017, as architect of record for one of the latest of the 100-plus showrooms that New York's CDR Studio has designed for Audi of America. The new four-story Fletcher Jones Audi is wrapped in a perforated corrugated grill placed in front of solid metal panels. Windows shaped like parallelograms cut into the cladding and sometimes turning the corner, giving the stolid building the feeling of movement.

122

1611 WEST DIVISION

Wheeler Kearns Architects, 2014
1611 West Division Street
Train: Blue to Division
Bus: #70 to Division Avenue at Ashland Avenue

Occupying a prominent spot catercorner to the Polish Triangle at Division, Ashland, and Milwaukee avenues, this eleven-story building is billed as the first transit-oriented development (TOD) within the City of Chicago. Since it is located within 600 feet of a CTA station (the Blue Line Division stop), the development eliminates parking entirely for the 99 rental apartments, while providing some surface parking in the rear for the ground-floor retail tenants. More TODs are set to follow this trailblazer which has seen high rates of oc-

The angled corner of the eleven-story building faces the Polish Triangle. (Credit Eric Allix Rogers, CAC Archive)

cupancy, though it remains to be seen if they will go to this extreme (the city allows one space for every two units in TODs). Some of this development's popularity can be ascribed to the architecture, which focuses on a jazzy pattern of vertical windows and gray metal panels overlapping dark horizontal spandrels. The pattern—or lack thereof—accentuates the chamfered corner and the subtle kinks in the elevations facing north and east, where glass is more prominent than metal.

C3PREFAB V1.0

Square Root Architecture + Design, 2011

1404 West Ohio Street

Billed as Chicago's first green prefab residence, this three-story house is composed of five modules that were built at a factory in Indiana, trucked to the site and then lifted into place in one day. As the name implies, Square Root continued its experimentation with prefabricated green design, building C3 v1.1 at 1650 West Huron Street.

PFANNER HOUSE

Zoka Zola Architecture + Urban Design, 2002

1737 West Ohio Street

This brick box that houses the home and architectural studio of Zoka Zola appears simple, but inside it is a complex intertwining of space that creatively responds to a building code that restricts single-family houses in the area to two stories. The studio, at the rear of the building, is set about four feet below grade, and above is the two-story residence that culminates in a sizable terrace around the corner.

(Credit John Hill)

123

BRICK WEAVE HOUSE

Studio Gang, 2009

1922 West Race Avenue

Bus: #50 to Damen Avenue at Ohio Street

While this house's West Town neighbors, like most in the city, present to the street some windows, a front door, and perhaps some steps, the aptly named Brick Weave House is fronted by a two-story enclosure of porous brick walls. It seems like this should be the back of the house, perhaps because the plan of the house is flipped from the norm. The garden (behind the brick walls) and garage that would typically be off the alley are instead off the street. Likewise, the living room is a double-height space at the very back of the house,

The porosity of the brick walls fronting the house is particularly pronounced in the evening. (Credit Steve Hall © Hedrich Blessing)

adjacent to a small side garden behind the garage. This "inversion" arose from the fact that the house is a complex renovation of a former horse stable from the late 19th century that was tight to the sidewalk, unlike its setback neighbors. Wishing to maintain that, Jeanne Gang's firm worked with masons to design custom brick ties that enable the steel-framed, single-wythe walls to stand, giving the clients privacy. At night, the house glows through the brick weave, making it one of the most distinctive facades of any contemporary house in Chicago.

2002 WEST OHIO
Filoramo Talsma, 2007
2002 West Ohio Street

This house for the family of Chris Talsma, co-owner of Filoramo Talsma, occupies a lot that is only 75 feet deep—50 feet less than the norm—and has no alley access. This pushed the architect to put the garage and entrance along Ohio Street, a long elevation of cedar planks that is layered in front of dark fiber cement panels.

124

UPTON'S NATURALS

UrbanLab, 2015
2054 West Grand Avenue
Bus: #65 to Grand Avenue at Hoyne Avenue

It is hardly an accident that this building on the northeast corner of Grand and Hoyne avenues looks industrial; after all, the three-story building houses a small factory. It is home to Upton's Naturals, which manufactures foods with seitan, a meat alternative. Yet, in addition to the factory, which occupies a double-height space on the east, the building has a café, offices, a yoga studio, and an apartment with roof deck on the top floor, where "vegan power couple"[3] Daniel Staackmann and Nicole Sopko live, like a modern-day version of the owner living above the store. UrbanLab's Martin Felsen and Sarah Dunn,

The precast panels are higher at the corner to open up the café to the street. (Credit Michelle Litvin)

Upton's Naturals manufactures vegan foods in a double-height space with a second-floor office overlooking the floor. (Credit Michelle Litvin)

The third floor is a calm, open living space with an enormous roof deck. (Credit Michelle Litvin)

an architectural power couple themselves, pulled off their first prefab building with this project where full-height concrete walls were made off site with integral insulation and finishes for both the exterior and interior. The walls are the main structure of the building, meaning that the interior can be adapted over time by, for example, adding floors or subfloors as needed.

W Grand Ave
Grand
N Ogden Ave
W Hubbard St
W Kinzie St
W Carroll Ave
Ace Hotel •
• 1K Fulton
• Fulton West
W Fulton St
CTA Morgan Street Station 125 •
W Lake St
Lake Street Studios •
N Ada St
N Elizabeth St
N Racine Ave
N Aberdeen St
W Randolph St
Chicago Public Library,
West Loop Branch •
N Morgan St
1/2-mile
radius
N Green St
N Halsted St (800W)
W Washington St
• Chicago Plumbers
Union Local 130
Skybridge 126 •
Kennedy Expy
W Madison St (0N/0S)
S Racine Ave (1200W)
727 West Madison •
S Throop St
S Morgan St
S Halsted St (800W)
W Monroe St
• Mark T. Skinner West
Elementary School
Mary Bartelme Park 128 •
W Adams St
Arkadia Tower •
W Jackson Blvd
• 129 Hubbard Street Dance Chicago
National Hellenic Museum 127 •
W Van Buren St
Racine
Dwight D. Eisenhower Expy
UIC Halsted

14 West Loop

Chicago's transformation from a place of industry to one of global services is no more evident than the West Loop, which has been in the midst of a development boom unlike anywhere else in the city since the mid-2010s. In such close proximity to the Loop, meatpacking and other industries existed side by side with hip bars, pricey restaurants, and lofts converted into apartments for families and offices for tech companies. In its heyday the Fulton-Randolph Market—oriented around these two east-west streets, the latter widened as early as 1850—was just one part of Chicago that handled the complex flow of foods in and out of the city. These places, such as the Union Stock Yards, the Maxwell Street Market, and the old South Water Street Market in the Loop, are now all gone. Today, Randolph is a foodie haven with world-class restaurants lining both sides.

Two big-name tenants are often highlighted when telling the story of changing demographics in this portion of the West Loop. First is Harpo Studios, the television studio that talk show host Oprah Winfrey opened on May Street (honorably named Oprah Winfrey Way in 2011) near Randolph in 1990, when skid row was an apt description for the area. By 2011, when Winfrey ended her talk show after its 25th season, the area had transformed from one to avoid to one to raise families in. Four years later, the TV mogul sold the studios (McDonald's opened its "Hamburger University" on the site of Harpo in mid-2018) to the same developer that transformed a nearby cold storage warehouse into the headquarters for Google, the second big-name tenant in the area's transformation. With the internet giant's move to the area, the industrial-global-service transformation appears to be complete, though the city's landmarking of the Fulton-Randolph market district will help to maintain the character of the industrial buildings even as their occupants are displaced in favor of the companies partaking in this century's digital economy.

While the Fulton-Randolph Market district gives the West Loop its most defining character, the neighborhood also includes Greektown to the south along Halsted Street, which was relocated here after the construction of University of Illinois at Chicago in the 1960s. Although the West Loop is often defined by the Chicago River on the east, the Eisenhower Expressway on the south, Ashland Avenue on the west, and Kinzie Street on the north, this chapter maintains the last three boundaries but pushes the east edge to the Dan Ryan Expressway. Buildings located between the river and the expressway can be found in Chapter 4.

125

CTA MORGAN STREET STATION

Ross Barney Architects, 2012
958 West Lake Street
Train: Green, Pink to Morgan

The steel-and-glass boxes of the new station fit into the industrial context. (Credit John Hill)

The intersection of Lake and Morgan streets is roughly the center of the Fulton-Randolph Market District, but as of 1994—when the area was in the midst of its profound transformation—the nearest CTA station was over a half-mile away, due to the closure that year of the Halsted Street stop on the Green Line. Pressure from businesses and residents moving to the neighborhood convinced the CTA in 2008 to build a new station at Morgan Street, which actually had a station from 1893 until 1949 when it was demolished due to low ridership. Since neither the street nor the "L" could be closed during construction, progress was slow. The new station didn't open until 2012, making it the first new elevated station in the system in over fifteen years.

Those familiar with older "L" stations will notice the number of ways this new one differs: in lieu of fare collection occurring on a mezzanine level between the street and tracks, this happens on the sidewalk level, cutting the number of elevators in half and streamlining the station's form. Ross Barney Architects' apparently simple design is made up of two slender rectangular boxes in glass and perforated stainless steel (with the same palette as their Cermak-McCormick Place Station [**47**]) that were sized to allow unencumbered traffic during construction. Canopies of translucent polycarbonate cover the platforms as well as a glass-enclosed bridge that connects the two sides above the trains; this last piece is another difference that comes from the elimination of the mezzanine while still allowing free movement from one side to the other after the tap of a Ventra card.

LAKE STREET STUDIOS
Harley Ellis Deveraux, 2014
727 West Lake Street

(Credit Lynn Becker)

About a dozen years into the new millennium, "microhouses" turned up as a trend in New York, San Francisco, and other US cities as a means of creating affordable housing. This slender ten-story building gives Chicago sixty-one 300-square-foot micro units behind a random checkerboard of white and blue metal panels. (Two years later, the Parker Fulton Market apartment tower with "luxury apartments" designed by Booth Hansen rose directly behind Lake Street Studios.)

(Credit Tom Harris Photography)

ACE HOTEL CHICAGO

GREC Architects, 2017
311 North Morgan Street

The trendy and super-popular Ace Hotel opened its Chicago location in the West Loop in summer 2017. Sitting across from Google HQ, the hotel occupies what appears to be three buildings but is just one. GREC renovated the facade of a landmark factory building on the south, putting a brick box behind it; to the south are two modern volumes, one low and one tall. The whole gives the impression of an evolving city rather than one tenant occupying one building.

(Credit Eric Allix Rogers, CAC Archive)

1K FULTON

Hartshorne Plunkard Architecture, 2016
1000 West Fulton Street

As sure a sign as any that Fulton-Randolph Market District has completed its transformation from industrial to tech comes with this conventional building, an addition and partial renovation of an old cold storage facility for Google's Chicago office.

FULTON WEST

Gensler, 2016
1330 West Fulton Street

Sterling Bay, developer of 1K Fulton and much of the West Loop, was banking on more tech companies moving to the Fulton-Randolph Market District when it built this new nine-story building. Glass floors are perched above a brick base with a pocket park sitting between it and its neighbors.

CHICAGO PLUMBERS UNION LOCAL 130

Gensler, 2017
1400 West Washington Street

A copper facade alludes to the plumbing trades being taught inside this training facility in the area of the West Loop known as "Teamster City." But this isn't old-school plumbing: greywater harvesting, solar-vacuum-tube water heaters, and other emerging technologies are taught and put on display through transparent panels.

CHICAGO PUBLIC LIBRARY, WEST LOOP BRANCH

Skidmore, Owings & Merrill, 2019
122 North Aberdeen Street

(Credit Courtesy of SOM | © Tom Harris)

Developer Sterling Mason donated two buildings that were formerly part of Harpo Studios for what would become the city's 81st public library. SOM renovated the adjoining one- and two-story buildings, maintaining their industrial interiors yet slapping handsome new facades on Aberdeen: Cor-Ten steel on the lower volume, and wood slats and painted graphics (that continue inside) on the taller volume.

126

SKYBRIDGE

Perkins and Will, 2003

737 West Washington Boulevard

Bus: #8 to Madison Street at Halsted Street

To appreciate the design feature that gives this 39-story condo tower its name, Skybridge is best seen straight on from the east or west at a bit of a distance. From directly across the Kennedy Expressway to the east, for example, the 30-foot-wide glass-enclosed walkways connecting the two halves of the slablike tower's top 25 floors are not only evident, they are completely transparent in the right light. From other vantage points, this vertical void between the stacked "villages," as architect Ralph Johnson likens them, is less evident, but the building is no less impressive; it is one of the best apartment buildings in Chicago this century. This praise shouldn't be surprising, given that Johnson is also responsible for the Contemporaine (**56**) and 235 West Van Buren (**27**), two other great multifamily buildings that this design predates.

The other formal flourishes that make Skybridge a welcome part of the neighborhood and West Loop skyline happen at the base and the top. In the case of the former, the tower is lifted upon a grid of round columns at the entrance, which is echoed in a four-story notch taken out of the building a few floors overhead. Around the corner (the weakest part of the full-block development, as a prominent area is given over to surface parking) on Halsted Street the low-rise garage-and-retail bustle that engages part of the tower is graced with a random checkerboard of opaque glass panes on Halsted Street. An abstract composition of horizontal louvered stripes faces the Dan Ryan Expressway. At the top, the tower is crowned by a large cantilevered steel trellis reaching out to the north, an exclamation point on top of a design worthy of one.

Opposite: An open steel trellis caps the north end of the 39-story tower. (Credit John Hill)

727 WEST MADISON

FitzGerald Associates Architects, 2019

727 West Madison Street

This 45-story tower with nearly 500 rental units is the second of two towers designed by FitzGerald Associates that are located south of Skybridge (**126**) and start to define a streetwall west of the Kennedy Expressway. The tower's elliptical plan makes it stand out, as does the two types of glass that appear to spiral up and around the exterior. The glass concealing the parking garage along Halsted is also a standout.

ARKADIA TOWER

Fitzgerald Associates Architects, 2015

765 West Adams Street

The earlier FitzGerald tower is 33 stories with 350 rental apartments. Here, it's all about the parking garage facing Halsted, with a memorable, if kitschy, perforated screen adorned with an image of the Parthenon, a nod to the small Greektown neighborhood.

127

NATIONAL HELLENIC MUSEUM

RTKL (now CallisonRTKL), 2011

333 South Halsted Street

Bus: #126 to Jackson Boulevard at Halsted Street

Chicago's Greektown is synonymous with the stretch of Halsted Street west of the Loop, a natural location of the only museum in the country devoted to Greek history and culture. The National Hellenic Museum sits on a trapezoidal lot on the northeast corner of Halsted and Jackson streets, across the street from a miniature Greek temple (built ca. 1996 when Chicago hosted the Democratic National Convention at the nearby United Center and pumped

Limestone walls cantilever over the museum's transparent first floor. (Credit Eric Allix Rogers, CAC Archive)

money into the West Loop) that marks the southern entrance to Greektown. The dignified design, by RTKL principal Demetrios Stavrianos, wraps the top floors in limestone panels with a running bond pattern that is broken up by two tall windows on the south and west elevations. The whole ground floor is transparent, and the distinction between the glass and stone is accentuated by the gallery floors cantilevering over the sidewalk along Halsted to subtly but effectively signal the museum's entrance.

128

MARY BARTELME PARK

site design group ltd., 2010
115 South Sangamon Street
Train: Green, Pink to Morgan
Bus: #126 to Jackson Boulevard at Morgan Street

"X" literally marks the spot in this much-needed park in the middle of the West Loop: diagonal paths cut across the site to define distinctive zones. There's a playground on the east, a dog-run opposite it on the west, a seating area with garden and lawn to the south, and the park's signature stainless steel fountain acting as a gateway from the northwest. This plan packs something

Diagonal paths cut across the West Loop park. (Credit John Hill)

A misting fountain acts as a gateway to the park. (Credit John Hill)

for everybody into the compact 1.4-acre park that is named for "Suitcase Mary," the first Cook County Public Guardian, a teacher who became the first woman judge in Illinois, in 1923. She devoted much of her life to helping young women coming out of the court system. While the leaning, misting gates that give the park its most distinctive image attract the most attention, the park's most ubiquitous detail is the angled Cor-Ten steel that boldly holds back the mounded prairie grasses and other plantings. Opposite the rusty steel walls in the southwest corner are stepped concrete benches that lend more history to the site through the incorporation of terra-cotta pieces from the state-owned infirmary that formerly occupied the site.

129

HUBBARD STREET DANCE CHICAGO

Krueck Sexton Partners, 2006

1147 West Jackson Boulevard

Bus: #126 to Van Buren Street at Racine Avenue

Although it is no longer found at LaSalle and Hubbard streets, the much-loved contemporary dance company that was started by Lou Conte in 1977 maintains this history through its Hubbard Street Dance Chicago (HSDC) name. The Lou Conte Dance Studio, among the company's other facilities, can be found inside its new home at Jackson Boulevard and Racine Avenue, a fairly anonymous low-scale building enlivened by Ron Krueck and Mark Sexton's facade renovation. Their design is multifaceted but strongly focused

Yellow tile anchors the far corner of the otherwise gray building. (Credit William Zbaren)

on the corner, where large corrugated strands of perforated metal are layered over yellow tiles and graphics of dancers above the glass storefront near the entrance along Jackson Boulevard. Signage is displayed on gray metal panels next to the entrance as well as on Racine Avenue, where most of the frontage features smaller corrugated panels layered over brick painted gray. The various materials and shades of gray lend HSDC's home an industrial appearance while also accentuating the splash of color at the corner and the allusion to the dancers inside.

MARK T. SKINNER WEST ELEMENTARY SCHOOL
SMNG-A, 2009
1260 West Adams Street

(Credit John Hill)

This three-story school of brick, metal, and glass follows the Chicago Public School's "L"-shaped prototype design, here adapted slightly for a site facing Skinner Park and pedestrian-only Throop Street on the west. The main entrance with its steel canopy is on the south near a historic water tower. Ten years after completion, the Public Building Commission added a four-story annex along Monroe Street, turning the "L" into a "C."

W Chicago Ave (800N)
Chicago
W Grand Ave
Grand
Western Ave
Ashland
Morgan
W Lake St
California
W Madison St (0N/0S)
W Ogden Ave
Illinois Medical District
Dwight D. Eisenhower Expy
Racine
UIC-Halsted
Western
134
Academic and Residential Complex
W Harrison Rd
Rush University Medical Center
S Ashland Ave (1600W)
Grant Hall Renovation
130
UIC Student Recreation Facility
133
Taylor Street Apartments and Branch Library
W Polk St
Polk
S California Ave (2800W)
S Western Ave (2400W)
S Damen Ave (2000W)
W Taylor St
Jane Addams Hull House Museum
S Racine Ave (1200W)
S Halsted Ave (800W)
Site of West Side Grounds
1-mile radius
136
A Safe Haven Foundation
W Roosevelt Rd (1200S)
National Public Housing Museum
UIC Skyspace
132
135
Chicago Children's Advocacy Center
UIC Forum
131
Douglas Park
FBI Regional Field Office
W Ogden Ave
Dan Ryan Expy
Halsted St
S Blue Island Ave
Pilsen Gateway
Western Ave
18th St
18th
Western
California
W Cermak Rd (2200S)
Damen
Halsted
Instituto Health Sciences Career Academy High School
W 26th St (2600S)
Ashland

15 University Village, Medical District, Lawndale, & Pilsen

If there is one part of the city where the needs and desires of government and planning clashed with those of citizens and traditional neighborhoods, it is southwest of the Loop, where the University of Illinois at Chicago (UIC) now resides. Located at Navy Pier (**66**) at the time of the school's search for a permanent location in the mid-1950s, ten years later UIC landed near the Circle Interchange (initially it was called the Chicago Circle Campus due to this proximity) where the Dan Ryan, Eisenhower, and Kennedy expressways meet. Ironically, this was the same spot envisioned as a grand domed civic center in Burnham and Bennett's 1909 *Plan of Chicago*. This circle of on and off ramps surely emphasizes the importance of the automobile in postwar America, but also its impact on the urban landscape: expressways sliced up neighborhoods in Chicago, and in this case they delivered students commuting by automobile to a brand new campus on land obtained through the clearance of more than one hundred acres of "slums" in the name of urban renewal. This approach echoes what Mies van der Rohe and university officials did at the Illinois Institute of Technology on the city's South Side (discussed in the next chapter), but on a much larger scale.

Referred to as "an academic oasis in the center of a great city"[1] upon its 1965 completion, UIC's campus, designed by Walter Netsch of Skidmore, Owings & Merrill, was the antithesis of the traditional city that it displaced. Large concrete buildings sat upon superblocks covered with parking lots and green space, connected by elevated walkways. Only Hull House—created in the late 19th century by Jane Addams as a service for new immigrants entering the city—remains, both a form of education and urbanism that was displaced by the new campus. The ensuing evolution of theories of architecture and urbanism is evident in UIC's expansion south of Roosevelt Avenue (the southern edge of its initial footprint), where neo-traditional school buildings and residences predominate. Nevertheless, this expansion also involved the demolition of "blighted" land and the displacement of residents in the late 20th century.

West of UIC is the large Illinois Medical District (IMD), made up of four hospitals and other medical facilities on nearly six hundred acres, on what is considered the nation's largest medical district. Its origins go back to 1919, when the state of Illinois bought land for a research and medical hospital from the Chicago Cubs after they moved to Wrigley Field from the West Side Grounds, where they won two World Series championships. Between UIC and the IMD is what remains of Little Italy, the neighborhood that was largely devoured by UIC. Much of the land south of Roosevelt was given over to public housing in the last century, hand in hand with the federal funding that helped to pay for the Circle Campus. Like public housing elsewhere in the city, it is being redeveloped as mixed-use communities with low-scale residential buildings in neotraditional garb. Further south is Pilsen, a traditionally Czech neighborhood that is now predominantly Mexican but saw an influx of artists displaced from Wicker Park and is now noticeably gentrified in parts. Its colorful and eclectic mix of buildings and residents is perhaps a 21st-century incarnation of the neighborhood Jane Addams served.

130

UIC STUDENT RECREATION FACILITY

Moody Nolan/PSA-Dewberry, 2006
737 South Halsted Street
Bus: #8 to Halsted Street at Polk Street

Although the University of Illinois at Chicago (UIC) carries a history of displacement, this new recreational facility commendably replaced a parking lot and tennis courts—which once replaced 19th-century homes. It is located on the east edge of the East Campus catercorner to the Jane Addams Hull House, an explicit reminder of the built fabric that the modernist UIC campus replaced. As the school's new student recreational facility (one of two new facilities for the school, the other on the West Campus), the building faces the expressway on the east and the campus on the west. The fairly large three-story building was designed jointly by PSA-Dewberry (now Dewberry) and Moody Nolan, a firm that specializes in athletic facilities.

The design deals with its edge condition by opening up primarily to the west but closing itself off appropriately on the east; the latter expressway facade is primarily corrugated metal with some horizontal windows that hint at the locations of the large, four-court gymnasium. The long building is broken up on the Halsted Street side through overlapping materials: brick, metal panels, and glass. The last highlights the entrance and the internal street that connects the usual fitness spaces inside, which have only limited public access. The most unique aspect of the design is the pool tucked below the low butterfly roof at the south end of the building, its clear glass high enough to give only glimpses of the structure above but not the water below.

The pool and its butterfly roof anchor the south end of the building. (Credit Angie McMonigal Photography)

ACADEMIC AND RESIDENTIAL COMPLEX
Solomon Cordwell Buenz (SCB), 2019
940 West Harrison Street

This new complex near the UIC-Halsted Blue Line station comprises a ten-story residence hall on the east and a two-story classroom component on the west. SCB designed it with a "nod to Netsch,"[2] with geometric compositions of solid and void on the tall elevations facing both the campus and the Eisenhower, and a cylindrical volume for the classroom spaces.

GRANT HALL RENOVATION

SmithGroupJJR, 2011
703 South Morgan Street

Skidmore, Owings & Merrill served as master planner for UIC in the 1960s and '70s, so understandably they designed a number of buildings, including the interconnected Douglas, Grant, and Lincoln Halls, each one renovated separately. SmithGroupJJR's renovation of Grant Hall is the most dramatic, with a new curtain wall of energy-efficient glass replacing the narrow recessed windows. Its geothermal heating and cooling system is the first on campus.

131

UIC FORUM

HOK, 2008
725 West Roosevelt Road
Bus: #12 to Roosevelt Road at Halsted Street

When Walter Netsch of Skidmore, Owings & Merrill planned the Chicago Circle Campus in the early 1960s, the Forum occupied its heart. Sitting below the traversable roofs of the surrounding lecture halls, the circular space recalled a Greek amphitheater in form and name. But over the years the walkways were removed and the Forum was turned into a more traditional quad, a public space at grade. Although the new UIC Forum at Halsted Street and Roosevelt Road harks back to the school's origins in name only, not form, the building that houses a 3,000-seat convocation center also aims to serve as the school's heart, though now attuned to off-campus activities rather than those strictly on campus.

The Forum is part of a larger half-million-square-foot project that includes the 750-student James Stukel Towers, also designed by HOK and made up of four towers that increase in height from Halsted Street to the east. Therefore, the Forum acts as a gateway to campus from the Loop as well as one to the new South Campus, south of Roosevelt Road. More recently, UIC has developed both sides of Halsted Street as retail, commercial, residences, and

An extra-tall round column supports the Forum's roof trellis and serves as a local landmark. (Credit Anna Munzesheimer, CAC Archive)

parking in a neo-traditional garb (the area was home to the popular Maxwell Street Market that was relocated east of the expressway). HOK designed the dormitory tower in a fairly conservative manner, with brick piers predominating, but the Forum is thankfully a bit more progressive: the roof extends over the corner as a large trellis (designed with the structural engineers at Thornton Tomasetti) that is supported by a round column whose excessive height turns it from a piece of structure into a local landmark.

132

UIC SKYSPACE

James Turrell, 2006

Halsted and Roosevelt

Bus: #12 to Roosevelt Road at Halsted Street

Artist James Turrell is famous for his "skyspaces," most of them tucked into museums or sitting on private property. Each is a single room capped by a roof with a cutout—square, circle, or ellipse—that invites people to look at the sky and appreciate subtle changes of light and color. When finished

in 2006, the UIC Skyspace at Earl L. Neal Plaza was the first fully public, 24/7 skyspace from the artist. For safety reasons the design veers from its predecessors, namely in being open on the sides rather than fully enclosed. Since the open walls don't shield the sounds of traffic, and since Turrell's skyspaces invite a kind of meditative state, the 43-foot-diameter artwork incorporates walls of water that add some (but not necessarily enough) ambient sounds to the experience. Although looking through the elliptical opening here is not as serene an experience as other Turrell installations, it is a design that makes the most of its situation, giving Chicago a unique and truly *public* art.

A glass clerestory rings the space below the elliptical roof cutout. (Credit CAC Archive)

133

TAYLOR STREET APARTMENTS AND BRANCH LIBRARY

Skidmore, Owings & Merrill, 2019
1342 West Taylor Street
Train: Blue Line to Racine
Bus: #157 to Taylor & Throop

The Taylor Street Apartments and Little Italy Branch Library, carried out with Related Midwest, is one of three projects created by the Chicago Housing Authority and the Chicago Public Library in which mixed-income housing was paired with public libraries. (See **103** and Chapter 11 for the other two CHA/CPL projects.) Skidmore, Owings & Merrill (SOM) placed the one-story

The glass storefront gets taller toward the corner as if to accentuate the importance that branch libraries play in residential communities. (Credit Courtesy of SOM © Tom Harris)

library at the corner of Taylor and Ada Streets, where it will face the National Public Housing Museum once it's completed. Architecturally, the library is fully glazed while the 73 apartments (37 CHA, 29 affordable, 7 market-rate) sit behind facades where brick-colored, vertically striated metal panels randomly alternate with narrow and large windows.

NATIONAL PUBLIC HOUSING MUSEUM

Landon Bone Baker Architects

1322 West Taylor Street, anticipated completion in 2021

If any city deserves to host the National Public Housing Museum (NPHM), it is Chicago, which erected so much public housing only to tear it down decades later. One building from the 32-building Jane Addams Homes complex remains (an optimistic solution, these walk-ups were built as part of FDR's Public Works Administration program) home to the NPHM, which preserves the facades as well as an apartment it uses for exhibition space on a subject worth learning from.

134

RUSH UNIVERSITY MEDICAL CENTER

Perkins and Will, 2012

1620 West Harrison Street

Bus: #7 to Harrison Street at Ashland Avenue

The Illinois Medical District (IMD) consists of four major hospitals, two universities, and numerous other medical facilities covering a staggering 560 acres two miles west of the Loop. One of these four hospitals is Rush University Medical Center, which certainly has the greatest exposure of any IMD component given the sizable eye-catching building designed by Perkins and Will's Ralph Johnson for a site overlooking the Eisenhower Expressway.

The tall undulating building stands out in its location. (Credit John Hill)

The hospital is comprised of two parts: a five-story cloverleaf-shaped tower containing 386 patient beds and a seven-story rectangular base with diagnostic and treatment facilities. With this diagram of curved above rectilinear, it is reminiscent of an inflated version of the late Prentice Women's Hospital designed by Bertrand Goldberg. The entrance to Rush's massive new building is located to the south on Harrison Street, where the orthogonal base bows out to follow the curved tower above it. The highlight inside is the "reverse terrarium,"[3] as Johnson calls it, a glass-enclosed garden that brings some daylight and a little bit of landscape to the double-height lobby.

135

CHICAGO CHILDREN'S ADVOCACY CENTER

Tigerman McCurry Architects, 2001; Holabird & Root, 2015
1240 South Damen Avenue
Bus: #50 to Damen Avenue at 13th Street

The nonprofit Chicago Children's Advocacy Center (ChicagoCAC) investigates reports of child sexual abuse and provides family advocacy, among other services aimed at protecting children. Since opening its doors in 2001, the building has enabled efficient communication by housing a variety of agencies, such as the Chicago Police Department and Illinois Department of Children and Family Services. The 2001 building, designed by the firm of Margaret McCurry and the late Stanley Tigerman, fronts Damen Avenue and fills the width of the block. Although large, the one-story building was designed

The one-story original building has playful form and color palette. (Credit Angie McMonigal Photography)

with the child in mind, from its pastel color palette and playful forms to the internal courtyards (one a playground) and clear circulation inside.

Holabird & Root's expansion doubles ChicagoCAC's facility. The two-story addition that houses professional spaces, offices, and training areas, and a lunchroom is placed on the west side of the existing facility, which still contains the child-friendly spaces. Although taller than the original, the addition respects it through the rhythmic counterpoint of the roofline and some splashes of color. The architects found inspiration in rowhouses to give the addition a domestic scale, though the asymmetrical roofs and windows express the project's institutional heart.

FBI REGIONAL FIELD OFFICE

Lohan Anderson, 2005

2111 West Roosevelt Road

What is that anonymous-looking ten-story office building looming beyond the ChicagoCAC (**135**)? It's the post–September 11 home of the regional FBI, a secure building that, while admittedly un-fortress-like, isn't interested with engaging its urban context.

136

A SAFE HAVEN FOUNDATION

Krueck Sexton Partners, 2006

2750 West Roosevelt Road

Bus: #12 to Roosevelt Road at California Avenue

This building sits cater-corner to Douglas Park (one of the three original parks in the "emerald necklace" West Park System laid out by William LeBaron Jenney in the 1870s), a metal-and-glass mirage of sorts in Lawndale's urban landscape of diminished economic opportunities and slow recovery. The corporate-looking building was designed by the firm of Ron Krueck and Mark Sexton for the 100-year-old Chicago Christian Industrial League (CCIL), housing a varied program in its three wings: housing for families and single men

Curved brick walls (now covered by murals) occupy the corner of the glass-and-metal building. (Credit William Zbaren)

and women, social services, and training classrooms. The crisp, modern styling of the building is set off by the curving brick canvas for art at the corner.

Facing political and financial problems a few years after moving into its new headquarters, CCIL was taken over by A Safe Haven in October 2009, a nonprofit started in 1994 by husband-and-wife financial advisors who fell on hard times and realized the city lacked a place for those in need of recovery. A Safe Haven carries on the tradition of CCIL, offering housing and rehab services for those in need.

DRW COLLEGE PREP

Farr Associates, 2009

931 South Homan Avenue

Since 1905, a 14-story tower has stood over Homan Square, developed by Charlie Shaw after Sears shuttered its catalog facility that once employed over 22,000 employees. More than 100 years later, Farr Associates was tasked with transforming the nearby powerhouse into a high school and learning center. The catwalks overlooking the tracks on the south hint at the changes inside (some of the massive machinery inside was preserved as a reminder of the building's roots), which is sometimes accessible for community events.

DR. MARTIN LUTHER KING LEGACY APARTMENTS

Johnson & Lee, 2011
1550 South Hamlin Avenue

Forty-five affordable residential units and commercial space rose on a vacant lot that previously housed an apartment building known as the short-term residence of Dr. Martin Luther King Jr. The three-story buildings hold the streetline and create variety through bright yellow frames that playfully project from the facade. Polychrome masonry and limestone trim echo neighborhood buildings.

(Credit Steve Hall © Hedrich Blessing)

CAROLE ROBERTSON CENTER FOR LEARNING

Ross Barney & Jankowski (now Ross Barney Architects), 2002
3701 West Ogden Avenue

The Carole Robertson Center for Learning operates three locations in the city for fulfilling its mission of educating and empowering children and families. This one-story building with classrooms surrounding a courtyard is one of two Carol Ross Barney designed for them. It presents a patchwork of brick facing Ogden Avenue and the alley, while bold yellow walls and soffits face the other sides.

INSTITUTO HEALTH SCIENCES CAREER ACADEMY HIGH SCHOOL

JGMA with Ghafari Architects, 2011
2520 South Western Avenue

(Credit McShane Construction)

Before Juan Moreno of JGMA unleashed the colorful curves of his El Centro building (**104**) on the city, he renovated an abandoned four-story industrial building as a charter high school for the Instituto del Progreso Latino. Color is also an integral part of Moreno's design, here executed with a color-morphing rainscreen layered over existing brick walls with perforated panels in front of the windows to maintain daylight and natural ventilation.

PILSEN GATEWAY

Landon Bone Architects (now Landon Bone Baker Architects), 2002
1621 South Halsted Street

This project with residences and commercial space, uniquely developed by the architects, serves as an effective gateway to Pilsen from the north, sitting on the neighborhood's edge near railroad tracks and the Dan Ryan Expressway. Tall red-brick volumes bracket a central portion of corrugated metal and projecting balconies.

South Side

See Map 5 South Loop

27th Street South

Williams Park Fieldhouse

Lake Michigan

E 31st St (3100S)

31st Street Harbor 143

139 Ed Kaplan Family Institute for Innovation and Tech Entrepreneurship

Illinois Institute of Technology

137 McCormick Tribune Campus Center

138 State Street Village Domitories

S. R. Crown Hall

Burnham Park

Sox-35th

35th-Lou Jones

35th-Bronzeville-IIT

35th Street Pedestrian Bridge

E 35th St (3500S)

Arts and Rec Center at Ellis Park

140 35th Street Bridge and Station

U.S. Cellular Field

141 Park Boulevard

S Cottage Grove Ave

S Lake Park Ave

S Lake Shore Dr

E 37th St

142 Teen Living Programs Belfort House

1/2-mile radius

E Pershing Rd (3900S)

Engine Company 16

E Oakwood Blvd

Indiana

S Drexel Blvd

E 40th St

E 41st St

41st Street Pedestrian Bridge

S Wentworth Ave

Dan Ryan Expy

S LaSalle St

S State St (0E/0W)

S Wabash Ave

S Michigan Ave

S Indiana Ave

S Dr Martin Luther King Jr Dr

S Vincennes Dr

E 42nd St

43rd

E 43rd St (4300S)

Urban Green House I and Hybrid House

E 44th St

47th

47th

E 47th St (4700S)

See Map 17 Hyde Park

16 Bronzeville

Much of the story of Bronzeville can be described from one location. Stand at the intersection of State and 35th streets today and two distinct realms are apparent: to the north is the Illinois Institute of Technology (IIT), the bastion of Mies van der Rohe and his disciples; and to the south are fairly new, yet neo-traditional low-scale residential buildings lining the west side of State Street. Yet, during the Great Migration of the early 1900s, State Street was the dividing line between the rich and the poor: the rich toward the lake on the east and the poor to the west. The north-south street was also a racial divide, with white middle-class housing found along the boulevards to the east of it and the black slums running down Federal Street one block to the west, all the way from 22nd Street down to 55th Street. Calling someplace a "slum" was often a misnomer used by those in power eager to clear the land for new construction, but it was an accurate label here, since the city segregated the black population through restricted housing covenants and landlords demanded higher rents for substandard housing.

By the 1920s, the area was in the midst of an influx of African Americans migrating from the South. The intersection of 35th and State was the center of the city's black community, given the Bronzeville label in 1930 by James J. Gentry, a *Chicago Bee* editor. Functioning as a self-contained community, Bronzeville had its own bank, insurance company, and newspapers. A half-mile section of State Street from 31st to 35th streets was known as "The Stroll," due to its density of jazz and blues clubs. A blues favorite at the time was the "Mecca Flat Blues," a song inspired by the large courtyard apartment building erected at 34th Street and State Street in 1892, just in time for the 1893 World's Fair. Yet, like much of the area, the building was a victim of the Great Depression, and in 1941 the newly minted IIT (created by the merging of the Armour Institute of Technology and the Lewis Institute in 1940) obtained the building as part of Mies van der Rohe's plan for a modern campus on land cleared in the name of urban renewal. It took a little while, as opponents fought to save it, but the Mecca came down in 1952 and the land is now occupied by S. R. Crown Hall, one of Mies's masterpieces.

At the time of Crown Hall's construction in the mid-1950s, the city constructed Stateway Gardens just south of the intersection of 35th and State streets. As one of the city's many public housing projects, Stateway Gardens' eight towers would be accompanied by twenty-eight Robert Taylor Homes in 1962, south of 39th Street; combined they were the largest swath of public housing in the country. By 2007, each project was demolished and the blocks of cleared land are slowly being developed as mixed-income communities following the federal government's HOPE VI program. But large swaths of land are not limited to the traditionally "poor" side of Bronzeville, because the shuttering of Michael Reese Hospital in 2009 north of 31st Street near Lake Shore Drive gave the South Side another large site for redevelopment.

137

McCORMICK TRIBUNE CAMPUS CENTER

Office for Metropolitan Architecture with Studio Gang and Holabird & Root, 2003
3201 South State Street
Train: Green to 35th-Bronzeville-IIT
Bus: #29 to State Street at 33rd Street

This student center for the Illinois Institute of Technology (IIT) is the first completed building in the United States by Rem Koolhaas and the Office for Metropolitan Architecture (OMA). Along with Helmut Jahn's dormitory (**138**) and John Ronan's academic building (**139**), it is only the third building on the IIT campus constructed since the 1960s. The McCormick Tribune Campus Center straddles Chicago's well-known "L" tracks to connect the educational and residential areas on the west and east sides, respectively, of the campus laid out by Mies van der Rohe in 1940.

Rem Koolhaas's design was chosen in a 1998 competition from a field of five finalists, which also included Peter Eisenman, Zaha Hadid, Helmut Jahn, and Kazuyo Sejima. A possible reason for OMA's selection is the way the design managed to balance the Modernist principles of Mies with contemporary,

The angled roofline gives the impression the building is being crushed by the wrapped elevated train. (Credit Eric Allix Rogers, CAC Archive)

avant-garde architecture; the other architects' designs were split between the Modernist (Jahn and Sejima) and the avant-garde (Eisenman and Hadid).

OMA's bold design is comprised of two elements: 1) a concrete tube clad in corrugated stainless steel that wraps the "L" to dampen the train noise; and 2) the main building, a one-story, 110,000-square-foot structure containing a welcome center, dining room, auditorium, meeting rooms, bookstore, cafe, post office, offices, convenience store, and campus radio station. These functions are contained in a dynamic form underneath the tube. With its angled roof, the building appears to have been crushed by the concrete tube. Movement through the main building happens along diagonal paths that were located according to analysis of the patterns of students walking from one side of campus to the other, called "paths of desire." The paths intersect to create island spaces and nodes of activity—color-coded according to activity—for the students and faculty.

Although these diagonals give the layout a complexity a Mies building would never have, the interior spaces are surprisingly easy to navigate, mainly due to the views across the spaces stretching both in plan and section. By seeing across and through to other spaces, one is always aware of their location in the overall building, with color playing a role: orange is prevalent on the west facade, green is used in the central dining area, and red saturates a

Orange glazing near the entrance on the west facade bathes the interior in an orange glow. (Credit Eric Allix Rogers, CAC Archive)

Diagonals predominate inside, following lines connecting buildings on campus. (Credit Eric Allix Rogers, CAC Archive)

narrow ramp of computer terminals, for example. Throughout the interior, a multitude of unique materials are used, including wire mesh between panes of glass that bends light, wall coverings that create the illusion of movement, and translucent fiberglass with a honeycomb core for walls and tabletops.

Koolhaas and his team at OMA directly confront Mies in two places: At the main entrance near the north end of the building is a patterned graphic of the architect's face; 2x4, the graphic design firm responsible for the building's consistent graphic language, based it on the international symbol for a human. When closed, Mies's visage is whole, but when the automatic parting doors open he becomes Koolhaas's humorous play on the master's lasting influence and stature at IIT. The other area is adjacent to Mies's 1953 Commons Building at the northeast corner of the student center. Koolhaas wanted to absorb the old building into the new, but preservationists protested and got their way, so the new building angles away from the predecessor's brick walls to respect it but also to create an odd-shaped, inaccessible green space and an even odder oversized foundation for the old building.

138

STATE STREET VILLAGE DORMITORIES

Murphy/Jahn (now JAHN), 2003
3303 South State Street
Train: Green to 35th-Bronzeville-IIT
Bus: #29 to State Street at 33rd Street

Taken together, Helmut Jahn's design for a 367-bed dormitory and Rem Koolhaas's design for IIT's student center (**137**) are a good lesson on divergent

A glass wall parallel to the "L" tracks extends past the building as if to accentuate its importance. (Credit Eric Allix Rogers, CAC Archive)

Glass and corrugated metal span across the courtyards between dormitory volumes. (Credit Eric Allix Rogers, CAC Archive)

ways of dealing with Chicago's "L" structure. Koolhaas wraps the elevated tracks as a way to muffle the sound of passing trains and create a strong image in the process (a tactic that Carol Ross Barney executed to similar effect one station to the north [**47**]). Jahn, restricted to a narrow site to the east of the tracks, incorporates a continuous glass wall paralleling the tracks to alleviate the train noise to both the dorm rooms and the courtyards in between, achieved with triple-pane, laminated glass. Unlike Koolhaas's project, the transparency of Jahn's design celebrates the trains and the structure they ride atop, rather than celebrating his own building.

Although the glass wall hasn't been kind to birds (necessitating the installation of mesh screens at the courtyards so birds can "see" the plane of glass), the dorm is more than this west facade. On State Street, corrugated metal curves up and over the roof to shelter terraces atop the six parallel "teeth" of the block-long building. The corrugated metal extends across the five courtyards, though it is perforated to let some sunlight through to the plantings below. The steel structure needed to support these curved sections of metal is on display, just as the concrete structure behind the glass and metal walls is left exposed. With other details, such as glass-enclosed elevator shafts, the building displays how it works (unlike the Koolhaas student center, which hides most everything, not just the "L") and serves as a lesson for the future architects and engineers studying at IIT.

139

ED KAPLAN FAMILY INSTITUTE FOR INNOVATION AND TECH ENTREPRENEURSHIP

John Ronan Architects, 2018

3137 South Federal Street

Train: Green to 35th-Bronzeville-IIT

Bus: #29 to State Street at 33rd Street

The newest building on the IIT campus—the first since the one-two, Koolhaas-Jahn punch (**137**, **138**) in 2003—sits on a former green space just north of Grover M. Hermann Hall, a building designed by SOM's Walter Netsch in 1962. While Netsch's design follows the campus grid and the glass-and-steel palette established by Mies van der Rohe in the decades previous, Ronan's design is a dramatic departure thanks to its facade of lightweight ETFE (poly-Ethene-co-TetraFluoroEthene, a strong polymer) and white (not black) surfaces throughout.

The large, two-story low-slung building is organized around two courtyards: the southern one is accessed from the campus's main pedestrian promenade on the east, while the smaller courtyard to the north is accessed from Federal Street on the west. These spaces give back a little bit of the green space taken by the new building and bring sunlight to the tech studios, classrooms, offices, and other spaces occupying the building's deep floor plates.

The glow of the ETFE facade makes for a dramatic contemporary statement on Mies's historic IIT campus. (Credit Steve Hall © Hall+Merrick)

In their scale, though, these two courtyards are reminiscent of Ronan's earlier Poetry Foundation (**61**).

The 72,000-square-foot building (named after IIT alumnus and donor Ed Kaplan and his wife, Carol) exists to foster collaboration, innovation, and entrepreneurship between IIT students, faculty, and alumni and serves as the new home for the Institute of Design, which was founded by László Moholy-Nagy in 1937 as "The New Bauhaus." Flexible collaboration spaces allow

Open stadium seating has become de rigueur in higher education; at Kaplan it's called the Victor Morgenstern Pitch. (Credit John Ronan Architects; James Florio)

Even with its differences, Ronan's design has very Miesian moments. (Credit John Ronan Architects; James Florio)

students, for instance, to fabricate prototypes and then team up with industry partners interested in similar innovations. The innovation of the project's name extends to its second-story ETFE facade: the amount of sunlight entering the building can be controlled through pneumatic adjustments. Although Mies did not have access to this material and technology in the 1940s and '50s, he would probably embrace their use on the progressive campus he laid out.

WILLIAMS PARK FIELDHOUSE
STL Architects, 2019
2850 South State Street

This small fieldhouse sits in Williams (Daniel Hale) Park and serves the residents of Dearborn Homes and others in the area north of IIT. Although petit, the building is a standout: the facades are wrapped in iridescent stainless steel shingles in a dragon scale pattern, while inside, the gymnasium and other spaces are capped by glulam beams.

140

35TH STREET BRIDGE AND STATION

Gensler with Ross Barney + Jankowski (now Ross Barney Architects), 2003

142 West 35th Street

Train: Red to Sox-35th

Bus: #29 to State Street at 35th Street

Much as the city spruced up the bridges (among other things) connecting the Loop to all parts west when the United Center hosted the Democratic National Convention in 1996, the 35th Street bridge and "L" station got some much needed attention when U.S. Cellular Field hosted baseball's All-Star Game in 2003. Previously an anonymous overpass, the bridge now sports the names of the prominent institutions that sit on either side of the yawning, fourteen-lane interstate—the home of the Chicago White Sox to the west in Bridgeport and the Illinois Institute of Technology to the east in Bronzeville. While the names are visible to cars zooming by (or crawling) north and south, people walking over the bridge are treated to steel canopies that extend

The architects worked with Schuler Shook to light the canopies at night. (Credit Anna Munzesheimer, CAC Archive)

from the angled guardrails and another large canopy spanning the street that clearly signals the Red Line entrance. Planted medians are a last element that works with the architecture to transform a utilitarian bridge into a pedestrian-friendly space spanning the expressway.

141

PARK BOULEVARD

VOA Associates (now Stantec), 2013
3622 South State Street
Train: Green to 35th-Bronzeville-IIT
Bus: #29 to State Street at 36th Street

For decades the view down State Street from 35th Street was an unending vista of one public housing block after another, starting with Stateway Gardens and extending to Robert Taylor Homes until 55th Street. Mayor Richard M.

An alternating checkerboard of projecting windows animates the State Street elevation. (Credit Courtesy of Stantec Architecture Inc., Mark Ballogg Photography)

Daley's controversial and prolonged "Plan for Transformation," which used federal HOPE VI funds for demolition and relocation in all of the city's public housing projects, started in 2000. By 2007 all of Stateway Garden's eight high-rise buildings were demolished. Now State Street is fronted by low-scale neo-traditional buildings that express the ambitions of mixed-income, mixed-race neighborhoods—the anathema of public housing policies based on segregation. VOA designed many of the replacement buildings in the Park Boulevard development, including the first one across the street from the Chicago Bee building, now Chicago Public Library branch. It is a playful five-story apartment building marked by projecting windows in a shifting grid.

142

TEEN LIVING PROGRAMS—BELFORT HOUSE

Hartshorne Plunkard Architecture, 2010
3745 South Indiana Avenue
Bus: #39 to Pershing Avenue at Indiana Avenue

The nonprofit Teen Living Programs (TLP) offers services to homeless youth aged 14 to 24 with the goal of providing them stability through housing, education, and opportunities. TLP is based in River North and has two locations on the south side, a drop-in center in a church basement in Englewood, and this three-story building in Bronzeville. The building approaches the domestic through a scale that re-

The domestic-scaled building overlooks a garden to the north. (Credit Angie McMonigal Photography)

calls the city's traditional three-flat dwellings and precast concrete panels with a color resembling brick. Its institutional nature is expressed in the expanses of glass facing the street, a slight angle at the front and back of the building, and the articulation of the concrete panels, which are staggered and pulled in and out to create shadow patterns. The building overlooks a parking lot on the south for a nearby church, but it has its own garden to the north where the main entrance is located.

(Credit Eric Allix Rogers, CAC Archive)

ENGINE COMPANY 16

DLR Group with Interactive Design Architects, 2012
3901 South Wabash Avenue

For a new 20,000-square-foot fire station at 39th and Wabash, DLR Group (working with architect of record Interactive Design Architects) redesigned the city's fire station prototype with a focus on reducing energy usage. The high-performance building envelope, geothermal system, green roof, water recycling for washing trucks, and increased daylighting led to a LEED Platinum Certification.

ARTS AND REC CENTER AT ELLIS PARK

Booth Hansen, 2016
535 East 35th Street

Booth Hansen, the firm responsible for the Chicago Park District's prototype field houses, designed a site-specific two-story building with gymnasium, pool, and arts center for Ellis Park. The building's location at the north end of the triangular park positions it near the new bridge connecting the Bronzeville and Oakland neighborhoods to the lakefront.

35TH STREET PEDESTRIAN BRIDGE

exp, 2016

Lake Shore Drive at 35th Street

(Credit Jeffrey Parfitt)

This pedestrian and bicycle bridge that connects Bronzeville and Oakland residents with the lakefront is a long time coming—Teng & Associates (now part of exp) won a design competition held by the city in 2005 to replace an old non-ADA-compliant bridge. The new design is an elegantly simple curved bridge suspended by cables from a single "A"-shaped mast between the Illinois Central tracks and Lake Shore Drive.

143

31ST STREET HARBOR

EDAW AECOM, 2012

3155 South Lake Shore Drive

Best accessible by car

When EDAW AECOM was selected by the Chicago Park District in 2007 to design a new harbor at 31st Street, the city was in the early throws of Olympic fever. Even before Chicago was named one of the four finalists for the 2016 Olympic Games in 2008, the city developed locations for various events, including sailing competitions to be held on Lake Michigan east of Bronzeville. Although Chicago lost its bid to Rio in 2009, the city built the 31st Street Harbor, which consists of a 2,700-foot-long breakwater, around 1,000 new boat slips, a parking garage tucked below approximately four acres of new park space, a playground, promenade, open lawn areas, and a harbor building housing a restaurant and community space.

From the east, the harbor facilities are purely a building in concrete and glass. (Credit Eric Allix Rogers, CAC Archive)

The project is equal parts building to the east and landscape to the west. Glass walls and concrete beams face the water and the lakefront walkway, while from the green space or playground above one would be hard pressed to realize they are standing upon a building. This approach recalls the DuSable Harbor Building (in Chapter 2) near Lakeshore East, though here the scale is increased to match the number of amenities (more than twice as many slips) and the failed ambitions of the city's Olympics bid.

41ST STREET PEDESTRIAN BRIDGE

Cordogan, Clark & Associates with AECOM, 2018

Lake Shore Drive at 41st Streets

This pedestrian bridge, like the one at 35th Street, replaces an old non-ADA-compliant bridge over the Illinois Central tracks and Lake Shore Drive. The new bridge is structured as a double-curved arch mono truss to create an "S"-shaped plan. Another span by the same team is slated at 43rd Street.

URBAN GREEN HOUSE I AND HYBRID HOUSE

IIT Design-Build Studio, Ray/Dawson, 2007

448 East 44th Street, 454 East 44th Street

Students at the Illinois Institute of Technology, under professors Eva Kultermann and Thomas Gentry, designed and built this compact, two-story house with a central atrium that acts as a solar chimney for ventilating

Urban Green (Credit Eric Allix Rogers, CAC Archive)

Hybrid (Credit Eric Allix Rogers, CAC Archive)

warm air. The similarly ambitious neighbor with the solar panels facing the street is the three-bedroom, two-bath Hybrid House, designed by Ray/Dawson as a hybrid between a net-zero house and more traditional house.

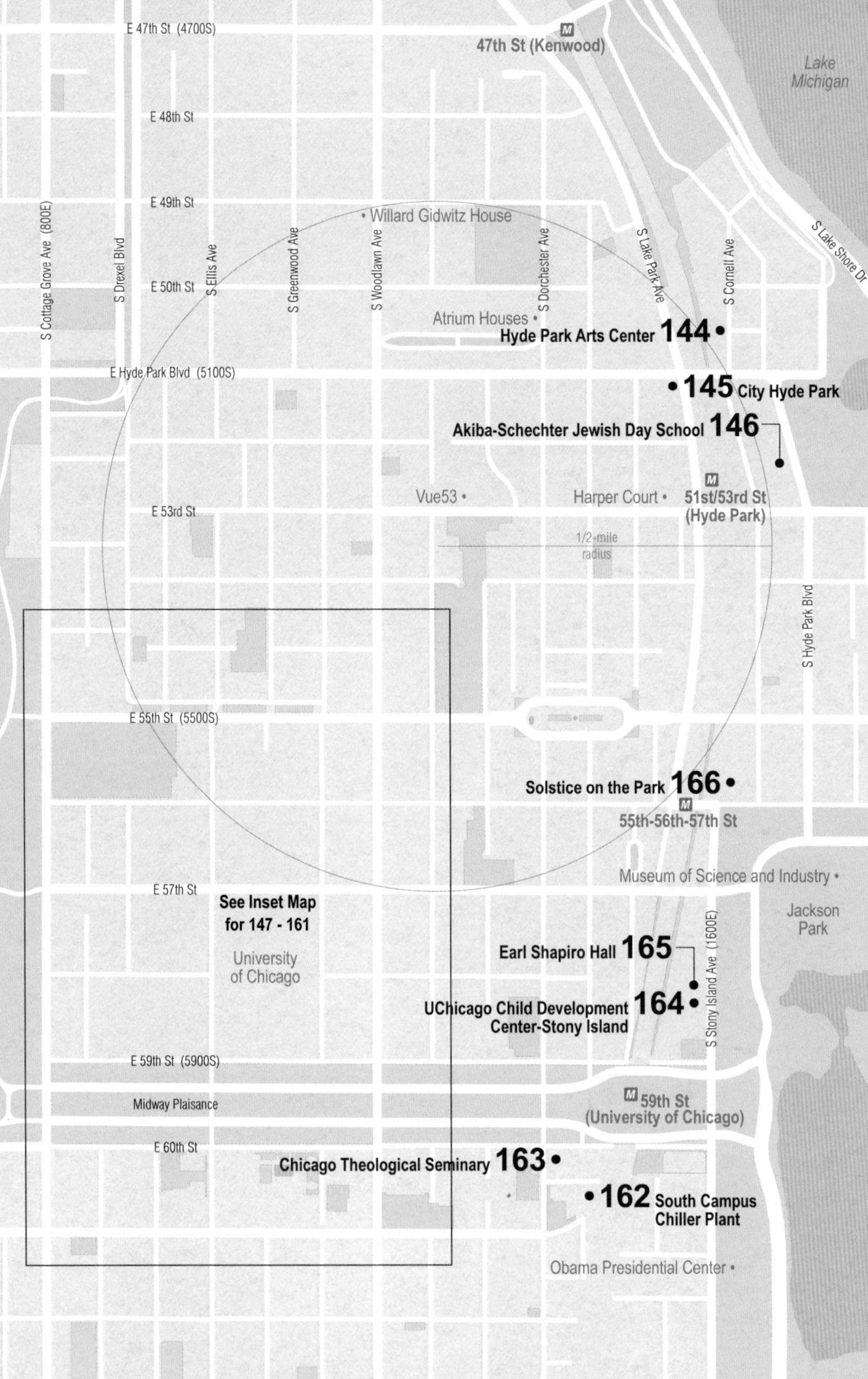
E 47th St (4700S)
47th St (Kenwood)
Lake Michigan
E 48th St
E 49th St
Willard Gidwitz House
S Cottage Grove Ave (800E)
S Drexel Blvd
S Ellis Ave
S Greenwood Ave
S Woodlawn Ave
S Dorchester Ave
S Lake Park Ave
S Cornell Ave
S Lake Shore Dr
E 50th St
Atrium Houses
Hyde Park Arts Center 144
E Hyde Park Blvd (5100S)
145 City Hyde Park
Akiba-Schechter Jewish Day School 146
Vue53
Harper Court
51st/53rd St (Hyde Park)
E 53rd St
1/2-mile radius
S Hyde Park Blvd
E 55th St (5500S)
Solstice on the Park 166
55th-56th-57th St
Museum of Science and Industry
E 57th St
See Inset Map for 147 - 161
University of Chicago
Jackson Park
Earl Shapiro Hall 165
UChicago Child Development Center-Stony Island 164
S Stony Island Ave (1600E)
E 59th St (5900S)
Midway Plaisance
59th St (University of Chicago)
E 60th St
Chicago Theological Seminary 163
162 South Campus Chiller Plant
Obama Presidential Center

17 Hyde Park

Hyde Park *is* the University of Chicago. Certainly this isn't an exclusive condition, but the school's size and influence make it the largest landowner in the area and give it more power than most institutions anywhere in Chicago. Given an endowment of over $7 billion, it's not surprising that under university President Robert J. Zimmer the campus has seen some of the densest—and best—recent architecture in the city, ranging from renovations and expansions of existing buildings to new school buildings, dormitories, and even power plants. Therefore this chapter is the thickest in the book, such that a visit to the neighborhood might have to be made over multiple days.

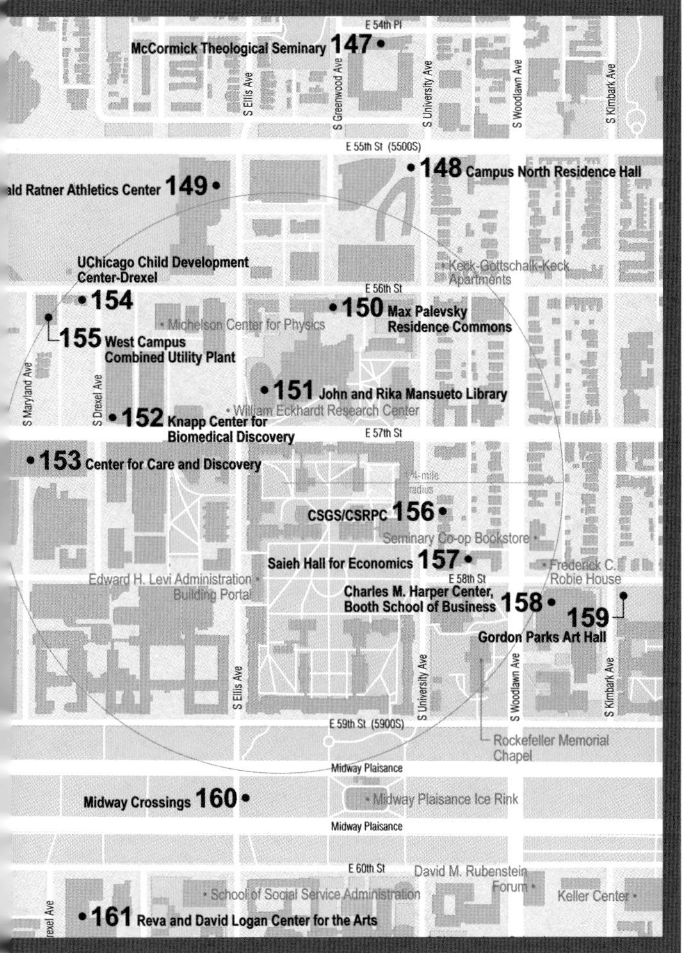

Founded in 1890 by oilman John D. Rockefeller—one year after the town of

Hyde Park was annexed by Chicago—the University of Chicago held its first classes two years later on land donated by Marshall Field. Henry Ives Cobb laid out the main quadrangle, a 27-acre area bounded by 57th Street on the north, Ellis Avenue on the west, 59th Street on the south, and University Avenue on the east; in the ensuing 130 years the university has grown to 215 acres. Cobb, the versatile architect of the Newberry Library and Chicago Varnish Company Building (now Harry Caray's), selected a neo-Gothic style for the campus. He designed buildings with limestone walls and red-tile roofs fronting a large central quadrangle and smaller quads to the north and the south that are reached between and sometimes through the buildings.

The prevalence of limestone in a Gothic guise earned the campus the "Gray City" nickname, which certainly was meant as a counterpoint to the nearby "White City" of the 1893 World's Fair. That influential fair, planned by Daniel H. Burnham and espousing neoclassical architecture and City Beautiful planning, was located to the east and south of the university campus in Jackson Park and along the Midway Plaisance, which Frederick Law Olmsted and Calvert Vaux originally laid out in the 1870s and was later redesigned by successor firms after the fair. Architecturally, all that remains of the fair is the Museum of Science and Industry, which was built as the Palace of Fine Arts but then modified from stucco to stone after the fair (the only other architectural survivor is the Art Institute [**8**] in Grant Park). The University of Chicago bridged the Midway in the 1960s, adding buildings by Mies van der Rohe and Eero Saarinen on its southern edge, just as it partook in urban renewal plans north and east of the campus to "fix" the then-declining neighborhood.

To the north of Hyde Park is the residential Kenwood neighborhood, noted here because it was home to the great architect Louis Sullivan and more recently it was where Barack and Michelle Obama resided with their family before their move to the White House. In 2015, about a year and a half before leaving office, the Obamas selected Hyde Park as the location of the Obama Presidential Center.

(Hyde Park and the University of Chicago are best reached by the Metra Electric District Line from Millennium Park: to 51st / 53rd Street [Hyde Park] for entries between Hyde Park Boulevard and 55th Street; and to 55th—56th—57th Street for those south of 55th Street. As an alternative, bus lines are included with each entry.)

144

HYDE PARK ARTS CENTER

Garofalo Architects, 2007

5020 South Cornell Avenue

Bus: #6 to East Hyde Park Boulevard at Cornell Avenue

On the occasion of the Hyde Park Arts Center (HPAC) opening the first home of its own in 2006, the organization put out a retrospective book called *Perpetually Strange*. The title fittingly describes an organization whose exhibitions and educational programs have been on the cutting edge ever since it was founded in 1939. The renovation of an old Army warehouse (leased long-term by the University of Chicago for $1) by architect Douglas Garofalo subtly extends this strangeness, bringing art to the street through a glass wall with an integral digital projection screen facing Cornell Avenue. Transparent during the day, the wall comes alive after sunset based on the whimsy of the artist controlling it. The wall, propped up by angled columns in front of a quintet

The elevation on Cornell Street comes alive through art installations. (Credit Eric Allix Rogers, CAC Archive)

Behind the glass wall is a mezzanine overlooking the main gallery. (Credit John Hill)

of garage doors, leans out slightly beyond the brick walls of the warehouse. Behind the glass wall is a catwalk linking second-floor galleries, and beyond it still is the museum's main gallery, a double-height space that is bare bones (not surprising, given the $3 million budget) yet which cleverly engages the street through the overhead doors.

Five years after the HPAC's completion, Garofalo died at the age of only 53, making this his only building in the city; he built a number of suburban houses and codesigned a church in Queens, New York. A champion of digital technologies and architecture's "perpetual strangeness," Garofalo's potential is evident in this low-budget yet creative design. It is a shame he wasn't able to continue his explorations on further commissions in the city.

145

CITY HYDE PARK

Studio Gang, 2016
5105 S. Harper Avenue
Bus: #6 to South Lake Park Avenue and East Hyde Park Boulevard

Jeanne Gang's Aqua Tower (**14**) is one of the most creative articulations of a coveted and increasingly common component of urban living: the balcony. Her firm continues their exploration of private outdoor space with this 15-story, 182-unit apartment building that sits on a prime spot across the street from a Metra station and two blocks north of Hyde Park's main commercial thoroughfare. Eleven stories of rental apartments occupy a slab oriented east-west, with one floor of amenities and a roof terrace above a two-story podium fitted with parking, a grocery store, and other retail. Serrated facades face all directions on the residential floors, but the elevation facing south has

Balcony "stems" climb the south side of City Hyde Park's residential slab. (Credit Eric Allix Rogers, CAC Archive)

a layer of balconies structured in what Gang calls "stems." Made of concrete slabs and wall panels that alternate as they ascend the building, the angled balconies are independent, self-supporting structures that add some visual interest to the project, provide some southern shade, orient views obliquely, and, like Aqua, encourage neighbors to interact with each other while outside.

HARPER COURT
Hartshorne Plunkard Architecture, 2013
5235 South Harper Court

(Credit Leslie Schwartz Photography)

Consisting of an office tower, retail, parking, and a hotel (the last designed by Legat Architects), this mixed-use development was created to spur the revitalization of Hyde Park's commercial corridor along 53rd Street. The multiple buildings are oriented along—appropriately enough—Harper Court, an "L"-shaped street with a pedestrian scale that makes it seem like a mall.

146

AKIBA-SCHECHTER JEWISH DAY SCHOOL

John Ronan Architects, 2005

5235 South Cornell Avenue

Bus: #6 to 5200 S South Hyde Park Boulevard

In 1972, the Akiba South Side Jewish Day School and Solomon Schechter South Side School merged to form the Akiba-Schechter Jewish Day School, operating out of two neighboring Hyde Park buildings from that time. In 2003, the elementary school tore down one of its structures and built a two-story addition designed by John Ronan, which connects to the renovated 1950s building with a glass link. Two exterior wall types cover the new building: oxidized copper with horizontal glazing toward the existing school and tilt-up concrete panels finished with an exposed limestone aggregate facing the parking lot and the neighbors to the south. The concrete pieces, notched for narrow vertical windows, include cast Hebrew letters that break up their sizable expanse and turn them into devices for communication.

Precast concrete with Hebrew letters covers part of the addition. (Credit © Nathan Kirkman 2004)

VUE53

Valerio Dewalt Train Associates, 2016

1330 East 53rd Street

This development with 267 apartments overlooking Nichols Park to the south was a long time coming, having been delayed by neighbors who sued due to the bulk of the building. The design by the firm of Joe Valerio breaks down the building to make it appear less massive and to give more residents sunlight and park views.

(Credit Steve Hall © Hall+Merrick)

147

McCORMICK THEOLOGICAL SEMINARY

M+W Zander Architects, 2003

5460 South University Avenue

Bus: #55 to 55th Street at University Avenue

The McCormick Theological Seminary was one of the oldest institutions in the Lincoln Park neighborhood, where it was originally established in 1859. In the early 1970s, the Seminary decided to move, selecting Hyde

Glass walls line the elevation that forms a courtyard with a 1960s Perkins and Will building. (Credit Eric Allix Rogers, CAC Archive)

Park where a cluster of theological institutions already thrived. One of these, the Lutheran School of Theology of Chicago, is housed in an impressive 1960s "U"-shaped building designed by Perkins and Will, which the Seminary's 2003 administrative building connects to, creating an enclosed courtyard in the process. The Seminary's new three-story building designed by M+W Zander (now M+W Group) has a kinked brick facade overlooking a small parking lot on the north, while the south courtyard elevation is all glass, just like the bridges connecting new and old.

148

CAMPUS NORTH RESIDENTIAL COMMONS AND THE FRANK AND LAURA BAKER DINING COMMONS

Studio Gang, 2016

5500 South University Avenue

Bus: #55 to 55th Street at University Avenue

The University of Chicago's first new dormitory since the one designed by Ricardo Legorreta (**150**) on East 56th Street both follows and departs from the campus's traditional architecture. The exterior's grid of flowing precast panels and three-story-tall expanses of glass with steel grilles would hardly be confused for the school's neo-Gothic origins—or even Legorreta's playful brick-and-metal contribution. Yet the way Jeanne Gang, Todd Zima, and the rest of Studio Gang Architects sculpted the precast panels implies vertical movement in a manner that recalls the spire of Rockefeller Chapel, whose height the new dorm respects.

The Campus North Residential Commons is located on East 55th Street, the campus's northern edge. The nearly full block was formerly occupied by Harry Weese's inelegant, ten-story Pierce Tower, which housed 320 students. Gang's 800-student complex is made up of four buildings that range in height from two to fifteen stories. The two-story piece is devoted to a dining commons, while the other three buildings—bar-shaped buildings that are kinked in the middle to give shape to the spaces between them—are devoted to dorm rooms that follow from the University of Chicago's traditional "house system." Each house consists of about seventy students, and here they are organized

Seen from the corner of East 55th Street and University Avenue, the kinked slabs draw visitors toward campus. (Credit John K. Zacherle)

The quad is located at the block's southwest corner, close to the Smart Museum of Art. (Credit Steve Hall © Hall+Merrick)

The dining commons overlooks the diagonal portal that cuts across the site. (Credit Steve Hall © Hall+Merrick)

in three-story "hubs" that are expressed through the triple-height glazing and concrete panels on the facade.

More than the exterior elevations and the stacking of floors, the complex's site plan most strongly relates to the campus's historical architecture while also taking it in a new direction. Like the original campus between the Midway Plaisance and East 57th Street, Gang provides a quad at the site's southwest corner, on land taken from closing a one-block stretch of South Greenwood Avenue. But the orthogonal definition of the quad is eschewed through the diagonal lines of the dorm bars and the circular layout by landscape architect Walter Hood with Terry Guen. A small plaza at the northeast corner funnels students into the building and allows the public to move diagonally across the site to the quad and the rest of the campus beyond.

149

GERALD RATNER ATHLETICS CENTER

Pelli Clarke Pelli Architects, 2003
5530 South Ellis Avenue
Bus: #171 to Ellis Avenue at 55th Street

Though not quite as tall as the 200-foot-tall bell tower of the Rockefeller Memorial Chapel in the middle of the University of Chicago campus, the 120-foot-tall masts of the university's new athletic complex stand out in the campus's northwest corner. Five steel masts with thick bundled cables support two undulating roofs over the pool to the north and the gymnasium to the south. The building also contains a practice gym, a dance studio, weight rooms, exercise rooms, locker rooms, and offices. Both the masts and the glass walls next to them lean out slightly, as if to express the resistance of the cable structural system at play. Between the pool and gym are an east-facing plaza and the main entrance, which is housed in a round volume whose brick wall ascends toward a trio of the masts, reinforcing their importance.

The curling entry wall rises up toward the masts over the natatorium. (Credit Anna Munzesheimer, CAC Archive)

150

MAX PALEVSKY RESIDENCE COMMONS

Legorreta + Legorreta with VOA Associates (now Stantec), 2001

1101 East 56th Street

Bus: #171 to Ellis Avenue at 55th Street

Limestone walls and red tile roofs predominantly make up the University of Chicago's traditional neo-Gothic campus. Therefore, this addition to the campus by Mexican architect Ricardo Legorreta is a bit of an odd fit, given that the limestone and red roofing were eschewed in favor of, respectively, orange brick and purple standing seam metal. The project caps the north end of a

The "Barbie" pavilion at the corner of East 56th Street and South Ellis Avenue. (Credit Eric Allix Rogers, CAC Archive)

block occupied primarily by the Regenstein Library, another building clearly at odds with the campus's traditional architecture. To provide some scale and distinction, the dormitory is broken down into three four-story buildings, each one distinguished by full-height glass pavilions with window frames rendered in pink, purple, and yellow—Barbie, Barney, and Big Bird, to students.[1]

151

JOE AND RIKA MANSUETO LIBRARY

Murphy/Jahn (now JAHN), 2011

1100 East 57th Street

Bus: #171 to Ellis Avenue at 55th Street

Before the completion of this addition to the 1970 Regenstein Library, designed by Skidmore, Owings & Merrill's Walter Netsch, architect Helmut Jahn

Steel tubes structure the glass dome. (Credit John Hill)

had designed and realized two power plants for the University of Chicago (**155**, **162**). Each one is a glass-and-steel design that puts the mechanical equipment housed inside on display. While glass and steel are also prevalent in the domed design of "the Egg"—the affectionate name for the Joe and Rika Mansueto Library that is connected to "the Reg" by a glass walkway—the addition takes the opposite tactic and hides the library's equipment.

Tucked below the glass dome and reading room is a sophisticated automatic retrieval system that stores up to 3.5 million volumes. Twelve full-height metal racks holding 24,000 bins are located fifty-five feet below grade to help maintain appropriate temperature and humidity levels for the books. Patrons request a book from a computer and a robotic crane retrieves the bin and book within five minutes.

The decision to build a state-of-the-art storage system on campus gives students and researchers access to the university's books as needed, unlike the day or more it would take if the volumes were located offsite, a popular option in our digital age. Capping the below-grade storage with the glass dome also gives students a grand reading room and it provides librarians, behind glass walls, spaces for two tasks that would seem to be at odds with each other: the conservation and digitization of books. Yet in its decision to locate physical books within easy reach, the university has acknowledged information's hybrid physical/digital state in the 21st century and created its own architectural icon.

WILLIAM ECKHARDT RESEARCH CENTER

HOK, 2015

5640 S. Ellis Avenue

This five-story addition to University of Chicago campus houses a number of science research groups as well as the new Institute for Molecular Engineering. Glass predominates, with the serrated east- and west-facing facades, designed with glass expert (and designer of the Midway Crossings [**160**]) James Carpenter, being the most distinctive.

152

GWEN AND JULES KNAPP CENTER FOR BIOMEDICAL DISCOVERY

ZGF Architects, 2009

900 East 57th Street

Bus: #171 to Ellis Avenue at 57th Street

Some architects in the early 20th century theorized glass as a transparent material that would create a truly open and modern architecture connecting people to nature. But the material's reality made that utopian dream impossible, since glass is reflective, transmits heat, and can kill birds in large numbers. Nevertheless, glass has retained its status as the most important modern material. It is now seen in a more multifaceted manner, as witnessed by this new ten-story medical and research building that is part of the University of Chicago Medical Center. Glass is the predominant exterior material (all but a contextual limestone base), but most of it is opaque, in white and green panes. Clear glass is limited to horizontal clerestory windows at the labs and vertical sections that correspond to circulation spaces. But inside, out of sight to the public, is where that dream of transparency prevails, as clear-glass partitions allow researchers to see each other while encouraging them to interact.

Serrated glass of clear and opaque glass covers the west side of the building. (Credit Eric Allix Rogers, CAC Archive)

153

CENTER FOR CARE AND DISCOVERY

Rafael Viñoly Architects with CannonDesign, 2013

5700 South Maryland Avenue

Bus: #2 to Cottage Grove Avenue at 59th Street

While the 200-foot-tall bell tower of the Rockefeller Memorial Chapel looks out over the original neo-Gothic campus of the University of Chicago, the 225-foot-tall Center for Care and Discovery stands above everything at the west campus's Medical Center. But where the neo-Gothic tower punctuates the skyline above the trees, this ten-story, one-million-plus-square-foot hospital building looms over campus like a cruise ship run aground. The building, which houses high-technology research and advanced patient care, spans two city blocks, from Drexel Avenue on the east to South Cottage Grove on the west where it overlooks Washington Park.

The stacked layers of the building are evident on each side. (Credit Eric Allix Rogers, CAC Archive)

Although the largest building on campus, Rafael Viñoly's design breaks down the bulk into stacked layers that he calls the factory, the garden, and the house. From bottom to top, the building features four stories of horizontal windows punctuated by raking metal panels, a one-story gap on the seventh floor with recessed glass walls and orange metal panels, and three stories with more horizontal windows alternating with metal panels, this time corrugated. A generously sized mechanical penthouse caps the building, punctuated by two vertical core extensions that most contribute to the cruise ship metaphor. Interior highlights are found on the seventh floor: the sky lobby, the curving wood-lined chapel, and the dining area with great views toward downtown.

154

UCHICAGO CHILD DEVELOPMENT CENTER—DREXEL

Ross Barney Architects, 2013
5610 South Drexel Avenue
Bus: #55 to 55th Street at Drexel Avenue

In 2013, the University of Chicago opened its first two childcare centers, this one located on Drexel Avenue adjacent to the West Campus Combined Utility Plant (**155**) and the buildings of the Medical Center (the other childcare center is located on Stony Island Avenue [**164**]). Given the expansion of this part of campus, where professionals outnumber students, it makes sense to provide daycare, just as it makes sense to hire the firm of Carol Ross Barney, which has executed a number of buildings for early education. Their design of the one-story building focuses on color and light: yellow panels brighten the exterior walls, while selective expanses of glass—some of it treated with frits in treelike patterns—bring plenty of sunlight inside.

Yellow panels enliven the exterior by the center's entrance. (Credit Kate Joyce Studios)

155

WEST CAMPUS COMBINED UTILITY PLANT

Murphy/Jahn (now JAHN), 2010

5617 South Maryland Avenue

Bus: #2 to Cottage Grove Avenue at 56th Street

Helmut Jahn opted for a softer, more rounded, form when designing the South Campus Chiller Plant (**162**) for the University of Chicago, but faced here with a site hemmed in by other buildings on the west campus, he built taller and stuck to the rectilinear. The same idea that worked in the earlier plant works here: clear glass is used to put the boilers, pumps, and chillers on display, while perforated metal is used when needed, such as at the top of the building where the cooling towers require air movement. Although the West Campus Combined Utility Plant, which serves the Medical Center, is not as striking as the South Campus Chiller Plant's rounded corners, its less-out-of-the-way location gives it a prominence that is befitting the top-notch architecture it displays.

Glass walls put the boilers, pumps, and chillers on display. (Credit Rainer Viertlböck, courtesy of JAHN)

MICHELSON CENTER FOR PHYSICS

Perkins Eastman, 2017

933 East 56th Street

Perkins Eastman renovated and expanded Skidmore, Owings & Merrill's two-story, concrete-framed Laboratory for Astrophysics and Space Research from 1965, doubling the building's height and wrapping the whole in glass and stone. A hint of the former's deep-set structure can be grasped at the first floor facing 56th Street and in two stories across its side elevations.

EDWARD H. LEVI ADMINISTRATION BUILDING PORTAL

Krueck Sexton Partners with Gensler, 2014

5801 South Ellis Avenue

The University of Chicago's original 27-acre neo-Gothic campus has little to no room for contemporary architecture, which makes this small walkway piercing a 1948 building on the western edge of the quad such a great surprise. Glass walls above the portal give views into the second floor, while the glass walls lining the sides of the walkway are angled and tapered in plan, providing some visual interest while also mitigating a wind-tunnel effect.

156

CSGS/CSRPC

David Woodhouse Architects (now Woodhouse Tinucci Architects), 2013

5733 South University Avenue

Bus: #171 to University Avenue at 57th Street

This building on the University of Chicago campus expands the facilities of the school's Center for the Study of Gender and Sexuality (CSGS) and the Center for the Study of Race, Politics, and Culture (CSRPC), which share a small three-story brick building built in 1901 as a townhouse for a professor.

The corrugated, copper-colored addition seen from the alley. (Credit Mike Schwartz)

The three-story addition is placed behind the brick building and is accessed by a walkway between the pair and the neighbor to the north. (It is best seen from the mid-block alley, which also gives a view of the addition to the Saieh Hall for Economics [**157**].) Even as the new does not try to mimic the old, the skin of corrugated metal in a copper color melds well with the existing brick building. Some of the exterior panels are perforated, meaning that the building takes on a slightly different character at night when "hidden" windows make their presence known.

157

SAIEH HALL FOR ECONOMICS

Ann Beha Architects with Gensler, 2014
5757 South University Avenue
Bus: #172 to Woodlawn Avenue at 58th Street

In 2008 the University of Chicago bought the impressive 1928 Chicago Theological Seminary building in order to turn it into the Department of Economics and the Becker Friedman Institute for Research in Economics. The seminary moved south of the Midway Plaisance in 2011 (**163**) and the Seminary Co-op Bookstore moved across the street on Woodlawn, but the Saieh Hall for Economics is a complex project that actually involves four buildings, three of which were existing.

The illuminated "cuts" by the new ramp hint at the below-grade lecture hall. (Credit Tom Rossiter)

An addition at the rear of the old seminary buildings adds a contemporary flourish. (Credit Tom Rossiter)

The renovation of the substantial seminary building is the main piece in the project, though much of the sensitive transformation by Boston architect Ann Beha isn't visible from the outside but is hinted at by the light flooding out through the replacement windows. The most overt change is visible at the front of the building to the right of the bell tower and entrance (the seminary formerly fronted 58th Street, but as part of the plan it now looks onto a pedestrian mall). A series of ramps, planters, and clerestory windows for the new below-grade seminar room now front a new first-floor glass wall while providing wheelchair access to the raised entrance.

The other two existing buildings are row houses on Woodlawn Avenue that previously served as part of the Laboratory Schools but have been renovated and linked to Saieh Hall. The fourth and last piece is a three-story addition, a research pavilion that sits behind the seminary building and is oriented perpendicular to it along the mid-block alley-turned-pedestrian-way. Here is the project's contemporary flourish: glass walls face east and west on the top two floors, while a metal wall caps the north end, all sitting above a base of masonry and glass.

SEMINARY CO-OP BOOKSTORE

Tigerman McCurry Architects, 2012
5751 South Woodlawn Avenue

As the name indicates, this stalwart Hyde Park bookstore (it has another location on 57th Street) was formerly housed in the Chicago Theological Seminary, now Saieh Hall for Economics (**157**). That mazelike basement space finds contemporary expression in the new space across the street, which is full of custom bookcases set at a forty-five-degree angle to the walls. The project, in the ground floor of an unremarkable late-1950s building, also includes a café overlooking Frank Lloyd Wright's neighboring iconic Robie House.

158

CHARLES M. HARPER CENTER, UNIVERSITY OF CHICAGO BOOTH SCHOOL OF BUSINESS

Rafael Viñoly Architects, 2004

5807 South Woodlawn Avenue

Bus: #172 to Woodlawn Avenue at 58th Street

Gothic meets Prairie in Rafael Viñoly's competition-winning design for the University of Chicago's Booth School of Business, which was scattered about five buildings on campus before 2004. This melding of quite different architecture styles comes from the Argentinian-born, New York–based architect finding inspiration in two neighbors: Rockefeller Memorial Chapel, built in a neo-Gothic style in 1928, and Frank Lloyd Wright's Robie House, a Prairie

The tall atrium sits in the middle, among cantilevered glass and stone boxes. (Credit Eric Allix Rogers, CAC Archive)

Style masterpiece from 1909. From the exterior, the asymmetrically stacked boxes and horizontal bands of glass and limestone seem akin to the much smaller Robie House with its strong horizontal rooflines. Inside, curved steel beams support the roof of the six-story winter garden (open to the public) at the heart of the 416,000-square-foot building, referencing the neo-Gothic vaults of the Chapel. One does not need to know about these precedents to realize that they work together to make a very large building less imposing—and even inviting.

159

GORDON PARKS ART HALL

Valerio Dewalt Train Associates with FGM Architects, 2015
5815 South Kimbark Avenue
Bus: #172 to Woodlawn Avenue at 58th Street

Since John Dewey founded the University of Chicago Laboratory Schools in 1896 as an experimental K-12 arm of the university, the Lab has occupied a block overlooking the Midway Plaisance. In need of more space this century, they hired Joe Valerio's firm for a master plan that included the off-site Earl Shapiro Hall (**165**), the renovation of the Lab's main campus, and a sizable new building to the north. The latter, home to the school's spaces for music and performing arts, opened in October 2015 as Gordon Parks Art Hall, named for the African-American director (*Shaft* his most well-known film), author, photogra-

Seen from the northwest, the Gothic inspirations of the contemporary creation are clear. (Credit Steve Hall © Hedrich Blessing)

Inside, circulation spaces flow around—and even penetrate—the circular assembly hall. (Credit Steve Hall © Hedrich Blessing)

pher, and poet, following a $25 million gift from the George Lucas Family Foundation. Valerio's design is like 21st-century Gothic, with exaggerated gable forms clad in limestone, vertical piers faced in glass, and angled glass walls knitting the two together. Through its formal rhythms and layering of materials, the building is like frozen music—a suitable expression for what happens inside.

160

MIDWAY CROSSINGS

James Carpenter Design Associates with BauerLatoza Studio and Schuler Shook, 2013

Ellis, Woodlawn, and Dorchester Avenues from 59th to 60th Streets

Bus: #59 to Dorchester Avenue at 61st Street

In 1870, Frederick Law Olmsted was hired to lay out South Park, which would later become Washington Park, Jackson Park, and the Midway Plaisance. By 1893, the sprawling Jackson Park and the linear Midway Plaisance would become sites of the World's Fair. Olmsted designed the Midway with bridges traversing a canal that would connect ponds in the other two parks, but this feature was put on hold by the Great Fire of 1871 and never built. Regardless, the low grade of the now grassy Midway makes traversing it feel like walking across bridges, something accentuated by the bowed walkways and lighting of the crossings designed by New York's James Carpenter with BauerLatoza Studio and the lighting designers at Schuler Shook. Connecting the University of Chicago campus on the north with the Woodlawn neighborhood and expanding campus to the south, the design's most dramatic feature is the 40-foot-high illuminated masts that light evenly from top to bottom so as to be seen at a distance and create a safe environment up close.

The pylons are illuminated to make the crossing safe and enjoyable. (Credit Tom Rossiter Photography)

The simple slender pylons look like lines of light at night. (Credit Tom Rossiter Photography)

161

REVA AND DAVID LOGAN CENTER FOR THE ARTS

Tod Williams Billie Tsien Architects with Holabird & Root, 2012

915 East 60th Street

Bus: #2 to Cottage Grove Avenue at 60th Street

New York–based, husband-and-wife architects Tod Williams and Billie Tsien bested four well-known architects—Hans Hollein, Daniel Libeskind, Fumihiko Maki, and Thom Mayne—in an invited competition in 2006 to design what the duo calls "a mixing bowl for the arts."[2] As completed six years later on a site overlooking the Midway Plaisance, the Logan Center contains facilities for visual arts, music, performance, and film, including classrooms, studios, media labs, rehearsal rooms, a screening hall, a performance space, a gallery, a café, and a courtyard—truly a mixing bowl.

From the beginning of the design process, the architects envisioned the building consisting of two parts: a tower and a field. This concept was based on the image of a silo sitting in a Midwestern field as well as one of the Chi-

The tower rises above the sawtooth skylights of the studios. (Credit © Tom Rossiter)

cago skyline—tall buildings rising from the flat landscape. The final result is faithful to this initial image: a ten-story tower sits next to a three-story base, with the main entrance off of 60th Street inserted between the two. The base, housing most of the program and capped by north-facing skylights (and solar panels facing south) for the studios, is of a similar scale to earlier university buildings south of the Midway: Eero Saarinen's Law School, Mies van der Rohe's School of Social Service Administration one block south, and the Midway Studios that form one edge of the Logan's courtyard.

It's the tower that makes the building stand out in its context, acting as a landmark in the south campus (much like the Rockefeller Memorial Chapel does on the main campus) and providing sweeping views of Hyde Park and the distant downtown skyline. Yet more than the café at its base, the stacked music rooms, and the double-height event/performance space at the top, the tower is a joy to walk up and down, thanks to stairs designed to be "beautiful, varied, and fun to use," in the words of the architects.[3] The same can be said about the rest of the building, which is full of sensuous materials, pleasing spaces, and surprises every step of the way.

The main entrance is inserted between the tower and the studios. (Credit © Tom Rossiter)

(Credit Kate Joyce, Hedrich Blessing Photographers)

UNIVERSITY OF CHICAGO HOSPITALS PARKING STRUCTURE AND CLINIC

Ross Barney Architects, 2009

6054 South Drexel Avenue

What looks like a glass office building is actually a narrow, "L"-shaped administrative center wrapping a large 1,010-car parking garage that serves the Medical Center north of the Midway Plaisance. The garage is taller, but set back from the administration spaces, so as to disappear when seen up close. Entry to the garage happens at the north and west ends of the office component.

DAVID M. RUBENSTEIN FORUM

Diller Scofidio + Renfro with Brininstool + Lynch, 2020

Woodlawn Avenue at East 60th Street

New York's DS+R was selected in 2015 to design a 90,000-square-foot building with meeting spaces for workshops, symposiums, lectures, and other events. The massing of a two-story base and eight-story tower recalls the nearby Logan Center (**161**), though here the metal-and-glass tower pushes and pulls to express the meeting rooms inside.

(Credit Courtesy of Diller Scofidio + Renfro)

THE KELLER CENTER, HARRIS SCHOOL OF PUBLIC POLICY

Farr Associates with Woodhouse Tinucci Architects, 2018
1307 East 60th Street

Farr Associates transformed a residence hall designed by Edward Durell Stone in the 1960s into a research and teaching center for the Harris School. At its heart is the Harris Forum, a four-story atrium carved from the original structure. Here, artist Theaster Gates worked with area residents to mill wood for the inviting space.

(Credit © Tom Rossiter)

162

SOUTH CAMPUS CHILLER PLANT

Murphy/Jahn (now JAHN), 2010

6035 South Blackstone Avenue

Bus: #59 to Dorchester Avenue at 61st Street

When Helmut Jahn was hired by the University of Chicago to design two power plants on campus—one south of the Midway and one by its expanding Medical Center (**155**)—he approached the former with soft lines and the latter with hard edges. Sited next to Metra Electric railroad tracks and the university's steam plant, the new South Campus plant is basically a glass-and-metal box with rounded corners, both in plan and section. The clear glass walls put the pumps, boilers, and chillers on display, heightened by a color coding that follows from their functions (blue for chillers, red for boilers, and so forth). Perforated metal is used elsewhere, where walls are solid or equipment is enclosed. It's a straightforward diagram that is elevated to elegance through materials and form.

The new chiller plant sits next to a brick-and-stone power plant. (Credit Eric Allix Rogers, CAC Archive)

163

CHICAGO THEOLOGICAL SEMINARY

Nagle Hartray Danker Kagan McKay Penney, 2012

1407 East 60th Street

Bus: 2# to 60th Street at Blackstone Avenue

The Chicago Theological Seminary (CTS) was founded in 1855, thirty-five years before John D. Rockefeller founded the University of Chicago, making it the oldest institution of higher education in Chicago. The Seminary's 1928 building was bought by the University of Chicago and turned into the Saieh Hall for Economics (**157**), so CTS headed south of the Midway and moved into a new four-story building designed by the firm that is now Sheehan Nagle Hartray Architects. Given the prominent location overlooking the Midway, the building is covered predominantly in a buff-colored brick that resembles the limestone of the university's neo-Gothic campus. Metal panels and a chapel housed in a round volume on the top floor add some visual interest, while the northeast corner of the ground floor has a small chapel that incorporates stained glass salvaged from its previous home.

The chapel is behind the curved walls visible atop the building. (Credit Tom Rossiter Photography)

OBAMA PRESIDENTIAL CENTER

Tod Williams Billie Tsien Architects, Interactive Design Architects, *estimated completion in 2023*

Jackson Park, South Stony Island Avenue at East 62nd Street

In 2016, the Obama Foundation selected the New York firm of husband-and-wife architects Tod Williams and Billie Tsien (who received National Medals of Arts from Barack Obama in 2013) and Chicago's IDEA to design a public campus with museum, classrooms, labs, and community facilities. Located on the western edge of Jackson Park west of Wooded Island, the initial design features a plaza formed by three buildings—one tall and two with landscaped roofs (by Michael Van Valkenburgh)—that attempt to blend the sizable project into the park.

164

UCHICAGO CHILD DEVELOPMENT CENTER—STONY ISLAND

Wheeler Kearns Architects, 2013

5824 South Stony Island Avenue

Bus: #2 to 5800 South Stony Island Avenue

Tucked between an apartment building and the Lab school (**165**), this is the second childcare center for the University of Chicago, having opened a few months after the Drexel location near the Medical Center (**154**). The one-story building with serrated roofline is made up of narrow volumes that make a stretched "Z" in plan. This creates two outdoor spaces: one oriented toward the Metra tracks to the west and one facing Jackson Park on the east. The latter sits behind a wire-mesh gabion fence that looks like a landscape painting made with rocks. Large boulders toward the entrance continue the nature theme, which is also picked up in the bark siding of one of the facades overlooking the playground.

Entry to the school is through a "fence" of boulders. (Credit Eric Allix Rogers, CAC Archive)

165

EARL SHAPIRO HALL

Valerio Dewalt Train Associates with FGM Architects, 2013

5800 South Stony Island Avenue

Bus: #2 to Stony Island & 59th Street

Founded by philosopher John Dewey in 1896, the University of Chicago Laboratory Schools provide education for children from nursery school to high school. The private Lab School is comprised of five schools (nursery, primary, lower, middle, and high), most of them situated on the main campus that fills two city blocks on 59th Street just east of the University of Chicago's main campus. As of 2013, the nursery and primary schools (to second grade) moved to the new Earl Shapiro Hall located just east of the Metra tracks and overlooking Jackson Park.

The school's design is based on the child-centered Reggio Emilia approach that is akin to Dewey's educational system developed more than one hundred years ago. The approach finds application in open and flexible layouts and in classrooms connected directly to the outdoors; the latter is visible in the small

The library cantilevers over the entrance at the south end of the school. (Credit Eric Allix Rogers, CAC Archive)

playgrounds at the front and back of the building and on the roof overlooking the park. The most striking feature of the building is the third-floor library that boldly cantilevers over the entrance and academic wing, all overlooking the childcare center to the south (**164**). The faceted glass and angled fins of the cantilevered volume indicate that, even in our digital age, the library is a space of creativity.

166

SOLSTICE ON THE PARK

Studio Gang, 2018

1616 East 56th Street

Bus: #2 to Stony Island & 57th Street

Unveiled in 2007, the Great Recession appeared to kill this 26-story condo tower just steps from Jackson Park, but in late 2016 construction finally started on the building, which had shifted to rental apartments—250 of them across 25 floors. Still in place, thankfully, is the design's unique southern facade,

The angled glass walls create kaleidoscopic reflections on the south facade. (Credit © Tom Harris)

where glass walls are cut back at 72 degrees to limit direct sunlight in the summer but welcome it in the winter.

Overlooking the Museum of Science and Industry at the northwestern corner of Jackson Park, the slablike form of Solstice on the Park resembles the unremarkable tower from the 1960s two blocks to the east. But with its checkerboard-like pattern of vertical and angled south-facing glass walls—in two-story bands across the lower half and three-story bands at top—the 272-foot-tall Solstice on the Park has a lovely, jewel-like appearance, especially when the sun rises over nearby Lake Michigan.

Seen from inside the building, the angled walls culminate in generous terraces for residents. (Credit © Tom Harris)

Cottage Grove
E 63rd St (6300S)
63rd Street
Jackson Park
E Marquette Rd
67th Street
E 67th St (6700S)
Stony Island Arts Bank
E 68th St
Oak Woods Cemetery
Dorchester Projects
S Dorchester Ave
S Dante Ave
S Harper Ave
E 70th St
167 Dorchester Artist Housing Collaborative
Stony Island
Bryn Mawr
E 71st St (7100S)
169 Gary Comer College Prep
1/2-mile radius
168 Gary Comer Youth Center
Greater Grand Crossing Library
E 73rd St
75th Street (Grand Crossing)
E 75th St (7500S)
South Shore International College Prep High School 170
E 76th St
S Cottage Grove Ave (800E)
S Greenwood Ave
Chicago Skyway
S South Chicago Ave
S Stony Island Ave (1600E)
S Jeffrey Blvd
E 79th St (7900S)
79th Street
CTA 95th/Dan Ryan Terminal
Method Manufacturing Facility

18 Grand Crossing & South Shore

The neighborhoods in the chapter are located south of Jackson Park and nearby Oak Woods Cemetery and east of the Skyway, which cuts a diagonal path across the South Side from Indiana until it meets the Dan Ryan Expressway. Like other parts of Chicago's South Side, the neighborhoods of South Shore and Grand Crossing were transformed in the 20th century by an influx of African Americans and the "white flight" of European and Jewish residents. Twenty-first-century investment in various forms is leading to a transformation of these neighborhoods that benefit from proximity to Lake Michigan, Jackson Park, and even the University of Chicago.

South Shore fills the area east of Stony Island Avenue from 67th Street to 79th Street. Its most famous historic architectural resident is the South Shore Cultural Center (formerly South Shore Country Club), a stately landmark from the early 1900s that is surrounded by a nine-hole golf course and fronts a beach on Lake Michigan. In addition to being a popular venue for weddings and other parties, the large building hosts cultural programs, classes, and other community-oriented events. About a half-mile west of the Center is Jackson Park Highlands, a historic district that was planned in 1905 and has traditionally been a middle- and upper-class neighborhood among the surrounding underserved neighborhoods of Woodlawn, Grand Crossing, and other parts of South Shore below 71st Street.

West of Jackson Park Highlands, between Stony Island Avenue and the Metra Electric railroad tracks alongside Oak Woods Cemetery, is a portion of Grand Crossing that is almost single-handedly being transformed by artist Theaster Gates and his Rebuild Foundation. Having moved into an old building on Dorchester Avenue in 2006, the artist invested in the area, creating an arts compound from old buildings, renovating an old bank, and creating housing for artists.

Immediately south of the cemetery—in a triangular section formed by it, the Skyway, and the Metra tracks—is an area that saw investment by another individual: Lands' End founder Gary Comer. Originally from the neighborhood, he donated funds to fix up his old elementary school, built a youth center, and posthumously—through his Comer Science & Education Foundation—built a high school and a library. Comer and Gates are examples of how individuals can make a difference, while also illustrating how public dollars haven't reached the places that need them most.

167

DORCHESTER ART + HOUSING COLLABORATIVE

Landon Bone Baker Architects, 2014

1456 East 70th Street

Bus: #73 to Stony Island Avenue at 70th Street

Chicago artist Theaster Gates founded the nonprofit Rebuild Foundation as a means of using cultural initiatives to redevelop underserved neighborhoods, focusing his efforts on the Grand Crossing neighborhood about one mile south of the University of Chicago in Hyde Park. That an artist would undertake such a "project" is not surprising considering he has a master's

An arts center sits in the middle of the two halves of the restored housing project. (Credit Mark Ballogg Photography)

The buildings for the 32 rental units were restored to their original modern designs. (Credit Mark Ballogg Photography)

degree in urban planning. Architecturally, his most ambitious project is this transformation of the former Dante Harper housing project into thirty-two mixed-income rental apartments with an art center inserted between them. The Rebuild Foundation worked with Brinshore Development to realize the project that is a few blocks south of the Dorchester Projects that were the beginning of Gates's slow and steady impact on the area.

Landon Bone Baker, a firm that specializes in affordable and supportive housing, used a subtle hand with the design, which restores the formerly boarded-up buildings to their modern design. The only flourish is the art center, which involved the demolition of a few of the units on the south-facing block, but which gives the multifaceted project a heart. The setback of the art center creates a landscaped plaza in the front and defines two landscaped areas in the rear adjacent to the alley and a row of surface parking.

DORCHESTER PROJECTS

Theaster Gates, 2011

6918 South Dorchester Avenue

Artist Theaster Gates renovated two buildings (originally a residence and a candy store) in the Grand Crossing neighborhood into what he calls the Listening Room and Archive Houses. The latter is covered in reclaimed wood and old windows in an arrangement that indicates something different is happening inside. Before being moved to the Stony Island Arts Bank, the Archive House (open to the public during events and by appointment) contained books from the late Prairie Avenue Bookshop, one of the best architecture bookstores that ever existed.

(Credit © Tom Harris)

STONY ISLAND ARTS BANK

Theaster Gates, 2015

6760 South Stony Island Avenue

Although Theaster Gates was able to purchase the majestic 1923 bank at 68th Street and Stony Island Avenue for one dollar, he and his Rebuild Foundation spent much more than that on renovating it as a cultural venue, artist and scholar residencies, and archive for his foundation's collections. The project was completed in 2015 just in time for it to be a South Side venue in the inaugural Chicago Architecture Biennial.

168

GARY COMER YOUTH CENTER

John Ronan Architects, 2006

7200 South Ingleside Avenue

Bus: #30 to South Chicago Avenue and Ingleside Avenue

The places of our childhood stay with us long after leaving. For Gary Comer, a competitive sailor and founder of the clothing retailer Lands' End, that place was Grand Crossing. After visiting his grade school, Paul Revere Elementary, in 1998 at the age of 60, the billionaire decided to invest in his old neighborhood, setting up the Comer Science & Education Foundation. From that he donated money to help fix up his old school and, a few years later, open a youth center one block away. Offering after-school programs for kids and serving as the home of the South Shore Drill Team, the Gary Comer Youth Center opened in 2006, the same year that Comer succumbed to cancer.

Comer's optimism and links to his childhood neighborhood find suitable expression in John Ronan's colorful design, a two-story rectangular box facing the diagonal South Chicago Avenue that parallels the adjacent railroad tracks and Skyway. Elevations covered in fiber-cement panels in reds, blues, and white were designed as a means of addressing graffiti—individual panels

The mesh-clad tower and LED signage give the school an evening presence. (Credit Steve Hall © Hedrich Blessing 2006)

Skylights pop through the urban garden atop the gymnasium. (Credit Steve Hall © Hedrich Blessing 2006)

could be replaced as needed, but to date that has not been necessary thanks to the neighborhood's fondness for the building. Glassy portions of the exterior cantilever beyond these walls to hint at the activity taking place inside. One glass box hangs over the entrance on Ingleside Avenue to the south, next to an 80-foot-high tower clad in mesh that is illuminated from the inside at night and capped by LED signage. In the center of the three-story building's plan is a gymnasium that is also used for performances; it is topped by a green roof designed by Hoerr Schaudt Landscape Architects as a place for children to learn how to grow food in the city.

169

GARY COMER COLLEGE PREP

John Ronan Architects, 2010

7131 South Chicago Avenue

Bus: #71 to 71st Street at Cottage Grove Avenue/South Chicago Avenue

Four years after the opening of the Gary Comer Youth Center (**168**), this charter high school opened on a lot north of the earlier building's parking lot. Together the two buildings form a campus, with the high school students in the College Prep School (run by the Noble Network of Charter Schools) using the gymnasium, cafeteria, music rooms, art rooms, and computer labs in the Youth Center. The space of the parking lot (used by the South Shore Drill Team at certain times) connects the two buildings via a walkway on its eastern edge.

Architecturally, one might be at a loss to decipher that the same architect designed the two buildings, although they exhibit similar rectangular massing. The patterning of red and blue fiber cement panels used at the Youth Center is substituted here with lime-green aluminum panels, some of them on display and some covered by perforated corrugated stainless steel. These panels are also found on the third floor of the Youth Center facing South Chicago Avenue, but here it covers the two-story building's whole street elevation, notched at the south end to open up access to the lobby.

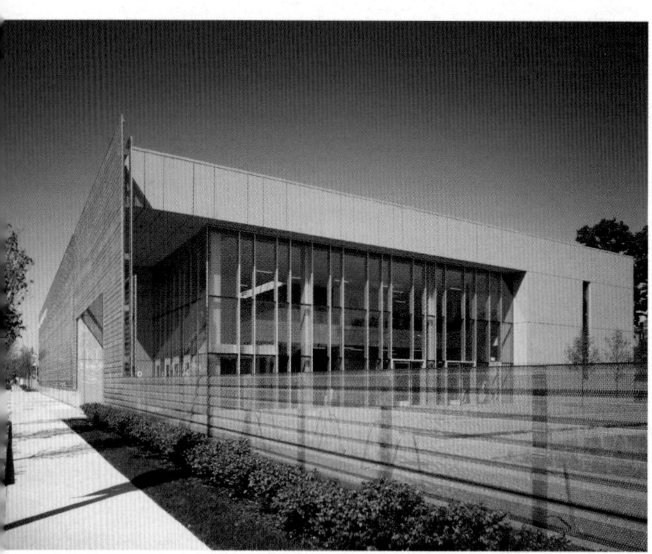

The glass-walled lobby faces the parking lot next to the Youth Center. (Credit Steve Hall © Hedrich Blessing 2010)

Inside the double-height lobby. (Credit Steve Hall © Hedrich Blessing 2010)

Large glass walls face the more secure parking lot side of the building, revealing the double-height lobby. What may appear dark from the outside is surprisingly light, thanks to two parallel rows of skylights that illuminate the corridors in the middle of the building.

GREATER GRAND CROSSING BRANCH LIBRARY

Lohan Anderson, 2011

1000 East 73rd Street

This small branch library is located one block south of the Gary Comer Youth Center (**168**) on land that the Lands' End founder donated to the city. The library, like others in the city that follow Lohan Anderson's prototype, has Prairie Style leanings that involve patterned brick walls, clerestory windows, and deep roof overhangs.

170

SOUTH SHORE INTERNATIONAL COLLEGE PREP HIGH SCHOOL

John Ronan Architects, 2010

1955 East 75th Street

Bus: J14 to Jeffrey Avenue and 75th Street

In 2004, John Ronan won a high-profile competition for a high school in Perth Amboy, New Jersey, besting finalists that included Peter Eisenman and Thom Mayne. The win gave some wider attention to Ronan, who had built little at the time. It also brought some attention to the strong design talent in the city a few months before Chicago hosted the American Institute of Architects (AIA) National Convention. While his winning design was not realized, the design's main elements—the Barscape, the Mat, and the Towers, as he called them—found fruition in Ronan's later educational projects. The Towers,

The glazed entrance is adjacent to a plaza between two masonry volumes. (Credit Steve Hall)

Behind the curtain wall at the entrance is a generous three-story atrium. (Credit Steve Hall)

vertical building elements that punctuated the winning design, can be seen in the Gary Comer Youth Center (**168**), and the other two elements are evident in the architect's design for the city's prototype high school.

Ronan's prototype CPS high school design, which was realized at the South Shore International College Prep, consists of three "bars"—rectilinear forms which include classrooms, gymnasium, and library with art and music spaces—that relate to body, mind, and spirit, respectively. These bars of varying widths and heights sit tangent to each other, creating open spaces through their relative placement. At South Shore, the middle bar is set back from the sidewalk to create an entry plaza facing the intersection of 75th Street and Jeffrey Boulevard; this plaza is raised about half a floor to give the school a ceremonial entrance. Toward the rear, a semi-enclosed landscape sits next to the library bar on Jeffrey

Boulevard, and on the other side of the building, the gymnasium overlooks the playing fields. While this general plan pervades in other high schools, tweaked per particular site conditions, it can also be seen as an evolution of an idea Ronan explored a decade beforehand, finally finding realization in the city he calls home.

CTA 95TH/DAN RYAN TERMINAL

exp, 2019
15 West 95th Street

At more than a quarter-billion dollars, the improvements and expansion at the southern end of the 24/7 Red Line comprise the most expensive project in the CTA system—ever. Architecturally, the bright red accents in the design by exp acknowledges the drivers zipping by on the Dan Ryan as much as it does the tens of thousands of bus and train riders that use the terminal every day.

METHOD MANUFACTURING FACILITY

William McDonough + Partners, 2015
1000 East 111th Street

(Credit Lynn Becker)

Two months after President Barack Obama named the Historic Pullman District a national monument, Method opened a new manufacturing facility on the site of a steel plant in Pullman that closed in 2006. The design by sustainability guru William McDonough is a clean-energy facility that gets its power from a large wind turbine and solar trees. Atop the large building is a 1.75-acre greenhouse; this partnership with Gotham Greens grows produce for local restaurants and farmers' markets.

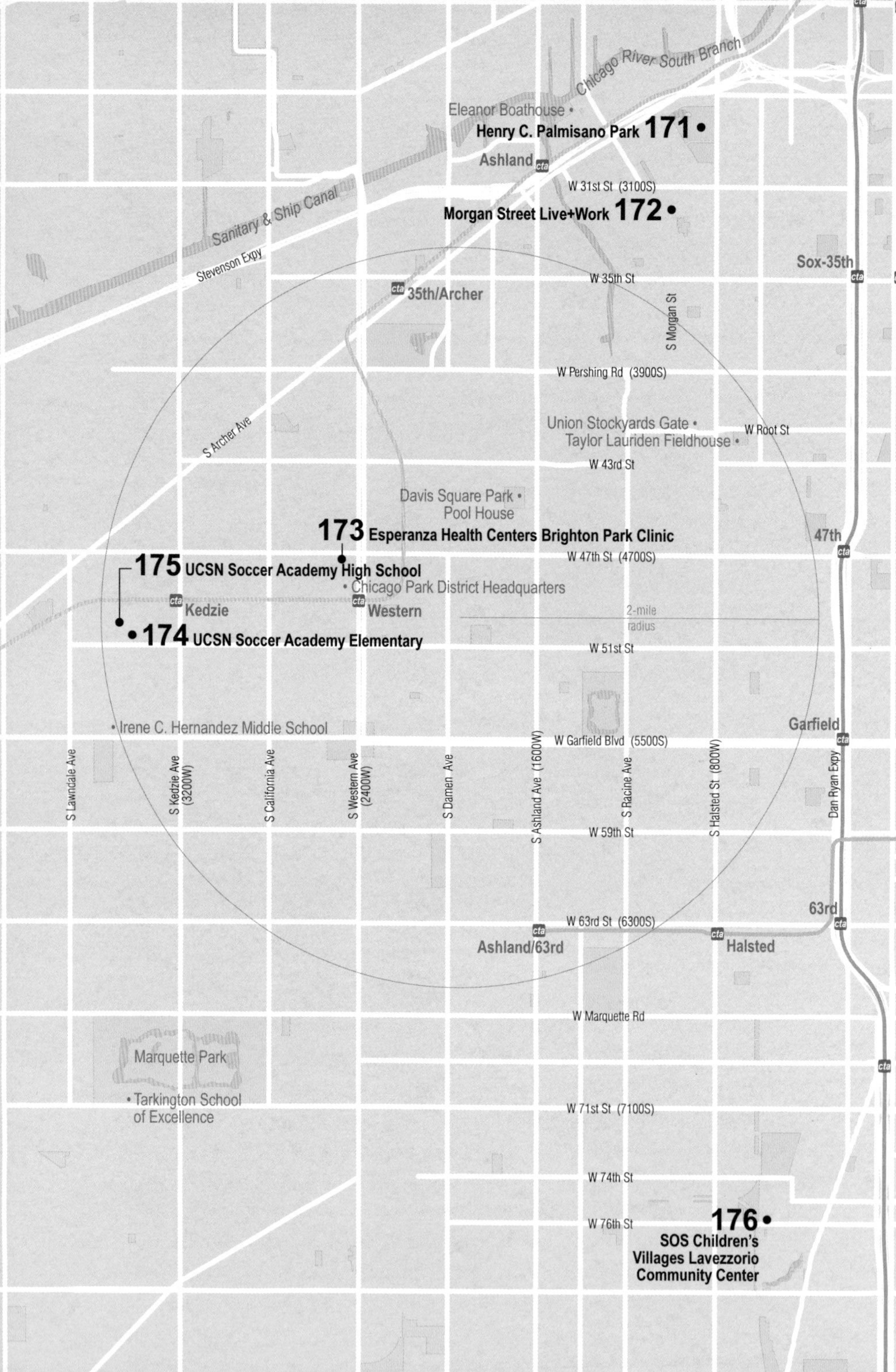

Chicago River South Branch
Eleanor Boathouse
171 Henry C. Palmisano Park
Ashland
W 31st St (3100S)
172 Morgan Street Live+Work
Sanitary & Ship Canal
Stevenson Expy
Sox-35th
W 35th St
35th/Archer
S Morgan St
W Pershing Rd (3900S)
S Archer Ave
Union Stockyards Gate
Taylor Lauriden Fieldhouse
W Root St
W 43rd St
Davis Square Park
Pool House
173 Esperanza Health Centers Brighton Park Clinic
47th
W 47th St (4700S)
175 UCSN Soccer Academy High School
Chicago Park District Headquarters
Kedzie
Western
2-mile radius
174 UCSN Soccer Academy Elementary
W 51st St
Irene C. Hernandez Middle School
Garfield
W Garfield Blvd (5500S)
S Lawndale Ave
S Kedzie Ave (3200W)
S California Ave
S Western Ave (2400W)
S Damen Ave
S Ashland Ave (1600W)
S Racine Ave
S Halsted St (800W)
Dan Ryan Expy
W 59th St
63rd
W 63rd St (6300S)
Ashland/63rd
Halsted
W Marquette Rd
Marquette Park
Tarkington School of Excellence
W 71st St (7100S)
W 74th St
W 76th St
176 SOS Children's Villages Lavezzorio Community Center

19 Bridgeport, Back of the Yards, Gage Park, & Auburn Gresham

The large area covered in this chapter contains neighborhoods located west of the Dan Ryan Expressway and south of the Stevenson Expressway. The most famous "tenant" of this swath of the South Side is gone, now just a symbol of Chicago's 19th- and early-20th-century industrial might and intelligence. From 1865 until 1971, when it officially closed, the Union Stock Yards covered 475 acres and handled more than one billion animals, making it the busiest meat processing facility in the world for most of its existence and famously earning Chicago the nickname "hog butcher for the world," as described by poet Carl Sandburg. Chicago was able to rise to the top of commercial meatpacking through its location in the middle of the United States, the web of railroad tracks leading to the city, and the efforts of packers like Philip Armour and Gustavus Swift, who furiously promoted their production and shipping methods. Although the Union Stock Yards forever changed the production and consumption of meat in the United States and beyond, the same methods that Armour and Swift promoted dispersed meatpackers outside of the city, leading to their demise. Physically, very little is left, including the landmarked Union Stock Yard Gate at Exchange Avenue and Peoria Street, now in the middle of Stockyards Industrial Park, home to just about every industry but meatpacking.

The area in and around the old stockyards is alternately called New City and Back of the Yards. To the north is Bridgeport, a traditionally Irish neighborhood. Irish immigrants working on the Illinois and Michigan Canal in the mid-1800s bought up land along the South Branch of the Chicago River where it met the canal, laying the foundation for the neighborhood. (Although the I&M Canal made Chicago an important major Midwestern trade hub, it was later abandoned in favor of the wider and deeper Sanitary and Ship Canal, which famously reversed the flow of the Chicago River.) The well-built-up residential neighborhood has been home to five mayors, including Richard J. Daley and his son Richard M. Daley.

Buildings in this chapter are found also in two neighborhoods that fall into Chicago's "Bungalow Belt": Gage Park, an Irish and Eastern European area that is now primarily Latinx, and Auburn Gresham, a once-Irish but now predominately African American area whose stock of bungalows was added to the National Register of Historic Places in 2012.

171

HENRY C. PALMISANO PARK

Site Design Group with D.I.R.T. studio, 2009
2700 South Halsted Street
Train: Orange to Halsted
Bus: #8 to Halsted Street at 26th Street

This park in Bridgeport occupies twenty-seven acres that served as a quarry from the 1830s until 1970, after which it was used as a landfill for construction debris for a little over thirty years. In its use as a stone quarry, the land was excavated to a depth of 380 feet—the equivalent of a 35-story building! Some of this depth is sensed in the new park, which retains some of the quarry walls adjacent to a fishing pond in the northwest corner of the park.

A fishing pond on the park's northwest corner gives a sense of the former quarry's depth. (Credit Eric Allix Rogers, CAC Archive)

There are numerous entrances to the park, but the best one is from the intersection of Halsted and 27th streets, where a line of boulders from the former Stearns Quarry lead to a fountain anchoring the park's northeast corner. This is the high point of a water retention system that keeps water out of the storm sewer and culminates in the fishing pond. From the fountain, the main path diverges: veering right leads past the cascading terraces to the pond and its walkways jutting

Walkways jut over the landscape and its tiered water retention system. (Credit Eric Allix Rogers, CAC Archive)

over the landscape, while heading left leads uphill to the park's mounded high point with native plantings and panoramic views toward the distant downtown skyline. The west edge of the park is given over to recreation and consists of an open grass field and a running track.

The park was named for the Bridgeport owner of Henry's Sports & Bait Shop who died in 2006. Like Millennium Park, Lakeshore East, and The 606 (**114**), Henry C. Palmisano Park is a 21st-century landscape built upon the industrial remains of the past two centuries. What sets Palmisano Park aside from these and other new parks is its remoteness. Sure, the skyline is visible in the distance, but there aren't many spots like this, where the urban surroundings fade away and one is left with the reclaimed nature of a not-too-distant past.

ELEANOR BOATHOUSE
Studio Gang, 2016
2804–72 South Eleanor Street

This boathouse is one of four proposed by Mayor Rahm Emmanuel for spots along the north and south branches of the Chicago River. Bridgeport's boathouse is a budget version of Jeanne Gang's WMS Boathouse at Clark Park (**96**), lacking some of the amenities and upscale materials but maintaining the serrated roofline inspired by the movement of rowing.

172

MORGAN STREET LIVE+WORK

UrbanLab, 2007

3209 South Morgan Street

Bus: #8 to Halsted Street at 32nd Street

Before Sarah Dunn and Martin Felsen founded UrbanLab in 2001, Dunn worked with Rem Koolhaas at the Office for Metropolitan Architecture (OMA) as lead designer on the McCormick Tribune Campus Center (**137**) at the Illinois Institute of Technology (IIT). One can grasp the influence of her former employer on this live/work building in Bridgeport for the couple and their office, specifically in synthesizing a methodological analysis, the given conditions of a site, and a building's program into a solution that is unexpected and

Cor-Ten steel covers the work volume and aluminum covers the live volume above it. (Credit Matthew Messner)

The rotated second floor extends to a mound built on debris of the old grocery store on the site. (Credit Matthew Messner)

a departure from the norm. Here, the project presents an almost blank, Cor-Ten steel facade to the street, concealing the creativity behind it.

The live/work building project sits on a parcel formerly occupied by a one-story grocery store, square in plan, which was in a deteriorated state and needed to be demolished. The duo took the same area of the store—3,000 square feet—but split it into two rectangular bars exactly half as large, one stacked upon the other. The office is on the ground, covered with the weathered steel panels on the sidewalk, an aluminum skin on its other sides, and a green roof on top. The second-floor living space, also wrapped in aluminum, is rotated 90 degrees, spanning from the sidewalk to a mound topped with native grasses in the backyard. Here, rather than the landfill, is where Dunn and Felsen dumped the debris of the old grocery store, using it as a base for a landscape that unites the two halves of the project: a constant backdrop for Dunn, Felsen, their employees, and their cats.

TAYLOR-LAURIDSEN FIELDHOUSE
Booth Hansen, 2010
704 West 42nd Street

Booth Hansen has designed two prototype fieldhouses for the Chicago Park District. This one at the five-acre Taylor-Lauridsen Park in the Back of the Yards neighborhoods is an example of the first prototype, while the second one can be seen at Haas Park in Chapter 12. The first prototype features curved roofs, insulated precast concrete walls, and an arcade entrance between the tall and low volumes.

(Credit Barbara Karant)

DAVIS SQUARE PARK POOL HOUSE

David Woodhouse Architects, 2001
4430 South Marshfield Avenue

Eight-acre Davis Square Park in the Back of the Yards neighborhood is particularly notable for its fieldhouse designed by Daniel H. Burnham in 1905. A blizzard at the tail end of the 20th century brought down one of the walls facing the pool. Instead of removing the park district's rudimentary replacement wall built of cinder blocks, David Woodhouse (now with Woodhouse Tinucci Architects) covered it with a rippling facade of fiberglass mounted on curved ribs.

CHICAGO PARK DISTRICT HEADQUARTERS

John Ronan Architects, estimated completion in 2022
Western Avenue between West 48th and West 49th Streets

A new 78,000-square-foot headquarters will anchor the 17-acre Park No. 596 that the Chicago Park District is creating in Brighton Park directly west of the Orange Line stop at Western Avenue and West 49th Street. Circular in plan, the two-story building will contain CPD offices but also a fieldhouse and two publicly accessible courtyards.

173

ESPERANZA HEALTH CENTERS BRIGHTON PARK CLINIC

JGMA, 2019

4700 S. California Avenue

Train: Orange Line to Western

Bus: #94 to California and 47th Street

Esperanza Health Centers teamed up with Mujeres Latinas en Acción to create the fourth location for Esperanza, which provides community health care in underserved areas and whose name translates as "hope." The provocative angular building features a glassy first floor and bright-orange upper

An angled corner creates a small plaza and invitation to enter the building. (Credit JGMA)

The rhomboid-shaped windows enliven the interiors. (Credit JGMA)

The bright orange palette outside continues inside the building. (Credit JGMA)

story with rhomboid openings and a large window facing California Avenue. A carved corner at the intersection welcomes neighborhood residents into the medical facility that adds life and hope to the formerly vacant industrial site.

174

JOVITA IDAR ELEMENTARY SCHOOL

JGMA with Ghafari Associates, 2011
5050 South Homan Avenue
Train: Orange to Kedzie

In 2010, the United Neighborhood Organization, a nonprofit focused on improving education in predominantly Latinx neighborhoods, held a design competition for an elementary school in Gage Park. Juan Moreno, working at Ghafari Associates at the time, won the competition with a swooping and angled design oriented toward the soccer field, the raison d'être of the charter school, which is now run by Acero Schools (formerly the UNO Charter School Network). Shortly after the competition win, Moreno started his own firm and subsequently was responsible for the school's design, while Ghafari handled the design-build mandate of the project, which had to be built within one year.

From the corner of 51st Street and Homan Avenue, the three-story building is fairly straightforward, with alternating bands of gray metal panels and greenish glass. Yet, toward the west the building rises in section as it curves in plan; its top two floors are propped upon circular columns to create a path un-

The swooping building is particularly dramatic seen from the soccer field. (Credit JGMA)

der the building. From the southwest, the building is a gateway to the soccer field, a key element in the school's focus on the sport as a tool for strengthening bonds in the community. Above the portal are a multipurpose room and community room with views of downtown Chicago, while the far western end of the building leans out as if to anticipate the neighboring high school (**175**) that would arrive two years later.

175

VICTORIA SOTO HIGH SCHOOL

Wight & Company, 2013
5025 South St. Louis Avenue
Train: Orange to Kedzie

The second piece in Acero Schools' campus arrived two years after the elementary school (**174**). The three-story glass-and-metal building curves away from Chicago's orthogonal grid, while the high school also departs from the rectilinear, taking a donut, or ring, as its shape. Covering the western side of the building is a red skin while the remaining facade consists of dark glass walls. The intersection between the two is angled, as if to reference the JGMA elementary school nearby.

A portal in the red building leads from the courtyard to the soccer field beyond. (Credit Angie McMonigal Photography)

176

SOS CHILDREN'S VILLAGES LAVEZZORIO COMMUNITY CENTER

Studio Gang, 2008

7600 South Parnell Avenue

Bus: #75 to 75th Street at Eggleston Avenue

Parnell Avenue south of 76th Street in the Auburn Gresham neighborhood includes something of an anomaly in Chicago: a cul-de-sac. This condition is due to two sets of elevated railroad tracks converging at about 78th Street, creating a triangular swath of land that is accessible only from the north. A mattress factory formerly occupied the site, but now it is home to the Chicago location of SOS Children's Villages, an international development organization. The townhouses and duplexes, for up to ninety children and their foster families, line both sides of Parnell Avenue with an island of trees and a paved plaza in the middle. South of the cul-de-sac is a community garden and a grassy area, while the site in the northwest corner of the "village" is given over for the community center designed by Jeanne Gang's firm.

Lots of glass and "V"-shaped columns face the entrance to the "village." (Credit Steve Hall © Hedrich Blessing)

When completed in 2008, the building brought international attention to Gang, who had previously realized only two buildings: a theater in Rockford, Illinois, with a retractable roof and a community center in Chinatown (**50**). Yet it would be hard to acknowledge the fuss of the Lavezzorio Community Center when approaching the building from 76th Street, particularly from the west where the building is simply a dark brick wall with punched openings. Things get interesting at the corner of Parnell Avenue though, where the brick at the top half of the building gives way to lots of glass and a simple concrete coping that is supported by "V"-shaped concrete columns on both the north and east sides. But it's at the rear where the building announces itself as something wholly unique.

Here, at the southeast corner, are two walls with six wavy layers of gray concrete. What looks like a purely artistic statement is an architectural response to a small budget: materials were donated, so what Gang calls the "strata-wall" expresses the different batches of concrete that made the project happen. This design feature also expresses the viscosity of concrete, which is poured as a liquid into forms and then hardens into a solid mass. The malleability of concrete is evident as well in the notch taken out of the corner for the glass walls of the lobby with some stepped seating inside. Rounding out the project is a playground to the side of the strata-wall, formed by the U-shaped plan.

Suburbs

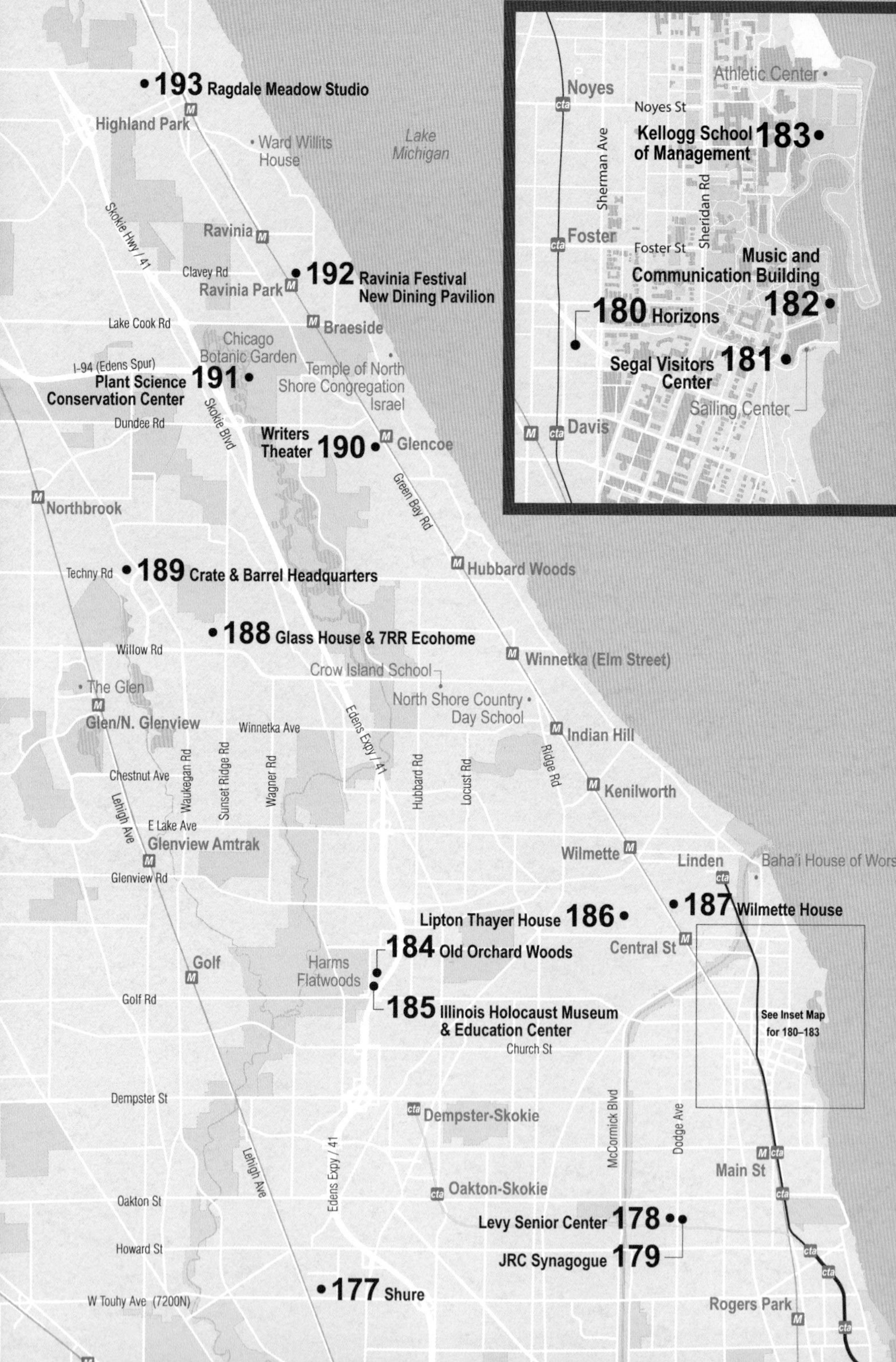

193 Ragdale Meadow Studio
Highland Park
Ward Willits House
Lake Michigan
Skokie Hwy / 41
Ravinia
Clavey Rd
Ravinia Park
192 Ravinia Festival New Dining Pavilion
Braeside
Lake Cook Rd
Chicago Botanic Garden
Temple of North Shore Congregation Israel
I-94 (Edens Spur)
Plant Science Conservation Center 191
Skokie Blvd
Dundee Rd
Writers Theater 190
Glencoe
Green Bay Rd
Northbrook
Hubbard Woods
Techny Rd
189 Crate & Barrel Headquarters
188 Glass House & 7RR Ecohome
Willow Rd
Winnetka (Elm Street)
Crow Island School
North Shore Country Day School
The Glen
Glen/N. Glenview
Winnetka Ave
Edens Expy / 41
Indian Hill
Chestnut Ave
Waukegan Rd
Sunset Ridge Rd
Wagner Rd
Hubbard Rd
Locust Rd
Ridge Rd
Kenilworth
Lehigh Ave
E Lake Ave
Glenview Amtrak
Wilmette
Linden
Baha'i House of Worship
Glenview Rd
187 Wilmette House
Lipton Thayer House 186
184 Old Orchard Woods
Central St
Golf
Harms Flatwoods
Golf Rd
185 Illinois Holocaust Museum & Education Center
See Inset Map for 180–183
Church St
Dempster St
Dempster-Skokie
McCormick Blvd
Dodge Ave
Lehigh Ave
Edens Expy / 41
Main St
Oakton St
Oakton-Skokie
Levy Senior Center 178
Howard St
JRC Synagogue 179
177 Shure
W Touhy Ave (7200N)
Rogers Park
Noyes
Noyes St
Athletic Center
Kellogg School of Management 183
Sherman Ave
Sheridan Rd
Foster
Foster St
Music and Communication Building
182
180 Horizons
Segal Visitors Center 181
Sailing Center
Davis

20 North Suburbs

Any architectural guide to Chicago would be incomplete without acknowledging the suburbs. As of 2019, 2.7 million people live within the city limits, but the larger metropolitan region totals 9.5 million people. In other words, for every four people living in the region, three of them live in the suburbs. Traditionally places to live, suburbs are now more diverse, no longer secondary to the city. Today, centers of work, culture, and play are found alongside the single-family houses that remain the driving characteristic of suburban life.

The suburbs in this chapter are located north of the city, what is often called the North Shore. Technically, the North Shore is made up of the suburbs situated along Lake Michigan, such as Evanston, Winnetka, Glencoe, and Lake Forest. The North Shore contains the most affluent suburbs in Chicagoland, as well as some of the oldest, dating back to the early 1800s and subsequently linked to the city through streetcar lines. Today, expressways and suburban trains connect these and other suburbs to the city, though it's just as common to find people commuting *from* the city to work in the suburbs, or even from one suburb to another. Further inland, the suburbs of Niles, Skokie, Glenview, Northbrook, and Northfield, among others, consider themselves part of the North Shore, testament to the area's cachet. Even those who have not visited the greater North Shore are surely familiar with it through the movies of John Hughes, who filmed *Ferris Bueller's Day Off*, *Sixteen Candles*, *Weird Science*, and other movies in these suburbs.

Given the generally dispersed nature of the suburbs, seeing the buildings in this and the next chapter is best done with a car. But a decent network of trains and buses serves the North Shore's "streetcar suburbs," so public transportation routes are given when applicable.

177

SHURE CORPORATE HEADQUARTERS

Murphy/Jahn (now JAHN), 2000; Krueck Sexton Partners, 2004

5800 West Touhy Avenue, Niles

This headquarters for the audio electronics company Shure is made up of two buildings: a seven-story building designed by Helmut Jahn that faces Touhy Avenue and a two-story building designed by Ron Krueck and Mark Sexton that sits behind it, parallel to the neighboring railroad tracks. Predating the KSP building by four years, Jahn's contribution was originally designed as the headquarters for Ha-Lo Industries, Inc., the company that specialized in putting commercial logos on mugs, t-shirts, pens, and other promotional items. But Ha-Lo filed for bankruptcy the same year its suburban building was completed (due to the unwise purchase of a dot-com company, not the Jahn building) and Shure snapped it up for its headquarters. With that building for

A mesh wall and trellis shield Jahn's south-facing glass wall from the afternoon sun. (Credit Rainer Viertlböck, courtesy of JAHN)

Krueck and Sexton's addition places louvers in front of the east-facing glass wall. (Credit © Hedrich Blessing)

The KSP addition is a layered composition of glass and metal. (Credit © Hedrich Blessing)

its administrative functions, Shure built the KSP addition to integrate offices with a technology center for the design and testing of their products, which include headphones, microphones, and the like.

When it was completed, Jahn's design was notable for being his first commission in Chicagoland since the 1980s, following the completion of the controversial James R. Thompson Center in the Loop. Yet all these years later, it's the formal and technical qualities of the building that garner the most attention, starting with the full-height, freestanding mesh screen that extends from the west wall, emblazoned near the top with the Shure logo facing the train tracks. Together with a large triangular trellis, the mesh wall shades the lobby and atrium space from the late afternoon sun and provides a memorable image to commuters taking Metra home in the evening.

A smaller version of the logo-covered mesh wall, trellis, and bowstring support is located at the back of the building where Krueck and Sexton hold their own with Helmut Jahn's skillfully layered composition of glass and steel. The addition has a similar palette, but given the studios and testing facilities contained inside, it includes more steel than glass. The west elevation overlooking the tracks has clerestory windows, while the north facade is all glass, and the east elevation facing the parking lot is layered with horizontal louvers in front of an all-glass wall on the second floor.

With so much glass and steel, these two kindred buildings—not accessible to the public, unfortunately—are best seen in the evening, when their walls glow to reveal something of what is going on inside.

178

LEVY SENIOR CENTER

Ross Barney + Jankowski (now Ross Barney Architects), 2002
300 Dodge Avenue, Evanston

James Park is a 55-acre open space in the southwest corner of Evanston that does not bring to mind the best associations for longtime residents, since its western edge is occupied by a recycling center and "Mount Trashmore," a former landfill that has been used as a sledding hill. In the southeast corner of the park, somewhat removed from these more noxious uses, is a City of Evanston senior center that was built with the help of the Levy Family Foundation. The one-story building houses classrooms, a multipurpose gymnasium/perfor-

Wood louvers wrap the classroom wings. (Credit Steve Hall, Hedrich Blessing Photography)

mance space, offices, and support spaces. Each component is expressed in the design by Carol Ross Barney's firm: classrooms face south and east in an "L"-shaped wing with wood louvers in front of glass walls; the multipurpose space is covered with translucent insulated fiberglass panels that face the park and the building's parking lot; and the offices form a brick volume between the other two parts.

Of these, the wood louvers (made from sustainably harvested sassafras) below the projecting roof give the strongest indication of the character inside. The entrance is through an all-glass wall facing the parking lot, and beyond it is a central courtyard ringed by a corridor wrapping the whole one-story building. Solid wood columns, combined with steel fittings and bracing, support the roof next to the courtyard, which is a comfortable, sun-filled space with areas of shade. The courtyard is a Zen-like respite within a building that keeps seniors active.

179

JEWISH RECONSTRUCTIONIST CONGREGATION

Ross Barney Architects, 2008

303 Dodge Avenue, Evanston

About a decade before the Jewish Reconstructionist Congregation (JRC) moved into its new "green synagogue," they had determined that their old building on the same site across from James Park was in need of repair. Rather than renovate their old building though, they opted to build anew, taking the Jewish principles of *bal tashchit* and *tikkum olam*—"do not destroy or waste" and "repairing the world," respectively—as their guide for the project. The design by the firm of Carol Ross Barney (whose earlier Levy Senior Center [**178**] is right across the street) took these principles to heart, resulting in an American Institute of Architects' (AIA) Committee on the Environment (COTE) award and bragging rights as the first house of worship to receive the US Green Building Council's Leadership in Energy and Environmental Design (LEED) Platinum certification.

A sustainable approach to the design is immediately evident. Conceptualized as a precious wooden box, the structure uses reclaimed cypress

Reclaimed wood and seemingly random openings face the native plantings on the west. (Credit Eric Allix Rogers, CAC Archive)

harvested from demolished barns to cover all sides of the square three-story building. A seemingly random grid of small openings are cut into the wall facing Dodge Avenue, which is surrounded by an indigenous landscape designed with Oslund & Associates. On the south side—the main approach to the building given the parking lot across the street—a large glass wall follows the main stair ascending to the third-floor sanctuary space. Breaking through the wood wall near the entrance is a thick wall covered in Jerusalem stone, the only material brought from afar, for symbolic and spiritual reasons. This stone wall continues inside and defines one edge of the stair. Although it shields the synagogue and classroom spaces from too much direct sunlight, the wall carries some meaning. The congregation and the students on the first two floors must pass through the openings in the Jerusalem stone wall when moving between floors.

Other sustainable features include low gabion walls—wire cages filled with waste brick and limestone from the old building—along the sidewalk and alley, reuse of the synagogue's old foundations, and an impressive stormwater management achieved by the landscaping and underwater cisterns. The JRC is proud of their building's green credentials and accordingly they offer docent-led tours of the synagogue.[1]

180

OPTIMA HORIZONS

Optima, 2004
800 Elgin Road, Evanston
Train: Purple to Davis; Metra UP-N to Evanston Davis Street

Glencoe-based Optima is a unique company since, in addition to providing architectural services, they also develop, build, sell, and manage their projects, most of them apartments and condos. Just as their firm structure is unique, so are their designs by founding architect David Hovey. Consistent across their portfolio of projects on Chicago's North Shore are low- or mid-rise massing, lots of glass, an emphasis on the horizontal, and splashes of color. This sixteen-story tower on the north edge of downtown Evanston just east

Splashes of red enliven the glass facade of the 16-story building. (Credit Angie McMonigal Photography)

of the Purple Line tracks exhibits these tendencies: the 248 condos have full-height glass walls; the retail and parking podium is covered in steel panels and translucent channel glass, both running horizontally; and red lines are found in the framing of the parking garage skin, the horizontal mullions of the units, and sunshades applied selectively. Optima originally planned the project as a 36-story tower, but neighborhood opposition resulted in a lower scale, meaning Hovey and company would have to wait another decade until they realized a building that tall, in the Optima Chicago Center (**63**).

181

SEGAL VISITORS CENTER

Perkins and Will 2014

1841 Sheridan Road, Evanston

Train: Purple to Davis; Metra UP-N to Evanston Davis Street

Northwestern University's Evanston Campus Framework Plan, prepared by Sasaki Associates and adopted in early 2009, included a number of proposals for the school's southeast campus that fronts onto Lake Michigan: a new green space next to then-proposed Music and Communication Building (**182**, now the Ryan Center for the Musical Arts), the reconfiguration of an existing parking garage to create the green space, a new boathouse for the sailing team, and a new visitors center appended to a new parking garage. Ralph Johnson of Perkins and Will was responsible for the Segal Visitors Center, which acts as a gateway to the campus on its southern edge and as an entry point for students considering Northwestern for their undergraduate studies.

Approaching the building from Sheridan Road on the south, it's hard to believe the building contains four hundred parking spaces. Its south and west elevations are covered in glass walls that are framed in ribbonlike limestone walls and lifted overhead on two-story round columns—it is more office building than garage. The west wall gracefully curves to follow Campus Drive and lead cars to the parking garage entrance at the north end of the building. People enter the visitors center on the south where a generous double-height reception hall looks out upon the lake. Behind it is a 160-seat auditorium. Rounding out the thoughtful design is an east facade of vertical fabric fins that relate to the sailing center that sits beside it and the water beyond.

The east wall is covered in nautical fabric fins. (Credit © James Steinkamp Photography)

SAILING CENTER

Woodhouse Tinucci Architects, 2015
1823 Campus Drive, Evanston

Just steps from Northwestern University's new Visitors Center (**181**) is this one-story building on the beach that offers sailing classes and a home for the school's sailing team. Folding and sliding doors in Northwestern purple are the only moments of color against the walls of board-formed concrete.

(Credit Mike Schwartz)

182

RYAN CENTER FOR THE MUSICAL ARTS

Goettsch Partners, 2015

70 Arts Circle Drive, Evanston

Train: Purple to Davis; Metra UP-N to Evanston Davis Street

Beginning in 2004, Sasaki Associates developed a master plan for Northwestern University's Southeast Campus, centered on a new building for the School of Music that would replace its outmoded facilities elsewhere on the Evanston campus. Four years later, Goettsch Partners was selected as architect in an invited design competition, with groundbreaking taking place another four years later. Their design places the new building tight to the Regenstein Hall of Music (designed in the 1970s by SOM's Walter Netsch, who designed a number of buildings on campus as well as the Regenstein Library at the University of Chicago) and adjacent to the Pick-Staiger Concert Hall, consolidating the university's Henry and Leigh Bienen School of Music and other music-related facilities in a corner of the campus dramatically overlooking Lake Michigan.

The limestone box houses the main performance space. (Credit © Tom Rossiter Photography)

The five-story building contains classrooms, offices, more than fifty practice spaces, and three performance spaces. The main venue is a 400-seat recital hall that is housed in a limestone-clad volume at the south end of the building; undulating wood walls wrap three sides of the space while a full-height glass wall on the south facade frames the downtown Chicago skyline as a backdrop for performances. Glass is used less sparingly elsewhere in the five-story building: the upper floors are wrapped in glass and sit above a limestone

The main performance space. (Credit © Tom Rossiter Photography)

The entrance and atrium features a glass roof. (Credit © Tom Rossiter Photography)

base, while the entry atrium features glass walls as well as a glass roof. The "S"-shaped plan culminates in angled, cantilevered glass walls at the southeast and northwest corners, giving the large building a dynamic flair befitting its musical purpose.

183

KELLOGG SCHOOL OF MANAGEMENT GLOBAL HUB

KPMB Architects, 2017

2211 Campus Drive, Evanston

Train: Purple to Noyes

Toronto's KPMB won an invited competition in 2011 to design the new 415,000-square-foot Global Hub for Northwestern University's Kellogg School of Management. The five-story, LEED Platinum building is located at the north end of a small lagoon not far from Lake Michigan. Shaped like a cloverleaf in plan, the building is made up of

The undulating lines of the building's exterior echo the bodies of water it sits near. (Credit John Hill)

four wings linked by a central atrium that is meant to foster collaboration. Outside, the curved glass walls reiterate the waves on the lake, while the heart of the building is given over to the aptly named "Collaboration Plaza," reached by the "Spanish Steps" from the building's entrance.

The central atrium is a popular space activated by plenty of seating, walkways surrounding it, and bridges traversing it. (Credit John Hill)

RYAN FIELDHOUSE AND WALTER ATHLETICS CENTER

Perkins and Will, 2018
2333 Campus Drive, Evanston

(Credit © James Steinkamp Photography)

Northwestern University selected the northeastern corner of its Evanston Campus for this athletics facility that contains a large indoor venue for practices and competitions, as well as offices, locker rooms, and training facilities. The elliptical fieldhouse dome allows football punting but stays within Evanston's strict height limitations. Glass walls facing north and east provide offices, student athlete lounges, and even the full length of the fieldhouse with dramatic views of Lake Michigan.

184

OPTIMA OLD ORCHARD WOODS

Optima, 2008

9739 Woods Drive, Skokie

For four decades, the buildings of Optima—the Glencoe-based company that designs, develops, builds, sells, and manages multifamily residential projects primarily in Chicago's suburbs—have steadily grown in size, from three-story townhouses in Oak Park in 1981 to this development with three 20-story towers. Old Orchard Woods is located less than a mile from the sprawling Westfield Old Orchard, sitting on a tapered lot tucked between the Edens Expressway on the east, a parking lot for adjacent office buildings on the north, and Harms Woods Forest Preserve on the west—architect David Hovey and his colleagues at Optima had nowhere to go but up.

What makes the project so exceptional is not its scale but the way the three towers are sited, shaped, and then connected to create a true vertical community. The Maple tower is placed to the north and runs east-west to

The large, three-tower development seen from the west. (Credit Angie McMonigal Photography)

The Optima development seen from the parking lot of the Holocaust Museum (**185**). (Credit Angie McMonigal Photography)

define this edge of the site. The Oak and Elm towers run north-south and are staggered relative to each other to follow the tapered site and give their units as much sunlight as possible. The three towers form one huge, west-facing forecourt with a fountain and a roundabout, both traversed by a trellis spanning from the east end of the Maple tower to a low-rise section of the Oak tower that includes a pool for the whole development. This low-rise section is indicative of how the towers are not simple slabs; they step in plan and are notched in section to break up the apparent mass of the project, aided by the splashes of red sunshades that Hovey has incorporated in other projects (**180**).

In addition to the parking garage and podium topped by landscaped roofs, the towers are connected at their upper floors, meaning that some units actually straddle the gaps between the buildings. Most interesting is the connection between Oak and Elm, which features two terraces suspended in the middle of the large opening and accessed from either tower. These gaps and multistory connections are like the visions of Fritz Lang's *Metropolis* and Antonio Sant'Elia's *La Citta Nuova* coming to reality. Who would have thought it would happen in a luxury housing development in the Chicago suburbs?

185

ILLINOIS HOLOCAUST MUSEUM & EDUCATION CENTER

Tigerman McCurry Architects, 2009

9603 Woods Drive, Skokie

If any Chicago architect was destined to design a museum about the Holocaust, it was the late Stanley Tigerman, who embedded Judaic scholarship into his writings and projects in ways both serious and humorous. Most

The museum is foreboding when seen from the parking lot to the west. (Credit Angie McMonigal Photography)

memorably, in the late 1980s he proposed rows of sycamore trees and a canal in place of the old Berlin Wall, placing two columns—Boaz and Jachin, from Solomon's Temple in ancient Jerusalem—on axis with the Brandenburg Gate. Here in Skokie, with its significant Jewish population, Tigerman designed the Illinois Holocaust Museum & Education Center and marked the entrance with columns similar to those found in Berlin but rendered here as steel cages with flared tops. The compact site is stuffed between the Edens Expressway, a forest preserve, and Optima's large Old Orchard Woods development (**184**).

This museum is all about movement and path, and for most visitors it starts at the parking lot across the street to the west. From here the museum is blank, foreboding even. A concrete wall with narrow windows at its top and an inaccessible steel gate at its base greets visitors; in the evening, uplights wash the wall to give it an ominous glow. The entrance is on the other side of the building, reached by a path next to a semicircular pool and curved concrete wall that are apparently at odds with the hard, orthogonal nature of the architecture but which foreshadow what lies inside. The cagelike columns are found on the east side of the building, sitting between two porches—one dark gray, one bright white. Entrance is through the dark porch in the foreground, and after the clockwise route through the building visitors exit through the

Twin columns sit between the entrance and exit wings on the east. (Credit Angie McMonigal Photography)

The voyage through the building culminates in the Hall of Reflection. (Credit Angie McMonigal Photography)

white porch—a journey from dark to light. Tigerman layered symbolism like this throughout the building: the dark wing is angled six degrees toward the West Wall in Jerusalem and the whole building is based on a roughly 18-inch-square cubit as mentioned in the Bible.

The experience inside is a careful balance between Tigerman's architecture of steel, concrete, exposed structure, and exposed ducts—what the architect called a German industrial aesthetic—and Layman Design's exhibition design. Together, the museum forces visitors to walk a dark and convoluted route through the first, dark wing, which fits appropriately with the stories of Jewish oppression during the Holocaust. In the narrow tapered void between the two wings is a German railcar, of the type used to transport Jews to concentration camps. From this midpoint, the journey through the light wing of the museum is brighter and softer, culminating in the circular Hall of Reflection that sits below bowstring trusses and is illuminated by glass walls. Here, more symbolism prevails: twelve cubit-sized stools represent the twelve tribes of Israel.

Visitors exit through the end of the light wing, now facing east toward the rising sun. The walk back to the parking lots is the reverse of the initial approach, but now the curved pool takes on a different meaning: the water and curved wall symbolize renewal, and the benches opposite allow visitors a moment of rest and reflection before returning to their daily lives.

186

LIPTON THAYER HOUSE

Brooks+Scarpa, 2018

2600 Thayer Street, Evanston

Brick is ubiquitous in Chicago and its suburbs, a fitting material for single-family houses in particular. This experiment in brick stands out clearly from the brook bungalows and other neighbors, yet it is rooted in the same traditional techniques. Designed by the Los Angeles studio of Angela Brooks and Lawrence Scarpa, the house resembles a cocoon, a porous wrap around the property's former bungalow. But it is new construction: a two-story glass box with a landscaped core that is screened by the innovative brick wall facing the street. The house was built at a time when robots laid bricks into undulating shapes elsewhere, but for this Chicago site Brooks+Scarpa developed a system with vertical rebars, horizontal plates, and a chart that helped masons in rotating the bricks by hand to achieve the architect's design. Recalling Studio Gang's Brick-Weave House (**123**), this house pushes two Chicago traditions—the glass box and brick exterior—enthusiastically into the twenty-first century.

The appearance of the openings between the rotated bricks changes as one moves up or down the suburban street. (Credit Margo Hill)

187

WILMETTE RESIDENCE

Tigerman McCurry Architects, 2016

1019 Linden Avenue, Wilmette

In American suburbs, the face a house presents to the street is paramount. On this brick-paved street in Wilmette lined with an eclectic mix of traditional-style houses, many with front porches, Margaret McCurry's modern design for a professional couple is an anomaly. Clad in white corrugated metal and punctuated with black window frames, yellow downspouts, and blue accents, it appears like a North Shore version of Gerrit Rietveld's famous Schröder House built nearly a century ago in the Netherlands. A red portal at the sidewalk simultaneously melds with and breaks from this modernist tradition, pointing to the clients' Eastern and Western backgrounds.

A red portal set into a row of beech trees imbues a sense of Eastern ceremony to approaching the house. (Credit Margo Hill)

Yet, the house's greatest departure from its neighbors is found in the two-story plan: an elongated "T" enabled by the extra-wide 50-foot lot and garage off the rear alley. The short leg of the "T" set perpendicular to the street houses a flow-through living space that opens onto a modern front porch and a rear deck. In an important gesture, this volume presents an exposed chimney flue to the street: a hint of the traditional hearth within the modern box.

188

GLASS HOUSE & 7RR ECO-HOME

Thomas Roszak Architecture, 2002, 2012

Rolling Ridge Lane, Northfield

Thomas Roszak, like many architects working in Chicago, is a graduate of the Illinois Institute of Technology. The rational ideals of structure, space, and technology that Ludwig Mies van der Rohe once championed at IIT as dean, are still instilled at the school of architecture. Two neighboring houses that Roszak designed are evidence of this. The first, the aptly named Glass House, was designed for the architect, his wife, and their three children. Like Mies's designs, it is based on a module that is repeated; in this case each room—kitchen, living room, bedrooms, and so forth—is sixteen feet square, giving the two-story house some flexibility over time. Columns and floor slabs are

The neighboring 7RR Eco-home is formally less rigid and covered in lots of wood. (Credit Jon Miller © Hedrich Blessing)

Roszak's own house is made of glass boxes on a regular grid. (Credit Scott McDonald © Hedrich Blessing)

concrete, beams are steel and painted yellow, walls are bright orange, and floors are wood. These materials combine with the all-glass walls and automated blinds throughout to create a house that is bright, open, and integrated into the landscape of the one-acre site.

Roszak departed from his own house in the design of the house next door for a married couple with three children. Wood and stone predominate over glass, giving the house a less classically modern appearance. And rather than a design of aligned boxes, the 7RR Eco-home, as Roszak calls it in reference to its sustainable attributes, splays across the site, angling as needed for solar orientation, views, and programmatic separation. Only a small portion of the large two-story house is visible from the street, but most distinctive is the covered terrace over the three-car garage, what the architect likens to a contemporary front porch. Not surprisingly, this raised outdoor space faces the earlier Glass House.

189

CRATE & BARREL HEADQUARTERS

Perkins and Will, 2002

1250 Techny Road, Northbrook

Techny Towers, a conference and retreat center, has been a landmark on Waukegan Road in Northbrook since it was completed in 1899 as a seminary. Today, it is accompanied by a much different landmark across the street—Crate & Barrel Headquarters. The massive old seminary and chapel is masonry and vertical, punctuated by the twin bell towers. In contrast, the Crate & Barrel Headquarters is a low-slung horizontal building covered in white brick and white metal panels. Given its scale and material palette, which echoes Crate & Barrel's line of products, as well as their former store on North Michigan

White metal panels, white brick, and glass predominate. (Credit © James Steinkamp Photography)

Avenue (now a Starbucks roastery), the building calls attention to itself *through* the trees along Waukegan rather than above them.

The south-facing end features a generous trellis shading the three-story glass wall. (Credit © James Steinkamp Photography)

The entrance to the headquarters is from Techny Road, which originally ran straight to Waukegan Road on axis with Techny Towers but was reconfigured to give Crate & Barrel more land for its 24-acre campus, mainly trees protecting its southern exposures. In plan, the building is like a door key, with the flat side facing the parking lot and the jagged side facing the trees. These edges that jut out from the main form contain conference rooms that cantilever from the building and are given glass on three sides. A gently curving roof caps the whole three-story building, culminating in a cantilevered trellis shading the generous glass walls that face southwest.

THE GLEN

Skidmore, Owings & Merrill

Glen of North Glenview

Skidmore, Owings & Merrill (SOM) master planned the old Glenview Naval Air Base loosely following New Urbanist principles, so houses have front porches, garages are located off of alleys, there is a walkable "town center," and the whole development has its own commuter train station. Some architectural highlights are pictured here.

Perkins and Will's American College of Chest Physicians, 2013 (Credit © James Steinkamp Photography)

Wight & Company's Evelyn Pease Tyner Interpretive Center, 2006 (Credit John Hill)

Adrian Smith + Gordon Gill Architecture's Willow Creek North Shore, 2016 (Credit © Adrian Smith + Gordon Gill Architecture)

NORTH SHORE COUNTRY DAY SCHOOL

CannonDesign, 2011
310 Green Bay Road, Winnetka

The North Shore Country Day School is made up of 12 buildings on 16 acres for grades kindergarten through high school. CannonDesign developed a master plan and renovated the Upper School, which is a bold addition that projects from the 1922 building toward the middle of the campus.

190

WRITERS THEATRE

Studio Gang, 2016
325 Tudor Court, Glencoe
Train: Metra UP-N to Glencoe

Seen from the south across Tudor Court, the raised wood trusses beckon theatergoers. (Credit Steve Hall © Hedrich Blessing)

The Writers Theatre was founded in 1992 to create an immersive experience between the audience and the performers. Its original venue, in the back of the Books on Vernon bookstore in downtown Glencoe, ensured this physical intimacy. About ten years later, the Women's Library Club of Glencoe donated its nearby, early-20th-century building to the theater, which used it for a decade and then hired architect

A second-floor walkway sits behind the wood trusses and overlooks the adjacent park. (Credit Steve Hall © Hedrich Blessing)

Jeanne Gang to design a new 36,000-square-foot building on the same site. Gang responded with what she describes as "a village-like cluster of distinct volumes"[2] that includes a 250-seat, thrust-style theater; a 99-seat black-box theater; a rehearsal room; back-of-house spaces; an event terrace; and a double-height lobby that doubles as a performance space. This last element is the key to Gang's design.

While the large theater and black-box theater are found behind walls of concrete and cedar (the concrete, perhaps an unfortunate detriment to the neighboring playground and historic house), the lobby sits behind glass walls and doors that literally open the space to the park on the east when weather permits. Framed in wood columns, beams, and Vierendeel trusses, the glazed lobby is shaded by a second-floor walkway with latticelike wood screens that recall Gang's unbuilt, competition-winning 2004 design for the Ford Calumet Environmental Center. In the evening, the space glows like a lantern, inviting people inside, while wood risers encourage visitors to sit and to ascend to the second-floor walkway and the adjacent roof terrace. More than a formal flourish, the lobby extends the Theatre and its intimacy to the street, beyond the confines of its traditional stages.

191

DANIEL F. AND ADA L. RICE PLANT SCIENCE CONSERVATION CENTER

Booth Hansen, 2009

1000 Lake Cook Road, Glencoe

Train: Metra UP-N to Braeside

Bus: Pace #213 to Chicago Botanic Garden

The Chicago Botanic Garden is a North Shore gem: 385 acres of flowers, trees, and shrubs among a network of lakes. Some highlights include the

Entrance to the symmetrical building is through a glass wall under an overhanging roof. (Credit Angie McMonigal Photography)

English Walled Garden, the Japanese Garden, and Evening Island; across the water from the last is the Daniel F. and Ada L. Rice Plant Conservation Science Center, which anchors the fifteen-acre campus along the garden's eastern edge. Designed by Booth Hansen (also responsible for the Garden's later Regenstein Foundation Learning Campus close to Lake Cook Road), the building is accessed by a curling footbridge that lands tangent to the circular Sun Evaluation Garden. Picking up on this, the symmetrical building is organized around a central two-story atrium that is on axis with the circular garden.

Labs are astride a generous central atrium that leads to green roofs. (Credit Angie McMonigal Photography)

Entrance to the publicly accessible building is through a glass wall that is shaded by a large overhanging roof with wood soffits. The building's nine labs (for ecology, soil, genetics, and other areas) are housed in brick wings on the sides of the central atrium, which is capped by the roof that floats above clerestory windows.

Visitors can watch the technicians at work through glass walls from this central space and then head up to the green roofs atop the labs by a stair at the back of the atrium (Oehme, van Sweden designed the green roofs and the grounds around the building). Each step of the way, the building is an architectural expression of the Chicago Botanic Garden's ideals of caring for the plants that people and other creatures depend on.

Although admission to the garden's grounds is free, there is a charge for parking. A bike path and the Pace bus are conveniently located right at the garden's entrance.

192

RAVINIA FESTIVAL DINING PAVILION

Lohan Anderson, 2007

418 Sheridan Road, Glencoe

Train: Metra UP-N to Ravinia Park

Summer in Chicago means hopping in the car or on the Metra to go to Ravinia, the oldest outdoor music festival in North America, dating back to 1904. While the outdoor pavilion has over 3,000 seats that provide shelter and views of the Chicago Symphony Orchestra or whoever is performing that evening, much of the crowd is spread across the lawn, most likely nibbling on bread and cheese and imbibing wine brought with them. For those without the desire to eat on the grass, Ravinia offers a two-story dining pavilion with four types of facilities: a to-go café and buffet dining room on the first floor, and a fine dining restaurant with bar and a banquet room for private dining on the second floor.

Wood siding and mullions give the building a horizontal emphasis. (Credit Angie McMonigal Photography)

The generous overhangs shield patios for outdoor dining. (Credit Angie McMonigal Photography)

The steel-frame building designed by the firm of Dirk Lohan and Floyd Anderson is covered in wood siding whose horizontal lines and deep-set mullions give it a Prairie-style aesthetic, aided by the generous overhangs that provide cover for outdoor dining. Opting for wood was a smart choice because it roots the building in its site, among the trees that bracket the west edge of the large lawn. The expansive windows give diners great views of the trees, the concertgoers on the lawn, and the sculptures that make Ravinia an outdoor museum as well as a one-of-a-kind music venue.

193

RAGDALE MEADOW STUDIO

IIT Design Build, 2008

1260 Green Bay Road, Lake Forest

Ragdale is an artists' retreat in Lake Forest, located about thirty miles north of the Loop. It takes its name from the summer retreat of Howard Van Doren Shaw, who built a house and barn on 33 acres in 1897. His granddaughter, the

The cedar and glass studio has a screened-in porch at the west end. (Credit John Hill)

late poet Alice Judson Hayes, started the Ragdale Foundation in 1976 to give artists, writers, architects, and other designers a respite from the busy world and a place to focus on their creative output. Hayes's mother, Sylvia Shaw Judson, worked in the Meadow Studio, which was built in 1943 west of the house and overlooking, appropriately, a large prairie meadow. The studio deteriorated over the years and was closed in 2003. Five years later, a dozen students from a design-build studio at the Illinois Institute of Technology (IIT) College of Architecture (under Professor Frank Flury and with local architect David Woodhouse) dismantled the old studio, designed its replacement, and then built it. Although the design of the 1,000-square-foot studio, which retains the original building's foundation, is a departure from the Arts and Crafts architecture elsewhere at Ragdale, the cedar siding integrates it well into its site that backs up against some trees. North light is brought in through floor-to-ceiling windows and a tall clerestory, while a screened-in porch gives the artist using the studio a usable outdoor space.

The 2015 Ragdale Ring by Design With Company. (Credit Design With Company)

Another contemporary reinterpretation of an old Ragdale element is the Ragdale Ring, which harkens back to Shaw's own Ring that he designed in 1912. Since 2013, the Ragdale Foundation has held an annual competition for a temporary performance venue next to the house. New York's Stephen Dietrich Lee won the first competition with a lacelike structure of wood pieces. Some later venues include Bittertang Farm's slumping amphitheater of earthen tubes that melded with the landscape in 2014, Design With Company's 2015 design that repurposed architectural elements from Shaw's buildings beyond Ragdale, and T+E+A+M's recreation of Howard Van Doren Shaw's 1912 garden stage design 105 years later.

Given their existence as an artists' retreat, the Ragdale Foundation is not open to the public all the time. Nevertheless, it is open for tours from May to September, and performances are held at the Ring during its annual summer tenure. Check the foundation website before visiting.[3]

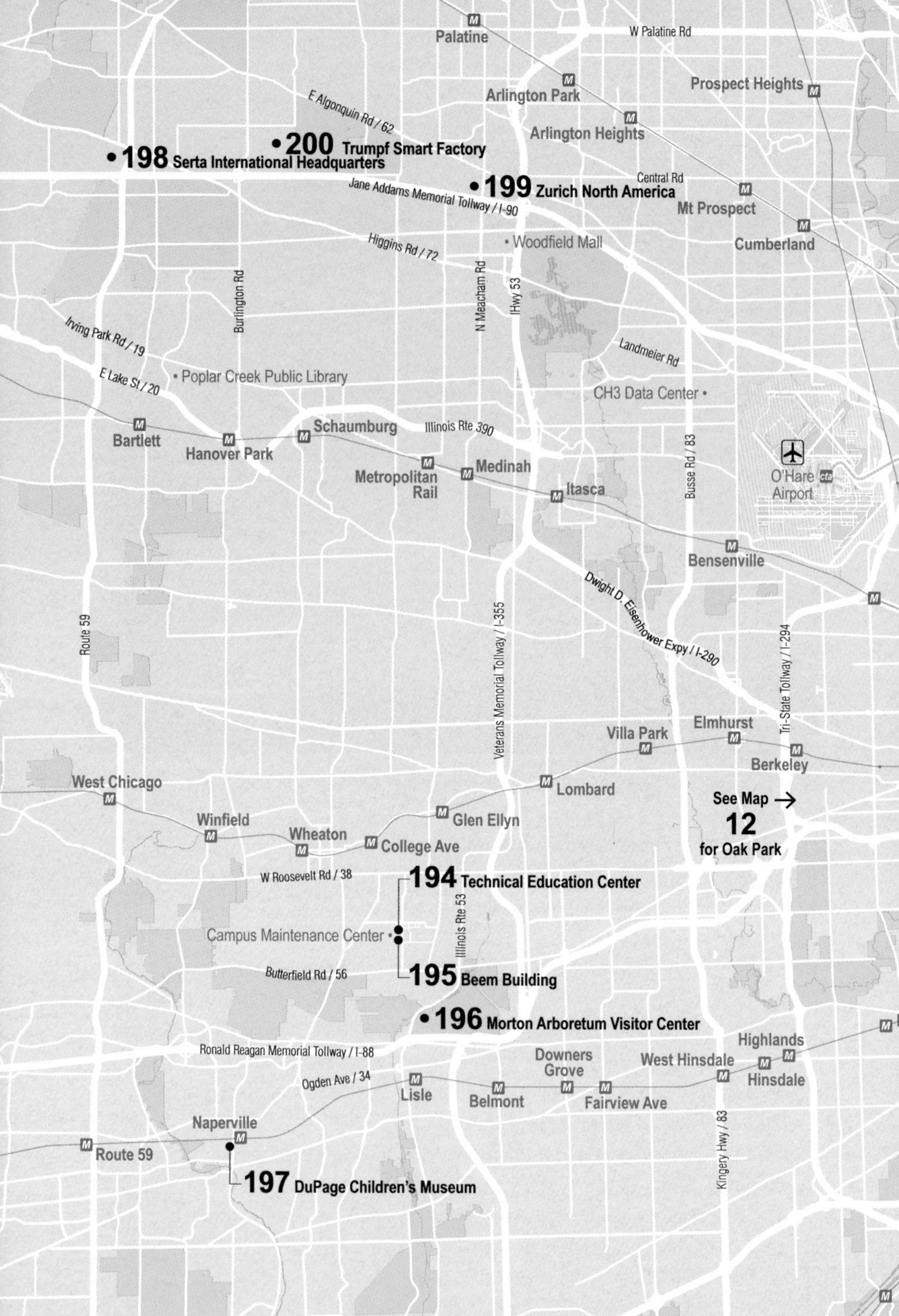
Palatine
W Palatine Rd
Arlington Park
Prospect Heights
E Algonquin Rd / 62
Arlington Heights
200 Trumpf Smart Factory
198 Serta International Headquarters
Central Rd
199 Zurich North America
Jane Addams Memorial Tollway / I-90
Mt Prospect
Cumberland
Higgins Rd / 72
Woodfield Mall
Burlington Rd
N Meacham Rd
IHwy 53
Irving Park Rd / 19
Landmeier Rd
E Lake St / 20
Poplar Creek Public Library
CH3 Data Center
Busse Rd / 83
Schaumburg
Illinois Rte 390
Bartlett
Hanover Park
Metropolitan Rail
Medinah
O'Hare Airport
cta
Itasca
Bensenville
Dwight D. Eisenhower Expy / I-290
Route 59
Veterans Memorial Tollway / I-355
Tri-State Tollway / I-294
Villa Park
Elmhurst
Berkeley
West Chicago
Lombard
See Map 12 for Oak Park
Winfield
Glen Ellyn
Wheaton
College Ave
W Roosevelt Rd / 38
194 Technical Education Center
Illinois Rte 53
Campus Maintenance Center
Butterfield Rd / 56
195 Beem Building
196 Morton Arboretum Visitor Center
Highlands
Ronald Reagan Memorial Tollway / I-88
Downers Grove
West Hinsdale
Ogden Ave / 34
Hinsdale
Lisle
Belmont
Fairview Ave
Naperville
Route 59
Kingery Hwy / 83
197 DuPage Children's Museum
M

21 Northwest & West Suburbs

Historically, Chicago's urban growth has been analyzed geographically with two models: the concentric-ring theory, in which zones of different uses and densities radiate from the Loop, and the sector model, in which the same occurs along wedges like pieces of pie. These are simplifications of complex factors and, as such, a synthesis of the two is more accurate than one or the other. Picture a dartboard, with its concentric rings and wedges; such is one way of looking at how the Chicago metropolitan region works, with certain uses following the wedges and density decreasing radially. For example, the North Shore, presented in the previous chapter, extends north of the city along the lake, from the density of Evanston and Northwestern University up to sprawling Lake Forest and its own Lake Forest College.

The northwest-suburb sector follows Interstate 90, which runs as the Kennedy Expressway from the Loop to O'Hare International Airport and then turns into the Jane Addams Memorial Tollway. (Improvements to O'Hare's infrastructure during the first two decades of the 21st century focused on runways, but in early 2019 O'Hare broke ground on an expansion to Terminal 5 designed by Muller+Muller, and a design team led by Studio Gang was selected for a new Global Terminal that would replace Terminal 2 and nearly double the airport's square footage as part of a huge $8.5 billion expansion.) Given the proximity of this transportation hub for passengers and freight, suburbs such as Hoffman Estates and Schaumburg are home to corporate headquarters, while Schaumburg's Woodfield Mall is the largest shopping mall in Illinois. Nearby Elk Grove Village, located just west of the airport, boasts of the largest industrial park in North America. I-90 is intersected by two north-south interstates—I-290/IL 53 and I-294—that are radial arteries connecting suburbs. As built, they roughly follow the "encircling highways" proposed by Daniel H. Burnham and Edward H. Bennett in their *1909 Plan of Chicago.*

These two radial expressways are integral for the sector of the west suburbs, which are oriented along Interstate 90 that extends westward from the

Loop. The west suburbs featured in this chapter (Lisle, Naperville, and Glen Ellyn) are located in DuPage County, which is also home to the largest community college in Illinois.

194

TECHNICAL EDUCATION CENTER, COLLEGE OF DUPAGE

DeStefano Partners, 2010

425 22nd Street, Glen Ellyn

Campus building sprees this century have not been limited to Northwestern University, University of Chicago, and other traditional universities. The College of DuPage, founded in 1967 as a community college, boasts of more undergraduate students (circa 2015) than any other institution in the state of Illinois besides the University of Illinois at Urbana-Champaign. In turn, the Col-

Classrooms in a variety of technical programs are behind a random-patterned glass wall. (Credit John Hill)

Entrance to the building is under a large armature for signage. (Credit John Hill)

lege has added buildings to its Glen Ellyn campus and opened facilities in other western suburbs, including Carol Stream, West Chicago, and Naperville. The most striking addition to the 273-acre main Glen Ellyn campus is the Technical Education Center (TEC) with 31 classrooms, 16 laboratories, a greenhouse, and other spaces for programs such as architecture, interior design, automotive technology, HVAC-R (Heating, Ventilation, Air Conditioning, and Refrigeration), welding technology, and emerging tech courses in wind and solar energy.

Designed by Avram Lothan (now with Lothan Van Hook DeStefano Architecture), the large four-story building sits on the west side of South Lambert Road, which most students will cross to approach the building, given the large parking lot to the east. The different parts of the building can be best grasped from here: classrooms sit behind the glass curtain wall with random patterns of clear and opaque glass, and labs are behind the lower concrete walls that gain light from narrow windows. Between is the entrance, generously called out by a large armature for signage that is supported by an oversized column. A stroll around the outside of the building reveals that the plan works like a pinwheel, so the classrooms and labs switch position on the rear while still maintaining their exterior expressions.

195

BEEM BUILDING, COLLEGE OF DUPAGE

Ross Barney Architects, 2007

425 Fawell Boulevard, Glen Ellyn

When built in 2007, the Louise M. Beem Early Childhood Center (ECC) was one of four new College of DuPage buildings west of South Lambert Road (most of the campus lies to the east). Catering to the children of students and faculty, the ECC responded to its site between parking lots on the south and a pond on the north by orienting its entrance toward the parking and locat-

Colored panels cap the east and west ends of the building. (Credit Kate Joyce © Hedrich Blessing)

ing outdoor play areas for children to the east and north, away from cars. The building has a shallow roof covered in standing seam metal that turns down to the angled walls on the long north and south elevations, while the shorter ends come alive with a random grid of glass and colored panels. The ECC closed in 2018 due to a decline in enrollment, but the College of DuPage moved administrative spaces to give the 22,500-square-foot building a second life.

(Credit John Hill)

CAMPUS MAINTENANCE CENTER, COLLEGE OF DUPAGE

Legat Architects, 2013

West College Road, Glen Ellyn

Formerly housed in an old gymnasium, the Campus Maintenance Center (CMC) brings together the College of DuPage's facilities and operations departments into a new 35,000-square-foot building in the southwest corner of campus. The highlight of the design by Legat Architects (which was also responsible for the Homeland Security Education Center (HEC) just north of the TEC [**194**]) is the textured precast concrete that adds visual interest to the utilitarian building.

196

MORTON ARBORETUM VISITOR CENTER

David Woodhouse Architects (now Woodhouse Tinucci Architects), 2004
4100 Illinois Route 53, Lisle

At 1,700 acres (more than four times as large as the Chicago Botanic Garden in Glencoe) there is much to explore at the Morton Arboretum located in Lisle just west of where I-88 and I-355 overlap. Much of the land, which bridges Illinois Route 53, is given over to woods with over 222,000 labeled trees and shrubs that are navigated by primary routes and secondary trails. Additionally, the arboretum has an education center, children's garden, maze garden, and research center. The last few are located near the visitor center that overlooks Meadow Lake and is a great starting point for exploring the arboretum.

The hull-like wood ceiling covers most of the public spaces. (Credit Eric Allix Rogers, CAC Archive)

Architect David Woodhouse is something of a local expert on building for nature preserves. He has designed numerous pavilions and visitors centers in and around Chicago; notable projects in the suburbs include the Independence Grove Visitor Center in Libertyville, the Gardens at Ball Pavilion in West Chicago, and the Morton Arboretum Visitor Center. Here in Lisle, he splits the building into two so it acts as a literal gateway to the arboretum, aided by a curved stone wall that funnels people from the adjacent parking lot. The smaller volume to the west is typically used for private events, but the more substantial portion on the east contains bathrooms, a gift shop, and—at the far end—a café and restaurant that overlook the lake through glass walls supported by glass fins. Connecting the building's two halves, and covering most of the interior spaces, is a wooden ceiling that curves like the underside of a boat, extending past the glass wall and trellis to provide shade and shelter for those enjoying their meal outside.

197

DUPAGE CHILDREN'S MUSEUM

Architecture Is Fun with Nagle Hartray Architecture, 2002; renovated 2015

301 North Washington Street, Naperville

Just as the DuPage Children's Museum appears to be a one-of-a-kind place from the outside, there is something oddly familiar about it. Fronting a large parking lot, it feels like a mall or big box retail store. This makes sense considering that the museum is the renovation of a former retail lumber warehouse. The aptly named firm Architecture Is Fun, headed by husband-and-wife duo Peter and Sharon Exley, turned the commercial eyesore into a riot of color that announces itself with signage along Washington Street that both engages and detaches itself from the building. Through the "big red door" (a wall that is detailed with windows and ornaments to look like an oversized door) visitors find even more color in a multitude of environments that are geared for fun but also education.

The signage at the east end of the building hints at the fun inside. (Credit Architecture Is Fun/Doug Snower Photography)

EQUINIX CHICAGO CH3 DATA CENTER

Sheehan Partners, 2006

1905 Lunt Avenue, Elk Grove Village

(Credit John Hill)

Just west of O'Hare International Airport is Elk Grove Village, which boasts the largest industrial park in the United States, totaling over five square miles. Block after block of warehouses and fairly anonymous tilt-up concrete buildings makes the area architecturally abysmal, but this data center designed by a firm that specializes in them stands out for the cantilevered glass volume toward the street and the textured concrete walls that face the street and the large parking lot.

POPLAR CREEK PUBLIC LIBRARY

Frye Gillan Molinaro Architects, 2009

1405 South Park Avenue, Streamwood

This renovation and expansion of a 1960s Brutalist library in a residential area looks different from every angle. Most distinctive is the new south elevation, with bellowlike windows above a glass storefront. Inside, the most interesting space is "the Amoeba," a mezzanine within a double-height space at the rear of the library.

(Credit John Hill)

198

SERTA INTERNATIONAL

Epstein | Metter Studio, 2009

2600 Forbs Avenue, Hoffman Estates

Like their urban counterparts, suburban office buildings make their mark on the public realm through their external form and appearance. Far too often the buildings located near expressways are a combination of mirrored glass and chunky masses that detract from their surroundings rather than enhance them. This headquarters for mattress manufacturer Serta is an exception to that rule. The low-slung building designed by Andrew Metter of Epstein | Metter Studio sits on 17 acres fronting an 80-acre wetland preserve in the Prairie Stone development, whose largest landholder is Sears but which also includes a shopping center, a sports center, and a plethora of less distinguished office buildings.

The narrow S-shaped building appears to hover above the surrounding prairie grasses, a visual deception that happens by cantilevering the floor plates and glass walls of the raised first floor from the recessed foundations. (Jacobs/Ryan Associates handled the landscape design.) Most dramatic is the southern wing, which tapers in plan toward a small pond and is propped upon circular columns to accentuate the sensation of being above the landscape.

A large trellis, at center, sits over the second floor and its roof terrace. (Credit John Hill)

The southern leg of the "S"-shaped building is cantilevered from small round columns. (Credit John Hill)

All around the building, the glass envelope is alternately clear and translucent, depending on the orientation, and is shaded by horizontal louvers—no mirrored glass here! Combined with a trellis that floats above a roof deck next to the lunchroom, the building is unmistakably modern, but it is one that manages to feel like it belongs to the prairie and improves the character of its suburban development.

199

ZURICH NORTH AMERICA

Goettsch Partners, 2016

I90 and Meacham Road, Schaumburg

This corner of Chicagoland—west of O'Hare Airport along I90—appears to be a breeding ground for attention-getting corporate headquarters. Serta's

The asymmetrical stacking of bar-shaped volumes is the result of a concerted effort to define the exterior spaces, often an afterthought in the suburbs. (Credit James Steinkamp Photography)

S-shaped building (**198**) hugs the landscape and cantilevers over it at select points, and this newer headquarters for Switzerland's Zurich Insurance takes an even more daring approach: stacking a five-story, bar-shaped volume atop two splayed, offset five-story volumes, like an homage to the nearby IKEA and its flat-pack boxes. Visible behind the top bar's glass facade are the diagonal braces that enable this gesture and, in effect, turn it into a five-story truss that points toward the distant lake and Loop.

Goettsch Partners went this atypical route for the 783,800-square-foot building to give Zurich's 3,000 employees better views and daylighting than typical center-core towers. Further, on the exterior, it creates two distinctive outdoor spaces: a sunken courtyard that sits between the lower buildings and adjacent to the triple-height dining room, and a roof terrace in the 180-foot-wide void between the three-story entrance volume and the five-story bar overhead. But for the majority who will only drive past the building, never to venture inside, the stacking gives Zurich's global brand a strong image and presence in this suburban corner remote from downtown.

200

TRUMPF SMART FACTORY

Barkow Leibinger with Heitman Architects, 2017
1900 West Central Road, Hoffman Estates

With the late-2017 completion of the Trumpf Smart Factory, there now exists an inadvertent triumvirate of buildings (with **198** and **199**) along a ten-mile stretch of Interstate 90 west of O'Hare that just might reverse the prevailing trend of unexceptional suburban commercial architecture. Most unique about the Smart Factory, designed by the German architecture firm of Frank Barkow and Regine Leibinger, is that it combines factory and showroom into one, allowing the production facilities to double as exhibition set pieces for Trumpf, a machine tool and laser manufacturer based near Stuttgart. The plan is divided into two volumes, like a blocky figure 8: production facilities to the south; offices, auditorium, and courtyard to the north; with the lobby located where the two volumes overlap.

Covered in full-height glass and corrugated Cor-Ten steel, Trumpf Smart Factory immediately recalls Eero Saarinen's design for the John Deere Head-

The building slopes down from the south, facing I-90, to the wetlands on the north. (Credit Steve Hall © Hall + Merrick Photographers)

A courtyard brings daylight to the offices. (Credit Steve Hall © Hall + Merrick Photographers)

Each truss was assembled by Trumpf from more than 200 pieces. (Credit Simon Menges)

quarters in Moline, Illinois. Notably, that complex includes a display space for the company's tractors and other wares. In the Smart Factory, the company's production process is put on display via an open bridge that traverses the factory floor by running through eleven huge tapered trusses that are nearly 150 feet long and as deep as around 20 feet. Made with Trumpf machines, these beefy trusses might just be a better sell than the facilities downstairs—for those fortunate enough to get inside and go for a walk on the bridge.

Notes

Introduction

1. Becker, Lynn. "Stop the Blandness!" *Chicago Reader* (January 16, 2003).

2. Kamin, Blair. "Monuments to Mediocrity," *Chicago Tribune* (August 10, 2003).

3. Kamin, Blair. *Why Architecture Matters.* Chicago: University of Chicago Press, 2001, 3.

4. Sassen, Saskia. "A Global City" in *Global Chicago*, Charles Madigan, editor. Chicago: University of Illinois Press, 2004, 34.

Millennium Park

1. Gilfoyle, Timothy J. *Millennium Park: Creating a Chicago Landmark*. Chicago: University of Chicago Press, 2006, 223.

2. The Art Institute of Chicago. *Zero Gravity: The Art Institute, Renzo Piano, and Building for a New Century*. Chicago: The Art Institute of Chicago, 2005, 10.

3. From the architect's website, Michael Van Valkenburgh Associates, www.mvvainc.com.

Lakeshore East

1. Gang, Jeanne. *Studio Gang Architects: Reveal.* New York: Princeton Architectural Press, 2011, 163.

2. Kamin, Blair. "340 on the Park a Welcome Breath of Fresh Design," *Chicago Tribune* (July 22, 2007).

3. Gang. *Studio Gang Architects*, 145.

The Loop (East)

1. The City of Chicago. *A Vision for State Street, Wabash Avenue and Michigan Avenue*. Chicago: City of Chicago, Department of Planning & Development, 2000, 3.

2. The City of Chicago. *The Chicago Central Area Plan: Preparing the Central City for the 21st Century*. Chicago: City of Chicago, Department of Planning & Development, 2003, 115.

3. Ibid., 91.

4. Ibid., 90.

5. Miller, Ross, in Grossman, James R., Ann Durkin Keating, Janice L. Reiff, editors. *The Encyclopedia of Chicago*. Chicago: The University of Chicago Press, 2004, 81.

6. Noone, Peter, Gary Klompmaker, Crista Sumanik. "Residential Towers in Central Business Districts," in *CTBUH Journal, 2011 Extracts: The Legacy*, 2011, 3.

7. Weiner, Lynn Y., in Grossman, James R., Ann Durkin Keating, Janice L. Reiff, editors. *The Encyclopedia of Chicago*. Chicago: The University of Chicago Press, 2004, 722.

The Loop (West)

1. Website of Handel Architects: www.handelarchitects.com/projects/type/residential/a111-w-wacker-residential.html.

South Loop & Chinatown

1. Website of the City of Chicago, Chicago Landmarks: webapps1.cityofchicago.org/landmarksweb/web/districtdetails.htm?disId=12.

2. Kent, Cheryl. *The New Spertus Institute: A Study in Light by Krueck & Sexton Architects*. Chicago: Spertus Institute of Jewish Studies, 2008, 22.

3. Website of Columbia College, Chicago: about.colum.edu/archives/college-history/buildings/.

4. Anderson Economic Group. *2014 Study on Higher Education in the Loop and South Loop*. Chicago: Chicago Loop Alliance, 2014.

5. Website of Holabird & Root: holabird.com/work/detail/east-west-university/living/.

River North

1. Mayor's Press Office. Press release, "Mayor Emanuel Announces Proposed Ordinance to Establish a Chicago River Corridor Special Sign District," September 17, 2014.

2. Lubell, Sam. "Upcoming Building Projects Help Establish a New Design Tradition," in *Architectural Record* (May 2004): 95.

3. Kamin, Blair. "Unwrapped, Godfrey Comes to Life Beautifully," in *Chicago Tribune* (March 22, 2014).

4. Website of the Poetry Foundation: www.poetryfoundation.org/foundation/about.

Streeterville

1. Kamin, Blair. "Apple Store Stylishly Reinforces Brand," *Chicago Tribune* (June 29, 2003).

2. Kamin, Blair. "Apple's New Flagship Store an Understated Gem on the Chicago River" *Chicago Tribune* (October 20, 2017).

Near North Side

1. Zorbaugh, Harvey. *The Gold Coast and the Slum*. Chicago: University of Chicago Press, 1929; as quoted in Solzman, David M. *The Chicago River: An Illustrated History and Guide to the River and Its Waterways*. Chicago: Wild Onion Books, 1998, 94.

2. City of Chicago. *Near North Tax Increment Redevelopment Plan and Project*. Prepared by Camiros, Ltd., et al., June, 1997.

Lincoln Park

1. Sinkevitch, Alice, and Laurie McGovern Petersen. *AIA Guide to Chicago*. Urbana: University of Illinois Press, 2014, 198.

2. From the architect's website, Ross Barney Architects: www.r-barc.com.

3. From the architect's website, John Ronan Architects: www.jrarch.com.

Lakeview & North Center

1. Faulkner, Wayne. "No High-Rise for Choice LSD Parcel," *Chicago Tribune* (August 14, 2005).

2. Website of Center on Halsted, www.centeronhalsted.org.

3. Website of Heartland Alliance, www.heartlandhousing.org.

Lincoln Square, Ravenswood, Bowmanville, Edgewater, & Rogers Park

1. Hendershot, Steve. "The Nation's Greenest House, Three Years Later," *Chicago Magazine* (April 2012).

Irving Park, Avondale, Kilbourn Park, Logan Square, Hermosa, Galewood, Oak Park, Austin, Garfield Park, & Humboldt Park

1. Website of Intrinsic Schools: intrinsicschools.org.

2. Website of Flexhouse2: www.flexhouse2.com.

Bucktown, Wicker Park, & West Town

1. Zukin, Sharon. *Loft Living*. Baltimore: Johns Hopkins University Press, 1982.
2. Gorlin, Alexander. *The New American Townhouse*. New York: Rizzoli, 2000, 10.
3. Website of Mercy for Animals: www.mfablog.org.

University Village, Medical District, Lawndale, & Pilsen

1. *Chicago Circle Overview: A New Kind of Community*, 1965, quoted in Haar, Sharon. *The City as Campus: Urbanism and Higher Education in Chicago*. Minneapolis: University of Minnesota Press, 2011, 97.
2. Website of Solomon Cordwell Buenz (SCB): www.scb.com.
3. Gerfen, Katie. "Rush University Medical Center, Designed by Perkins+Will" in *Architect Magazine* (February 20, 2013).

Hyde Park

1. Kamin, Blair. "Ricardo Legorreta, 1931–2011," in *Chicago Tribune* (January 4, 2012).
2. Building of the Week feature on Reva and David Logan Center for the Arts: www.world-architects.com/en/architecture-news/reviews/reva-and-david-logan-center-for-the-arts.
3. Ibid.

North Suburbs

1. Visit jrc-evansont.org to arrange a tour.
2. Web page of Studio Gang: studiogang.com/project/writers-theatre.
3. ragdale.org.

Glossary

See also: www.architecture.org/architecture-chicago/visual-dictionary/.

ADA—The Americans with Disabilities Act of 1990 is a federal law that requires accessibility to buildings and spaces, with some exceptions; the most overt expression of the requirements is ramps at building entries.

air rights—Unused development rights (area above a building) transferred from one property to another, not necessarily contiguous, property.

avant-garde—A term applied to artists/architects working outside of conventions; ultimately their output is assimilated into the mainstream, like 20th-century modernism.

Bilbao effect—Coined in relation to the success of Frank Gehry's design for the Guggenheim in Bilbao, Spain, in which the architecture of a major cultural institution revitalizes a city in its move from industrial to postindustrial.

brise-soleil—French term, "sun break," used in architecture to describe the assembly of elements on a facade that shade the interior and add texture to the exterior.

Brutalism—The late style of influential Swiss-French architect Le Corbusier (1887–1965), marked by raw concrete walls and the impression of weight or heft; derivative architecture briefly popular in the late 1960s bears this term.

building code—A legal document setting the minimum requirements for construction, focused on public health, safety, and welfare.

butt-glazing—An inelegant term for glass wall assemblies without exterior mullions; interior mullions combine with structural silicon on the outside to hold the glass in place and give the wall an extremely flat appearance.

cantilever—A horizontal projection (such as a balcony, beam, or canopy) that is fixed at one end.

channel glass—U-shaped self-supporting glass system, translucent in appearance; it is increasingly popular for the diffuse light it enables and the reduced need for intermediate structural members.

Chicago Landmark—The legal designation of a building, structure, site, or district within the City of Chicago as determined by the Commission on Chicago Landmarks; intended to ensure protection against demolition and/or mitigate alterations to the character and historic construction materials of a property.

Chicago window—A window with one large fixed pane of glass that is flanked by narrow double-hung windows on each side.

cladding—Protective and aesthetic cover over a structural frame; typically watertight and airtight, they are increasingly ventilated, as in **rain screens**.

cornice—A decorative band across the top of a building that projects beyond the wall, usually found in traditional more than modern or contemporary architecture.

curtain wall—A non-**load-bearing** wall hung in front of a structural frame, it is usually made of glass and steel or aluminum (see also **window wall**).

elevation—The external face of a building, but also a two-dimensional drawing of a building exterior projected onto a vertical plane.

facade—A building **elevation** that faces a public way, such as a street.

fiber cement—A concrete that is reinforced by fibers instead of steel rebar, making them lightweight and rust-resistant; they are suitable for thin, prefabricated elements (facade panels, copings).

frit—Ceramic pattern baked onto glass, often used to filter sunlight entering a building while adding a distinctive appearance on the exterior.

geothermal—Literally the "heat of the Earth," geothermal technology is used to reduce the energy required to heat and cool water maintained at a constant temperature by circulating it in deep wells to take advantage of the Earth's natural heat.

GFRC—Glass Fiber Reinforced Concrete (see **fiber cement**).

green roofs—A generally flat roof that bears vegetation either intensively (at least six inches of soil, often in planters, to support plants) or extensively (a thin layer of soil with sedum, or similar plants). Used to help reduce the greenhouse effect in cities, green roofs absorb and release water at a slower rate than hard roofs, while also providing an aesthetically pleasing "fifth facade" to neighbors.

insulated glass—A glass unit made up of two pieces of glass and a sealed air space between; also referred to as IGU (Insulated Glazing Unit). Used many times in combination with a **low-E** coating.

LED—Light-emitting diode, a semiconductor device used in everything from small electronics to billboards.

LEED—Leadership in Energy and Environmental Design, a green building certification system developed by the U.S. Green Building Council (USGBC) in 1993. Projects earn credits based on building performance and other factors to gain certification in one of four categories, from least to most credits: Certified, Silver, Gold, and Platinum.

limestone—A sedimentary rock of fossilized shells and coral that is commonly found in Indiana and therefore has been commonly used for **facades** of Chicago buildings.

load-bearing—A method of construction in which exterior walls carry loads from above that consist of the wall, floors, and roof; in opposition to **curtain wall** construction in which the exterior walls are hung from a steel or concrete structural frame.

low-E—A low-emissivity coating applied to glass—in many cases **insulated glass**—that reflects infrared energy, keeping out heat in the summer and keeping it indoors in the winter, thereby reducing the need for air conditioning and mechanical heating, respectively.

masonry—Units of brick, stone, or concrete stacked into walls.

massing—The arrangement of a building's forms; individual forms are often called volumes.

Modernism—A 20th-century movement that broke with tradition in the arts (architecture, painting, sculpture, literature, music) and continues to influence Western culture.

mullions—The typically horizontal and vertical members that hold glass panes and metal panels in **curtain wall** and **window wall** assemblies.

neoclassical—A style of architecture popular in the 18th- through early-20th-centuries that strictly follows historical precedents, especially the Classical architecture of Ancient Greece and Rome.

patina—A tarnish that forms on copper and similar metals from oxidation, giving copper, for example, its distinctive green color.

photovoltaics—A solar cell that absorbs sunlight to produce electricity; its thin cross section enables it to be integrated into glass walls and roofs.

plan—The horizontal arrangement of rooms in a building, but also a two-dimensional drawing made from a horizontal plane cut through the building and seen from above.

podium—The wide base of a narrower tower or towers; in Chicago, a podium often extends to the sidewalk and contains parking and/or retail space, while above it is a setback tower for apartments or office space.

Postmodernism—Alternately seen as both a reaction to and extension of **Modernism**; in architecture, it was a style borrowing historical elements into hybrid and ironic compositions, popular in the 1970s and 80s.

precast concrete—Concrete poured into forms, usually off site, to create panels hung on building frames as **cladding** or used as structural elements, such as floors and walls.

prefab—A method of construction in which, typically, components are prefabricated as modules in a factory, shipped to the construction site, and then assembled like blocks. Proponents of prefab construction argue it results in less waste, is more cost and time efficient, and allows for more quality control due to the factory setting.

Pritzker Architecture Prize—Considered the Nobel Prize for architects, this annual prize is awarded by Chicago's Pritzker family, who started it in 1979. Its purpose is to honor "a living architect whose built work demonstrates a combination of those qualities of talent, vision and commitment, which has produced consistent and significant contributions to humanity and the built environment through the art of architecture."

program—The spatial and functional requirements of a building, often developed as a list of spaces, their sizes, and their adjacencies; all contemporary architecture is based on a program developed by or with the client.

rain screen—An exterior wall **cladding** system that controls water infiltration into buildings differently than traditional construction. It is made up of three layers: the siding—a panelized system made from a material like terra cotta—is open yet keeps out the majority of the water; the inner surface is an airtight layer that sheds moisture; and the air space between allows for drainage and evaporation through ventilation.

reinforced concrete—Concrete that gains strength from steel rods or mesh embedded within it, since concrete is a strong material in compression but steel is strong in tension; most reinforced concrete is poured on site into temporary formworks, but some is done off site as **precast concrete**.

section—A two-dimensional drawing of a vertical plane cut through a building and viewed from the side.

spandrel—A cover, usually glass or metal, that conceals the edge of a floor slab in a **curtain wall** or **window wall** assembly.

sustainability—By definition, the ability to sustain something over time; sustainable architecture aims to meet current needs without compromising the needs of future generations; aka *green building* (see also **LEED**).

TIF—Tax Increment Financing, a much-used, and overly complex, funding tool in Chicago for promoting public and private development that caps the property tax of an area deemed blighted to some degree, uses the incremental growth over the cap level to fund redevelopment projects in the area, and then distributes any revenues at the end of the 23-year period among the city's seven taxing bodies. TIFs are a popular means of everything from building and repairing roads and infrastructure to subsidizing corporations in building their headquarters in the city, since TIFs are seen as an alternative to raising taxes. In 2018, Chicago had 131 TIFs generating approximately $841 million in tax revenue.

truss—A number of members framed together to create a structure able to span long distances; most common are steel trusses made from two parallel beams connected by shorter perpendicular columns and diagonal bracing.

vernacular—Sometimes called "architecture without architects" (after Bernard Rudofsky's 1964 MoMA exhibit of the same name), it refers to buildings made from local materials and created without reference to style or theory; with a beauty that arises from "untainted" responses to functional needs, these buildings are increasingly mined as inspiration by contemporary architects.

window wall—Similar to a **curtain wall**, yet with the glass and metal spanning from floor to ceiling, between structural slabs.

zoning—Legal restrictions that determine land use, building bulk, setbacks, and other physical characteristics aimed toward public health and safety, quality of life, maintaining the character of residential neighborhoods, and numerous other concerns. Chicago's Zoning Code, first established in 1893 and revised most recently in 2004, applies districts citywide based on type of use and designated through a lettering system (R for residential, C for commercial, M for manufacturing, and so forth).

Selected Bibliography & Resources

It's impossible, and really unnecessary with a guidebook, to list every source that contributed to the text. What follows is a bibliography of selected recommended books and resources for people interested in gaining further information on the buildings and places in this book. It should be noted that architects' web pages are a very good, if partial, source for learning about individual buildings.

Books

Bennett, Larry. *The Third City: Chicago and American Urbanism*. Chicago: University of Chicago Press, 2010.

Bey, Lee. *Southern Exposure: The Overlooked Architecture of Chicago's South Side*. Evanston, IL: Northwestern University Press, 2019.

Bosch, Jennifer Marjorie. *A View from the River: The Chicago Architecture Foundation River Cruise*. Portland, OR: Pomegranate, 2008.

Burnham, Daniel H., and Edward H. Bennett. *Plan of Chicago*. Boston: Da Capo Press, 1970 (originally published 1909).

City of Chicago, Department of Public Works. *Chicago Public Works: A History*. Skokie, IL: Rand McNally & Company, 1973.

Condit, Carl W. *The Chicago School of Architecture: A History of Commercial and Public Building in the Chicago Area, 1875–1925*. Chicago: University of Chicago Press, 1964.

Cronon, William. *Nature's Metropolis: Chicago and the Great West*. New York: W. W. Norton, 1991.

Cutler, Irving. *Chicago: Metropolis of the Mid-Continent, 4th Edition*. Carbondale: Southern Illinois University Press, 2006.

d'Eramo, Marco. *The Pig and the Skyscraper: Chicago: A History of Our Future*. New York: Verso, 2002.

Dyja, Thomas L. *The Third Coast: When Chicago Built the American Dream*. New York: Penguin Press, 2013.

Eisenschmidt, Alexander, with Jonathan Mekinda. *Chicagoisms: The City as Catalyst for Architectural Speculation*. Zürich: Park Books, 2013.

Gilfoyle, Timothy J. *Millennium Park: Creating a Chicago Landmark*. Chicago: The University of Chicago Press, 2006.

Grossman, James R., et al. *The Encyclopedia of Chicago*. Chicago: University of Chicago Press, 2004.

Haar, Sharon. *The City as Campus: Urbanism and Higher Education in Chicago*. Minneapolis: University of Minnesota Press, 2011.

Harris, Scott Jordan. *World Film Locations: Chicago*. Bristol: Intellect, 2013.

Hayner, Don, and Tom McNamee. *Streetwise Chicago: A History of Chicago Street Names*. Chicago: Wild Onion Books, 1988.

Hudson, John C. *Chicago: A Geography of the City and Its Region*. Chicago: University of Chicago Press, 2006.

Hunt, D. Bradford, and Jon B. DeVries. *Planning Chicago*. Chicago/Washington, DC: APA Planners Press, 2013.

Kamin, Blair. *Terror and Wonder: Architecture in a Tumultuous Age*. Chicago: The University of Chicago Press, 2001.

———. *Why Architecture Matters: Lessons from Chicago*. Chicago: The University of Chicago Press, 2011.

Keegan, Edward. *Chicago Architecture: 1885 to Today*. New York: Universe, 2008.

Kitt Chappell, Sally A. *Chicago's Urban Nature: A Guide to the City's Architecture + Landscape*. Chicago: The University of Chicago Press, 2007.

Koval, John P., et al. *The New Chicago: A Social and Cultural Analysis*. Philadelphia: Temple University Press, 2006.

Lowe, David Garrard. *Lost Chicago*. New York: Gramercy, 1993.

Madigan, Charles. *Global Chicago*. Urbana: University of Illinois Press, 2004.

Maguire, Kathleen. *Cool Chicago*. London: Pavilion, 2014.

Mayer, Harold M., and Richard C. Wade. *Chicago: Growth of a Metropolis*. Chicago: The University of Chicago Press, 1969.

McBrien, Judith Paine. *Pocket Guide to Chicago Architecture, Third Edition*. New York: W. W. Norton, 2014.

Miller, Donald L. *City of the Century: The Epic of Chicago and the Making of America*. New York: Simon & Schuster, 1996.

Miller, Tom. *Seeking Chicago: The Stories Behind the Architecture of the Windy City—One Building at a Time*. New York: Universe Publishing, 2019.

Okrent, Lawrence. *Chicago from the Sky: A Region Transformed*. Buffalo Grove, IL: Chicago's Books Press, 2012.

Price, Virginia B., et al. *Out of the Loop: Vernacular Architecture Forum Chicago*. Evanston, IL: Agate Midwest, 2015.

Pridmore, Jay. *Building Ideas: An Architectural Guide to the University of Chicago*. Chicago: The University of Chicago Press, 2013.

Pridmore, Jay, and George A. Larson. *Chicago Architecture and Design, Third Edition*. New York: Harry N. Abrams, 2018.

Rast, Joel. *Remaking Chicago: The Political Origins of Urban Industrial Change*. DeKalb: Northern Illinois University Press, 1999.

Schulze, Franz, and Kevin Harrington. *Chicago's Famous Buildings, Fifth Edition.* Chicago: The University of Chicago Press, 2003.

Schwieterman, Joseph P., and Dana M. Caspall. *The Politics of Place: A History of Zoning in Chicago.* Chicago: Lake Claremont Press, 2006.

Schwieterman, Joseph P., and Alan P. Mammoser. *Beyond Burnham: An Illustrated History of Planning for the Chicago Region.* Lake Forest, IL: Lake Forest College Press, 2009.

Sharoff, Robert, and William Zbaren. *Last Is More: Mies, IBM, and the Transformation of Chicago.* Mulgrave, Australia: Images Publishing, 2014.

Sinkevitch, Alice, and Laurie McGovern Petersen. *AIA Guide to Chicago, Third Edition.* Urbana: University of Illinois Press, 2014.

Solzman, David. *The Chicago River: An Illustrated History and Guide to the River and Its Waterways.* Chicago: Wild Onion Press, 1998.

Thall, Bob, with Peter Bacon Hales. *The Perfect City.* Baltimore: The Johns Hopkins University Press, 1994.

Waldheim, Charles, and Katerina Rüedi Ray. *Chicago Architecture: Histories, Revisions, Alternatives.* Chicago: The University of Chicago Press, 2005.

Willis, Carol. *Form Follows Finance: Skyscrapers and Skylines in New York and Chicago.* New York: Princeton Architectural Press, 1995.

Zangs, Mary. *The Chicago 77: A Community Area Handbook.* Mount Pleasant, SC: The History Press, 2014.

Local Chicago Resources

These institutions and organizations host architecture-related lectures, exhibitions, tours, and other events. Chapter references are for maps where locations are included. Checking their websites for schedules and locations of events is recommended.

AIA Chicago, 35 East Upper Wacker Drive, #250 (Chapter 3; events held here but sometimes in other locations), aiachicago.org.

Art Institute of Chicago, 111 South Michigan Avenue (Chapter 1), artic.edu.

Chicago Architectural Club, (no address; members-only club that hosts open competitions and holds lectures and events at various venues around the city), chicago architecturalclub.org.

Chicago Architecture Biennial, 78 East Washington Street (held the end of each odd-numbered year since 2015; centered at the Chicago Cultural Center (Chapter 3) but with satellite events and exhibitions), chicagoarchitecturebiennial.org.

Chicago Architecture Center (CAC), 111 East Wacker Drive (Chapter 3; lectures held here but tours embark from here and other locations, including across Wacker Drive for their river cruises), architecture.org.

Chicago History Museum, 1601 North Clark Street (Chapter 9), chicagohistory.org.

Chicago Women in Architecture (CWA), (no address; events are held at various venues around the city), cwarch.org.

Council on Tall Buildings and Urban Habitat (CTBUH), The Monroe Building, 104 South Michigan Avenue, Suite 620 (events tend to be held elsewhere), ctbuh.org.

Graham Foundation for Advanced Studies in Fine Arts, 4 West Burton Place (Chapter 8), grahamfoundation.org.

Illinois Institute of Technology (IIT), 3360 South Federal Street (Chapter 16), arch.iit.edu.

MAS Context (no address; events and exhibitions are held at various venues around the city), mascontext.com.

Museum of Contemporary Art (MCA), 220 East Chicago Avenue (Chapter 7), mcachicago.org.

Open House Chicago (CAC's annual weekend of tours and open buildings that takes place in October), openhousechicago.org.

Richard H. Driehaus Museum, 40 East Erie Street (Chapter 6), driehausmuseum.org.

School of the Art Institute of Chicago (SAIC), 36 South Wabash Avenue, #1257 (Chapter 3), saic.edu.

Society for Architectural Historians (SAH), 1365 North Astor Street (Chapter 8), sah.org.

University of Illinois at Chicago (UIC), 845 West Harrison Street (Chapter 15), arch.uic.edu.

Volume Gallery, 1709 West Chicago Avenue, 2nd Floor (Chapter 13), wvvolumes.com.

Architect/Building Index

Note: Numbers refer to page numbers, not entry numbers; architect names are in plain text, while project names are in italics.

Building Type Index

Note: Numbers refer to page numbers, not entry numbers, and, where applicable, some entries are listed under more than one building type.

CHICAGO ARCHITECTURE CENTER is a nonprofit cultural organization that offers a variety of all-ages tours, exhibitions, programs, and events.

JOHN HILL is a registered architect and author of the *NYC Walks: Guide to New Architecture* and *Guide to Contemporary New York City Architecture*.

The University of Illinois Press
is a founding member of the
Association of University Presses.

Text designed by Dustin Hubbart
Composed in 11/13 Avenir 45 Book
with Avenir 35 Light display
by Jim Proefrock
at the University of Illinois Press
Manufactured by Versa Press, Inc.

University of Illinois Press
1325 South Oak Street
Champaign, IL 61820-6903
www.press.uillinois.edu